MW00800690

Hernando de Soto among the Apalachee

Ripley P. Bullen Series

Florida Bureau of Archaeological Research
Division of Historical Resources

University Press of Florida
Gainesville
Tallahassee
Tampa
Boca Raton
Pensacola
Orlando
Miami
Jacksonville

CHARLES R. EWEN

JOHN H. HANN

Hernando de Soto among the Apalachee

The Archaeology of the First Winter Encampment

Copyright 1998 by the Board of Regents of the State of Florida
Printed in the United States of America on acid-free paper
All rights reserved

03 02 01 00 99 98   6 5 4 3 2 1

LIBRARY OF CONGRESS CATALOGING-IN-PUBLICATION DATA
Ewen, Charles Robin.
Hernando de Soto among the Apalachee: the archaeology of the first winter encampment /
Charles R. Ewen, John H. Hann.
p. cm. — (The Ripley P. Bullen series)
Includes bibliographical references (p.) and index.
ISBN 0-8130-1557-X (c)
1. Tallahassee (Fla.)—Antiquities. 2. Soto, Hernando de, ca. 1500–1542. 3. Apalachee
Indians—Florida—Tallahassee—History—16th century. 4. Excavations (Archaeology)—
Florida—Tallahassee. I. Hann, John H. II. Title. III. Series.
F319.T14E94 1998   97-25212
975.9'88—dc21

The publication of this book is made possible in part by a grant from the Program for
Cultural Cooperation between Spain's Ministry of Education and Culture and United
States' Universities.

The University Press of Florida is the scholarly publishing agency for the State University
System of Florida, comprised of Florida A&M University, Florida Atlantic University,
Florida International University, Florida State University, University of Central Florida,
University of Florida, University of North Florida, University of South Florida, and
University of West Florida.

University Press of Florida
15 Northwest 15th Street
Gainesville, FL 32611
http: //nersp.nerdc.ufl.edu/~upf

We dedicate this book to B. Calvin Jones,
without whose effort the Governor Martin site
would not have been discovered, recognized for
what it was, or saved.
J. H. H.
C. R. E.

To my mother, Margaret S. Ewen, without whose love and
support this book would never have been written.
C. R. E.

Contents

Tables and Figures

Foreword

SITE MAY BE DESOTO'S CAMP shouted the headline in the *Tallahassee Democrat* on April 21, 1987. And so it became public, one of the most exciting archaeological discoveries of the decade. Leading up to the news story had been several months of quiet but intense archaeological investigation and speculation. What began as a routine look by state archaeologist Calvin Jones at a downtown property under development for office buildings quickly became a roller-coaster ride involving state agencies, property owners, developers, lawyers, the city commission, the city preservation board, archaeologists and historians around the country as well as overseas, hundreds of volunteers, media from local television to the *New York Times* and *National Geographic*, and a host of nonprofit organizations ready to assist.

No historical event was more crucial to the Native American people of southeastern North America than the de Soto *entrada*. The expedition, more than 600 strong, trekked through what are now 10 southern states from Florida to Texas, from its 1539 landing in Tampa Bay to its forlorn 1543 trip down the Mississippi River to eventual rescue in Mexico. Despite a 4000-mile journey, encounters with scores of native tribes, and the loss of hundreds of people and tons of goods—all of it chronicled by four separate accounts thoroughly studied by modern scholars—no de Soto archaeological site had ever been found.

In 1939, on the 400th anniversary of the landing, the United States De Soto Expedition Commission had collected, analyzed, and presented all the documentary and artifactual evidence for de Soto's expedition and had published a comprehensive report, along with a map of the supposed route. Since then, scholars had continued to search for de Soto sites, including the winter encampment of 1539–1540 in the Tallahassee area, but they turned up little more than de Soto–period artifacts at scattered Indian sites.

It was thus no small matter to claim the discovery of the first definite archaeological site representing de Soto's expedition, nor was the identity of such a site easy to confirm. Add to the mix a major construction project financed in such a way that each week of delay cost thousands of dollars in interest payments, a fascinated and excited public demanding that the site and its archaeological evidence be preserved, and the absence of funds for excavation or analysis of the site, and you have a modern archaeological crisis.

It is to the great credit of all the people involved in this exciting project that its story is now being told by Charles Ewen. More than any other project I know of, the de Soto winter encampment excavation depended on cooperation, commitment, sacrifice, and an unwavering faith that it was possible to succeed despite exceedingly trying conditions. The difficulties of the de Soto excavation were not those related in television specials and adventure books. There were no problems with transportation through thick jungle, dangerous plants and animals, or unhealthy food and water. Rather, the challenges were to confirm that the site was indeed that of de Soto and that it warranted an exceptional effort to save it, then to organize, staff, and fund a major excavation with virtually no time for planning or fund raising.

In scores of meetings and hundreds of phone calls, resources were sought and graciously offered. Archaeologists came to volunteer, to work for minimum wage, and to offer the services of their institutions. Other people arranged to raise funds through an amazing variety of strategies. Still others worked with the developers and the owners to modify schedules for constructing and occupying the proposed offices. Supporting their efforts were those who arranged public acquisition of part of the site so that it would not need to be excavated in advance of construction. And, in the middle of the excitement, the pressure, the difficulties, Calvin Jones and Charlie Ewen methodically and surely guided the excavation from tentative hints of connections with de Soto through complete recovery of all archaeological deposits that would have been impacted by the construction.

It was Jones's curiosity as well as his concern about the loss of archaeological remains that led him to look at the construction site during one lunch hour, and it was his persistence in searching for more evidence to explain the unusual artifacts from the site that led the rest of us to de Soto. With his decades of experience in Spanish Colonial artifacts from Florida sites, and his legendary knack for reading the land and finding the site, Calvin Jones was uniquely suited to recognizing the de Soto site and ensuring its complete excavation. Many others played important roles, as Charlie Ewen's fascinating account attests, but we would still be looking for the first de Soto site had it not been for the unique skills, commitment, and vision of Calvin Jones.

James J. Miller
State Archaeologist

Preface

Several years ago noted historian Michael V. Gannon published an article in the *William and Mary Quarterly* extolling the successes of archaeologists and historians in melding their disciplines to learn about the past and bring their information to the public. He was right. And nowhere is that success more apparent than in Florida, where the skills of people like archaeologist Charles Ewen and historian John Hann have been joined to bring us this extraordinary story of the Hernando de Soto expedition during the fall and winter of 1539–1540, when that Spanish *entrada* camped in an Apalachee Indian town in what today is Tallahassee, Florida.

The Native American town where the expedition was quartered is nearly in the shadow of the Florida capitol dome, yet it lay hidden for more than 450 years. Its discovery in 1987 by B. Calvin Jones, archaeologist with the Florida Division of Historical Resources' Bureau of Archaeological Research (BAR), whose headquarters are only a short walk from the site, would touch off a commotion rivaling that of the Florida legislature in the hours just before its annual adjournment. Journalists hailed the discovery; archaeologists sought time and funding to excavate the site before its owners developed it; government officials, private philanthropic and nonprofit organizations, as well as many volunteers and other individuals worked around the clock to save the site for future generations. The hullabaloo was tremendous.

Amidst all of this activity, James J. Miller, BAR chief, and his colleagues at the Division of Historical Resources worked quietly but effectively to assure that the site was both preserved and studied. They were successful, and the site is now in public ownership; Miller and the bureau and division staffs deserve accolades for their accomplishments. Rarely have governmental and private interests worked so fast and effectively to achieve so much. Charles Ewen recounts for us the clamor and its outcome, a story almost as interesting and exciting as the archaeological and historical discoveries themselves.

Much has been written about the Hernando de Soto expedition. De Soto remains an important historical figure not only in Florida, where both a Hernando and a Desoto county are named after him, but all across the southeastern United States from Florida to Texas, the route the expedition marched during 1539–1543. Despite that fame—some would say infamy—and distance, there is only one archaeological site that we can tie to the expedition with 100 percent certainty, the site reported here. As a consequence, the Tallahassee site takes on added significance, both as a symbol of the past and as a font of baseline information to guide all future researchers delving into sixteenth-century colonial America.

The Florida Museum of Natural History and the University Press of Florida are pleased to publish this final report and to acknowledge the many contributions of the Division of Historical Resources and the Bureau of Archaeological Research to the overall project.

Jerald T. Milanich
Series Editor

Acknowledgments

It is customary to begin this sort of section by proclaiming that the project could not have been accomplished without the help of many individuals, and so I shall. Nowhere is this more true than with the work at the Governor Martin site. Indeed, without the assistance of a great many individuals, businesses, and organizations, this project would never have been initiated, much less completed.

Of course the site would never have been recognized were it not for the keen insight of B. Calvin Jones. Though there were often disagreements in the field concerning interpretation and methodology, there was never any doubt that without Calvin the project would never have happened. His ability to enchant contractors, bureaucrats, and the general public was a marvel to behold and kept the project on the front burner when it might otherwise have been pushed to the back.

Much of the credit for the successful management of the project goes to Jim Miller, state archaeologist and chief of the Florida Bureau of Archaeological Research. He negotiated with developers, haggled for money, and ran interference with other agencies so that the site directors could keep their attention focused on the archaeology. This backing extended up the state hierarchy from State Historic Preservation Officer George Percy to Secretary of State Jim Smith to Governor Bob Martinez, and, especially, to Senator Bob Graham. All of these officials personally visited the site and worked to keep the project going. John Scarry (FBAR) lent incredible support in the field and at the computer, and K. C. Smith (Division of Historic Sites and Properties) labored tirelessly to drum up community support and made sure the site was interpreted to the widest possible audience. Many more in the various departments of the state government deserve individual recognition (e.g., Roy Lett, Herb Bump, James Levy, and Frank Gilson in the Conservation Lab and Kevin McGorty of the Historical Tallahassee Preservation Board), but space constraints and ignorance of the contributors behind the scenes does not permit more than an acknowledgment of their much appreciated contributions.

Our academic colleagues were supportive as well. Jerry Milanich and Mike Gannon were instrumental in staffing and funding the Governor

Martin dig as well as the subsequent De Soto/Apalachee Project. Jerry Milanich was also extremely patient and supportive as one of us took far longer than he should have to produce this manuscript. Our colleagues at Florida State University, especially Rochelle Marrinan and Glen Doran, helped out with advice and institutional support. The late William Maples, David Dickel, Clark Larsen, Rebecca Storey, and Randolph Widmer all assisted with the identification and interpretation of the human remains. Dolph Widmer also assisted in the field for a number of weeks. Russell Skowronek and Larry Conrad both volunteered weeks of their time at the dig when they could have been working on their own projects. Gary Shapiro, then director of archaeology at the San Luis Archaeological and Historic Site, made that site's archaeologists available for a brief period early in the Martin site excavations and acquiesced in John H. Hann's devoting work time at the San Luis site to preparing translations from the four major de Soto accounts and two Cabeza de Vaca accounts for the guidance of the archaeologists. And innumerable colleagues from other campuses dropped by the site to observe, kibbitz, and generally hobnob with their fellow wizards. Their support is gratefully acknowledged here.

As is detailed in the book, much of the funding and other support came from private sources. Sometimes this support came in the form of cash donations, other times as in-kind service (Goodtime's Pizza and Hobbit Hoagies fed the crew for much of the fieldwork). Dale Allen of the Trust for Public Land orchestrated the purchase of the site, and developers Jeff Allen, Steve Allen, Chuck Mitchell, and Gary Spangler graciously allowed the archaeologists to continue working while the negotiations were under way. Other contributors and supporters include Allen Cummings, Barbara McCrimmon, Robert Pierce, Eugenia Scott, and Bill Thomas.

The bead analysis was supported by a grant from the Bead Society of America and the De Soto/Apalachee Project by a grant from the National Endowment for the Humanities.

Over 250 individuals volunteered in various capacities at the site. Some were experienced archaeologists who helped dig. Others had little or no experience but performed invaluable assistance at the sifting screens recovering artifacts and in the lab washing the artifacts. Still others volunteered to give tours to the hundreds of visitors who mobbed the site each week. This allowed the archaeologists to devote their expertise to the site while not ignoring the public's interest in this significant site in their midst. While everyone who volunteered has the heartfelt thanks of the authors and archaeological crew, some contributed beyond what could have been expected. These include Charles Arant, Betty and Jennifer Ashlock, Larry Benson, Lora Chapman, Jean Coyne, Pete Cowdry, William DeGrove, Bea

Doran (winner of the coveted Golden Nozzle award), Linda Harkey, Louis Hill, Clay, Martha and Richard Hulet, Rich Johnson, Nan Koelliker, Vernon McCord, Dot Jean Owen, Mr. and Mrs. Fred Palmer, Bill Rayboun, Barbara Rodman, Bailey Thompson, Lula Threats, Earl Van Atta, Carrie, Mark, and Sue Weathersbee, and Carol Weber.

Finally, the professional crew deserve much praise. Most of them volunteered as much time as what they were paid for, and all endured bad weather, uncertain funding, and unending interruptions of their work without complaint (well, very little complaint). Many have gone on to work at other important archaeological sites. They include Greg Falstrom, Jennifer Lozowski, Marie Mathison, Phil Gerrell, Quincy Hamby, Sam Chapman, Bruce Byrd, Jim Cusick, Frank Keel, Allison Morris, Walter Crabbe, Jim Chafin, Yvonne McKinnon, Teresa Paglione, Doug Potter, Kathy Reichert, Richard Haiduven, Jean Wilson, Gerald Ferguson, and Elyse White.

This book was a long time in the writing, but the production went more quickly than I could have imagined. The staff at the University Press of Florida was a genuine pleasure to work with, especially Meredith Morris-Babb, Lynn Werts, and most of all, Judy Goffman. I would also like to acknowledge two students who helped with the production at ECU, Charles Heath with graphics and Tom Beaman with the index. The comments of the two almost-anonymous reviewers were very helpful in the revision of the manuscript and any errors or oversights in the text are no fault of theirs.

This list is by no means comprehensive, and the authors apologize for anyone who was inadvertently overlooked. Though many people contributed to the production of this book, the authors assume the responsibility for any errors or omissions.

Artifacts pictured in this book, as well as additional photographs of artifacts and features from the Governor Martin site, are available in the De Soto/Apalachee slide set from Pictures of Record.

Prologue: De Soto and the Apalachee

CHARLES R. EWEN

Computer games are the bane of those who are supposed to be engaged in serious research. However, every once in a while these distractions can actually prove thought provoking. One such game is "Seven Cities of Gold" (Electronic Arts). To play this game, you assume the role of a Spanish explorer granted funds from the Crown to take an expedition across the Western Sea. From your grant you must outfit an expedition (including food, equipment, trade goods, ships, and personnel) for an indefinite length of time (that is, as long as you can afford). You then sail into the unknown.

Throughout the expedition you are confronted with situations requiring decisions that will affect the next move. With each choice made (e.g., which direction to sail, where to land), time passes and supplies are slowly consumed. After a harrowing passage (there is always a storm, just as there was in the sixteenth century), you make landfall and encounter groups of native peoples of varying levels of social complexity. They range from hunter-gatherers to state-level societies and are usually cautious but not overtly hostile at the first meeting. You can trade with the natives (from your supply of trade goods) in order to gain additional food or gold. You have the option of establishing missions, trading posts, and forts in different territories or simply moving on and exploring. It is an easy game until supplies start to run low.

If you run out of food, the men begin to starve to death. The only option is to trade for food with the local natives. However, if you have already expended your trade goods, the natives won't give away food (and they won't exchange it for gold). Sometimes they are not interested in trading even if there are goods to trade. As the expedition begins to starve, you are faced with seemingly certain death—except for one important alternative. The natives are relatively easy to kill, and once you wipe out a village you get all their food and gold.

To win the game you must please the queen. She is impressed not only with the amount of gold you bring back but also with the number of souls you save and the size of the territory you gain for the Crown. Having played several different scenarios, varying from establishing a string of peaceful missions to straight plundering and killing anything that moves, I have found that the queen is unhappy with either extreme, and compromises are extremely difficult to engineer successfully.

The situations encountered in this simulation are not dissimilar to those faced by the early Spanish conquistadors whose responses resulted in similar reactions from the Crown. It is politically correct these days to consider these men as evil and their enterprises as moral travesties, and much history is being written from that perspective. I will not attempt to defend the characters of the conquistadors or their actions in the Americas. It is my intention instead to describe the setting in which these actions occurred and to try to understand something of the motivations of the explorers who came to the New World. In this book, the focus is on Hernando de Soto. However, the general setting and the imperial motivations here apply to many of the early European incursions into the New World.

HERNANDO DE SOTO: THE MAN AND HIS TIMES

When Christopher Columbus "discovered" the New World, he was actually searching for a quick route to the riches of Cathay. The enormous economic possibilities of his accidental discovery were not lost on Columbus, as is clearly demonstrated by his protracted legal dispute with the Crown (later pursued by his heirs) over hereditary titles and land claims. Although Columbus explored much of the Caribbean and the northern coast of South America during his four voyages, the end result of his struggles with the Crown for credit was that he was unable effectively to exploit his discoveries. The potential of the lands was quickly realized by other ambitious explorers, such as Hernan Cortés and Francisco Pizarro, to name but two. These men won great fortunes and became known as conquistadors.

Within the half century following Columbus's first voyage of discovery, the circum-Caribbean region had been overrun by Spain, and the native peoples systematically and often brutally reduced to subservience or driven to extinction. However, not every conquistador was as successful as Cortés or Pizarro. Some were thwarted by ignorance or their own incompetence, as may have been the case with the Pánfilo de Narváez (see Morison 1974). Sometimes, though, unforeseeable circumstances prevented even those who seemed the most able of these men from realizing their dreams.

What kind of place bred the conquistadors? At the inauguration of its colonial ventures, Spain could hardly be considered a unified nation. The first steps toward integrating the separate kingdoms had been taken in the latter half of the fifteenth century through the marriage of Isabella of Castile and Ferdinand of Aragon. The joint reign of these monarchs was a precarious coalition that defied the deep-seated suspicions of their respective subjects. Historian J. H. Eliott (1963:18) notes that "while a Castilian-Aragonese union had for some decades been an obvious possibility, it was far from being an inevitable development. There was no irrefutable economic or historical argument to bring the two Crowns together. On the contrary, the strong mutual antipathy of the Aragonese and Castilians made any prospect of union unattractive to both." To this John Lynch (1984:4) adds, "In so far as a sense of nationalism existed in Spain at the time, it was Castilian rather than Spanish in inspiration. . . . Most of the subjects of the Catholic Monarchs still thought of themselves as Castilians, Aragonese, Catalans, and Basques rather than as Spaniards." The political situation in Spain at the beginning of the sixteenth century was somewhat uncertain and often turbulent.

The Spanish Crown made a conscious effort to shore up the union by homogenizing the society. It was to be accomplished by abolishing all social deviation, under the auspices of the Catholic church. This policy led to the expulsion of the Jews and Moors and the establishment of the Inquisition, extreme measures that were essentially radical attempts to unify a diverse people. The doctrine of *limpieza de sangre* (purity of blood) required those who aspired to nobility to produce genealogies demonstrating no history of non-Christian blood. It even discriminated against those who had, in fact, converted to Catholicism. The conversos, as they were called, could not hold public or clerical office. Thus, Spanish society was polarized into elites and commoners. Ironically, the growing postmedieval middle class was composed primarily of conversos and so became a special target of elite discrimination and a source of social unrest in the sixteenth century. The near civil war over the question of succession after Isabella's death in 1504 demonstrates that the royal attempts to legislate social and political conformity were not entirely successful.

The Crown was not content to confine its attempts at social engineering to the Iberian peninsula. Through marriage and various other alliances, Spain came to control much of Europe. Efforts to maintain and expand this control resulted in Spain's almost constant state of war on at least one front and sometimes on as many as three. The expense of these conflicts in money and manpower impacted nearly every aspect of Spanish life.

Despite internal and external unrest, Spain came to be the leading power in postmedieval Europe. One reason for its success was the improved administrative abilities of the Crown after the ascension of the Hapsburg dynasty. A centralized government proved much better able to manage European affairs as well as those of the nascent New World colonial venture.

The circum-Caribbean region, at least during the sixteenth century, was wholly subservient to the Spanish Crown. Given Spain's need for capital to prosecute its imperial aims in Europe, it is not surprising that exploitation, rather than development, characterized Spanish Colonial policy. According to McAlister (1984:81), Spain and its colonies had similar, yet conflicting, motivations. "The Crown wished to convert and patronize the indigenous population, establish exclusive sovereignty in its American possessions and, at the same time gain a profit from the enterprise. Conquerors and settlers wanted to exploit the natives, acquire señoríos and become wealthy." It was in this milieu that Hernando de Soto came of age.

Hernando de Soto personifies the popular stereotype of a conquistador. Even the historian James Lockhart, while no fan of de Soto, characterizes him as "a knight of sorts, hasty, dashing, and gallant," although he quickly adds that de Soto "never seriously questioned the validity of the conquest of the New World, or his own right to govern a large part of it, and toward this end he killed as many Indians as the next man, resorting to torture and exemplary mutilation when he thought it necessary" (Lockhart 1972:191). The public image of de Soto ebbs and flows with the historical tide but seems always to be at the extreme end of the spectrum, either good or bad. Theodore Irving, nephew of *Legend of Sleepy Hollow* author Washington Irving, heads the knight errant camp. He paints a heroic portrait of the de Soto expedition. "Of the enterprises undertaken in this spirit, none has surpassed, in hardihood and variety of incident, that of the renowned Hernando de Soto and his band of cavaliers. It was poetry put into action; it was the knight-errantry of the old world carried into the depths of the American wilderness" (Irving 1835:2). Miguel Albornoz, 150 years later, refers to de Soto as the Amadís of Florida, Knight of the Americas.

Most recent scholarship takes a dimmer view of the Spaniard and his army. Alfred Crosby describes de Soto's impact on the native inhabitants of the New World in brutal terms. "They were the people through whose lands and bodies Hernando de Soto hacked a path from 1539 to 1542 in his search for wealth equal to what he had seen in Peru" (Crosby 1986:211). Henry Dobyns (1983:50) refers to the Spaniards as marauders.

Perhaps a more accurate picture of this man is found neither exclusively in *la leyenda negra* (black legend) or *la leyenda blanca* (white legend), but in a more human combination of both: *la historia grisácea* (the gray history). Oftentimes a person's actions are the result of, or constrained by, the course of events of the time. A brief look at de Soto's early life will give a better insight into his actions (a more detailed account is presented by Rocío Sánchez Rubio and Paul Hoffman in Clayton et al. 1993:383–460).

Hernando de Soto's early years are not well documented. The time and place of his birth are debated and little is known of his family. We can say that he was born around 1500 in the Extremadura region of western Spain. He was the son of a reputedly noble, though not exceedingly wealthy, family and expected little in the way of an inheritance, suggesting that he may not have been the eldest son (Duncan 1995:3–4). Yet for a hidalgo (a gentleman), it was considered by the elite of that time degrading to stoop to manual labor or even to engage in trade as a merchant. This may seem odd to our modern capitalistic way of thinking, but such behavior is well documented in both the fictional and historical literature of the period. Indeed, individuals often chose to live in abject poverty rather than work beneath their station (Defourneaux 1979:40–41). With no estates to support him, a hidalgo's options for making an honorable living were limited.

The New World must have been an attractive alternative to a young man with potential. So, as a teenager, de Soto ventured to the Darién region of Panama (where Central and South America join) in the company of Pedrárias Dávila (Pedro Arias d'Ávila), an early conquistador whom Morison (1974:204) characterized as "exceedingly rough, tough, and cruel, though not lacking in energy." Pedrárias is chiefly known in history for executing Blasco Núñez de Balboa and pursuing a brutal policy with the natives (Morison 1974:204). Under this stern tutelage, de Soto demonstrated an aptitude for soldiering and leadership and was soon a person to be reckoned with in the webs of power and intrigue of colonial society.

By his early thirties de Soto had maneuvered to become one of the chief lieutenants of Francisco Pizarro's expedition to Peru. As such, he was a key figure in the conquest of the Inca, personally leading the vanguard of the expedition through much of the Andes. Lockhart (1972:195) has characterized him as a "dashing, untrustworthy, but valuable forward rider." He received four shares of the loot gained from the Inca, the equivalent of either several hundred thousand dollars (Varner and Varner 1980:4n.) or four and a half million (Albornoz 1986:216), depending on the treatment of inflation and exchange rates. In any case, it was a sizable fortune. Ironically, de Soto was excluded by a justly wary Pizarro from any position of real power.

The ambitious de Soto was not satisfied with such wealth when much more was seemingly within his grasp. To validate his noble heritage, he desired hereditary titles and estates while increasing his purse. The surest way to acquire these trappings of nobility during the sixteenth century was by conquering rich new territory for Spain. Since Pizarro had an obvious lock on Peru, de Soto petitioned the Crown for lands to govern in what is now Ecuador and Colombia or, if that was not possible, in the region of Guatemala (Swanton 1985:75). Charles V, however, had other plans for this ambitious conquistador, as is evident in the following excerpt from a letter dated April 20, 1537.

> Inasmuch as you, Captain Hernando de Soto, set forth that you have served us in the conquest, pacification, and settlement of the Provinces of Nicaragua and Peru, and of other parts of our Indias and that now, to serve us further, and to continue to enlarge our patrimony and the royal crown, you desire to return to those our Indias, to conquer and settle the Province of Rio de las Palmas to Florida, the government whereof was bestowed on Pánfilo de Narvaez, and the Provinces of Tierra-Nueva, the discovery and government of which was conferred on Lucas Vázquez de Ayllón . . . I give you, the said Captain Hernando de Soto power and authority, for us and in our name, and in that of the royal crown of Castilla, to conquer pacify, and populate the lands that there are from the Province of the Rio de las Palmas to Florida . . . and further, the Provinces of the said Tierra Nueva. . . . (Clayton et al. 1993:359–60)

Thus, de Soto at last received an asiento, or royal charter, to explore and exploit his own share of the New World. There were terms of bestowal, and the Crown had developed a fairly standard contract by this point. For instance, de Soto or his men were obliged to pay all expenses of the expedition. These expenses included, beyond the mere outfitting costs, the salary of an officer of the royal exchequer, the support of priests, and the costs of constructing at least three stone fortifications at suitable harbors. De Soto invested most of his personal fortune to finance the expedition, which was "an unusual arrangement in an era when wealthy banking families in Seville fronted the funds for most expeditions, often at exorbitant interest rates" (Duncan 1995:219). Impulsive by nature, de Soto considered the potential payoff worth the gamble. If successful, he would receive land (200 leagues of coastline), titles (adelantado, governor, captain-general, and high constable), tax breaks, and the lion's share of any revenue generated by the colony. To ensure that de Soto did not dawdle, the Crown set a time limit of a year for preparing and launching the expedition.

If all went well, Spain gained territory and income at no risk to itself. De Soto, on the other hand, would receive hereditary titles, tremendous wealth, and a country to govern for Spain. The Crown also provided an additional incentive to make the venture successful, in an addendum to the asiento: "we promise and declare that to you will be kept these terms, and whatever therein is contained, in and through all; and you doing otherwise, and not complying therewith, we shall not be obliged to keep with you and comply with the aforesaid, nor any matter of it; on the contrary, we will order that you be punished, and proceed against you as against one who keeps not nor complies with, but acts counter to, the commands of his natural king and lord" (Clayton et al. 1993:365). Apparently social and economic ruin would not be punishment enough for a failed conquistador. Under one possible interpretation of the addendum, he could also have been charged with treason.

Three Spanish conquistadors had tried to subdue *La Florida* prior to 1539. Juan Ponce de León made the first attempt in 1521, followed by Lucas Vázquez de Ayllón in 1526 and Pánfilo de Narváez in 1528. All of these expeditions were led by seasoned campaigners who thought their supplies and preparations would be adequate. All three expeditions failed, their leaders dying in the attempts. Clearly, extraordinary measures were called for if de Soto's venture was to succeed. To this end, he assembled one of the largest, best-equipped, and most experienced armies to sail to the New World during the sixteenth century.

As part of the terms of the asiento, de Soto was made governor of Cuba. This appointment made it easier for him to assemble the personnel, livestock, and equipment necessary for the assault on *La Florida*. Cuba as a final point of departure was crucial since it greatly lessened the time that the horses, considered essential to the success of the endeavor, had to remain in the hold of a vessel.

The expedition set sail from its staging point in Havana on May 18, 1539, and made landfall off the west coast of Florida a week later. Curiously, de Soto decided to return to the same general area where León and Narváez had previously received a hostile reception. Juan Ponce de León had been mortally wounded by a native arrow shortly after he landed. Perhaps de Soto thought the Indians had riches worth protecting, or perhaps it was just hubris on his part. In any event, by the end of the month, the troops and supplies were being offloaded somewhere in Tampa Bay (Milanich and Hudson 1993:15, 53–61). Over 600 men and at least two Spanish women are recorded on the expedition roster. There may have been additional members (servants and so on) in the company not mentioned in the narratives or other documents associated with the expedition. Also transported were over 200 horses, a drove of swine, and specially trained war dogs. The pigs (the first to be introduced into what is now the mainland United States) were intended as insurance against the starvation that had been suffered by Ayllón and Narváez. (The latter expedition had been reduced to eating their horses.) The swine would serve as a self-sufficient, self-perpetuating mobile larder to be used on special occasions or when no other food was available.

The governor, as de Soto is referred to in the existing narratives of the expedition, established a base camp at the landing site and left 100 men to hold it. He and the bulk of his army marched inland and then turned north. The army was able to maintain a good pace despite the difficult terrain and hostile native encounters. Given the previous conquistadors' experiences with the Florida natives and his own reputation as an Indian fighter, it is not surprising that de Soto favored a policy of intimidation rather than negotiation in encounters with the natives. Often this took the form of holding a chief hostage or mutilating him as a warning to let the Spaniards pass unharmed. This policy of preemptive violence frequently had the opposite of the desired effect. Rather than cowing the Indians into submission, this tactic succeeded mostly in inspiring raids and ambushes against the expedition. These conflicts were won handily by the Spaniards, at least early in the expedition.

By early October the army had reached the territory of the chiefdom of the Apalachee. Although encountering stiff resistance, the Spaniards were eventually able to gain possession of the principal village of Anhaica Apalache. The village was large enough to quarter the army and amply supplied with maize as well. Since he had not found the gold he expected nor had any intelligence as to where it might be found, de Soto decided that his army needed to stop, regroup, and plan its future course. However, the time spent at the winter encampment was hardly recuperative. Infuriated over the capture of their village and winter stores, the Apalachee harassed the Spaniards at every opportunity, keeping the army essentially besieged for nearly five months.

The account of this bivouac by Rodrigo Ranjel, de Soto's personal secretary, describes the ordeal of the first winter in *La Florida*. "They [the Apalachee] burned the settlement on two occasions and they killed many Christians with ambushes on some occasions. And although the Spaniards pursued them and burned them, they never showed any desire to come to peace" (see Hann, chap. 9 of this book). It is difficult to have much sympathy for the Spaniards, considering what "coming to peace" with them meant for the native people. The report of the departure of the Spaniards from Anhaica Apalache in March of 1540 illustrates this point. "The horsemen carried their maize [taken from the Apalachee fields and stores] on their horses and those on foot on their backs because [of] the Indians that there were for work, most had died with the hard life that they had endured that winter, naked in chains" (see chap. 8).

This pattern of brutality toward the natives prevailed throughout most of the expedition. However, when it suited his needs, it appears that de Soto was not above giving gifts to or allying with an Indian group. Shortly after his arrival in Florida, de Soto spoke with the cacique Mocoço, who "complained to the Governor about the caciques Orriygua, Neguarete, Çapaloey and Eçita, all four of whom are caciques on that coast, saying that they menaced him because he took our friendship and was willing to give that Christian interpreter to the Christians. Using the same interpreter, the Governor told him that he should not be afraid of those caciques or of others, because he would help him, and all the Christians and many more who would come soon would be his friends and would help him against his enemies" (Ranjel in Clayton et al. 1993:256). The duplicity of presenting the arrival of reinforcements in the guise of assistance belies the calculating nature of de Soto's "friendship." It also demonstrates that he hadn't forgotten the "divide and conquer" lessons he had learned during the Inca campaign.

Unfortunately for de Soto, most of the chiefdoms of *La Florida* were dispersed and decentralized, so there were often no political factions (at least not on the scale of the Inca or Aztec states) to play off one another. Ironically, the cacique of Chicaça, from what is now the state of Mississippi, attempted to use this tactic to turn the tables on de Soto. This chief ostensibly allied with de Soto to make war on a rival cacique. In actuality this was a ruse to put de Soto's army off its guard so as to overwhelm it in a night ambush. The gambit did not prove wholly successful, as de Soto's army rallied after initial confusion to crush the Indians. However, the Spaniards did suffer substantial losses of equipment and livestock, and de Soto learned a harsh lesson (Duncan 1995:396-99).

By the time the army reached Arkansas, in June 1541, it must have been a dispirited lot that "discovered" the Mississippi River. They had suffered scores of casualties and lost much of their equipment, as well losing all of their stolen booty at Chicaça. However, the sight of a large, fortified town on the banks of the St. Francis River should have buoyed their spirits. Here at last, they thought, was a prosperous state like those encountered by other conquistadors. Surely this place would be the key to gaining the wealth that had eluded them for two years.

The fortified village was the principal town of the chiefdom of Casqui, identified by archaeologists as the Parkin Mound site (Morse and Morse 1983:164). Weary and beleaguered and in no position to enforce his request for aid, de Soto tried again to exploit the indigenous political situation. The Spaniards took the side of the chief of Casqui in a vicious raid on the neighboring chiefdom of Pacaha. Most of the atrocities on this particular raid, though, were committed by the Indians. In fact, de Soto paradoxically appears to have assumed the role of peacemaker and mediated a truce between the chiefs. The apparent paradox is resolved by the benefits to de Soto of helping settle the local rivalry: he in fact helped himself by gaining much-needed supplies and bearers.

The next year was spent zigzagging across Arkansas in a futile search for gold. The army entered into a few pitched battles with some of the groups of natives they encountered, but they were minor in comparison with those east of the Mississippi and nothing the battle-hardened Spaniards couldn't handle. At the winter encampment at the village of Autiamque, which archaeologists place in the vicinity of Little Rock, de Soto finally decided to contact his cohort in Cuba to resupply his force in *La Florida*. A risky decision, considering that his men might mutiny at the sight of a way home, this is the first clear indication that de Soto had had enough.

He moved to Guachoya on the Mississippi River to facilitate an investigation of a quick water route to the Gulf of Mexico. Although he was clearly on the right track, his scouting parties could not confirm that the river continued to the sea. Real despair began to spread throughout the ranks as even the dim hope of resupply was extinguished. Perhaps it was desperation that influenced the way de Soto and his men dealt with their situation from this point onward.

In mid-May 1542 de Soto fell ill. He was told that the great chief, Quigualtam, controlled the territory on the other side of the Mississippi. Desiring to cross into that territory to make his way back to the Gulf of Mexico, de Soto, claiming that he was the son of the sun, demanded that Quigualtam visit him at Guachoya. The chief declined this "honor" and mocked the Spaniards.

> . . . he [the cacique] answered him saying that with respect to what he [the governor] said about being the son of the sun, let him dry up the great river and he would believe him. With respect to the rest [that the governor said], he was not accustomed to visit any one. On the contrary, all of whom he had knowledge visited and served him and obeyed him and payed him tribute, either by force or of their own volition. Consequently, if he [the governor] wished to see him, let him cross there. If he came in peace he would welcome him with special good will; if he came in war, he would await him in the town where

he was, for not for him or any other would he move one foot back-ward. (Elvas in Clayton et al. 1993:134)

The Spaniards dared not attempt an assault across the river, as they were outmanned and de Soto himself ill, but he feared that inaction on their part would be interpreted as weakness. To demonstrate their might and the perils associated with defying them, the army conducted an unpro-voked assault on the lesser chiefdom of Anilco, just north of their camp at Guachoya. A detachment of Spanish foot soldiers and cavalry swept into that village and massacred more than a hundred men, women, and chil-dren. Even if the soldiers had exceeded their orders, as indicated by the reprimand for killing women and children that the officers later received, the attack illustrates the frustrations of the Spaniards and the loss of con-trol by de Soto.

The prospects for the army looked grim. The expedition had lost nearly a third of its complement and most of the equipment they had brought with them. More important, it had become obvious to everyone that there simply were no rich civilizations to plunder in *La Florida*. None of the conditions of the royal asiento had been met, which had dire implications for de Soto's political, and hence, social future. As de Soto had risked everything in outfitting the expedition, returning penniless and defeated would have been unthinkable (not to mention dangerous) to a man of his arrogance. De Soto was spared this dishonor, dying of a "fever" shortly after the raid on Anilco. The once-proud "Knight of the Americas" was furtively dumped into the Mississippi during the night to keep the knowl-edge of his death from the surrounding Indians.

The implied question "What would you have done in de Soto's place?" is probably best reserved for computer simulations and the idle specula-tions of armchair conquistadors. Most of us, I suspect, when confronted with de Soto's boyhood options, would have put on a black clerical robe or married the heiress down the street. The question of the proper tactics for leading an expedition in the New World is moot for the average per-son, who could never contrive to be in such a position in the first place.

Was Hernando de Soto typical of his day? Clearly not, any more than Donald Trump is typical of the present. Conquistadors such as Hernando de Soto belonged to an aspiring corps of venture entrepreneurs. They were extremely capable (read ruthless) men who possessed a variety of talents and the sangfroid to use them.

A successful conquistador had to possess certain diplomatic skills. To survive among the different political factions in the New World required an acute political acumen. It was also only by the Crown's favor that asientos were granted. Sometimes the Crown rewarded bold initiative, as in the case of Cortés. However, it was more common to gain recognition through favorable alliances and by securing friends in court.

De Soto also had to have extraordinary leadership skills. Members of these sixteenth-century expeditions were often hidalgos themselves. Usually they were paying part of the costs of the expedition in return for a share of the booty. As such, they followed the conquistador only so long as they thought it would profit them or saw that they could do no better. The threat of mutiny, as clearly seen in Cortés's precautions, was always present. Cortés burned his ships at the outset of the Aztec campaign to ensure that his men had no option but following him. Toward the end of his expedition, de Soto led by sheer force of will, since it was obvious that there was no gold nor other wealth.

Finally, the conquistadors had to have supreme confidence in their abilities. How else could they believe that with a relatively small, unruly force it was possible to sail into an unknown land and make it their own? De Soto's ego must have known no bounds, given his knowledge that three previous conquistadors had lost their lives attempting the same mission. In a nutshell, the conquistadors were ambitious men, in difficult circumstances, with a lot at stake.

Such blind ambition had its dark side. To be a successful conquistador required a certain ruthlessness, not only in dealings with the native inhabitants of the New World but with rival Spaniards as well. The conquistadors were not above hanging their own officers if they suspected treachery or thought that the example would bolster their authority. The torture of Indian captives was seen as a means to an end. The native inhabitants of the New World were simply another obstacle to be overcome by intimidation, negotiation, or warfare, whichever was most expedient. What this says of the conquistador's humanity is for the reader to decide.

The ironic fact is that, even though de Soto's entourage was well equipped for success in terms of supplies, organization, experience, and leadership, it was doomed to failure from the very outset. The goal of the expedition was to replicate the successes of Cortés and Pizarro—that is, to subjugate a wealthy native society possessing vast mineral wealth and to establish a prosperous colony that de Soto would govern. Unfortunately for de Soto, no such El Dorado existed in *La Florida*. There were prosperous agricultural chiefdoms, but nothing on the scale that would allow the expedition quickly to pay for itself, let alone make anyone rich. Even if de Soto had adopted a conciliatory policy toward the natives and had returned the whole expedition to Spain unscathed, he still would have been considered a failure. Farming colonies like those of *La Florida* would have merely produced food to support the more lucrative mining areas in

Mexico and elsewhere, a subordinate role that de Soto would not have relished.

However, even in failure de Soto achieved a remarkable feat. He led an army of 600 for three years, through hostile terrain, on little more than his strength of character. The ultimate tragic consequences of the expedition, the annihilation of the native societies he came in contact with, even de Soto did not foresee. Thus, Hernando de Soto earned a place in history, not because he was the shining Knight of the Americas or the genocidal Butcher of *La Florida* but because, by exploring the Southeast, he paved the way for its colonization and transformation from a native to a European-based society.

THE APALACHEE CHIEFDOM

Hernando de Soto and his army spent five months in the chiefdom of Apalachee. While recognized as a significant historical event, this was by no means the only occurrence of note in Apalachee province. This area of the Florida panhandle, between the Aucilla and the Ochlockonee rivers, has a long history of human occupation. Though this book focuses on the protohistoric period of Apalachee Province, it will take note of other events, particularly those at the Governor Martin site, the presumed location of the principal Apalachee village of Anhaica.

The Apalachee chiefdom arose nearly one thousand years ago during what archaeologists call the Fort Walton period. Based on changes in the material culture (primarily differences in pottery styles), this period is subdivided into shorter archeological phases, which presumably reflect changes in native political regimes or lifestyle. For the Fort Walton period in the Tallahassee Red Hills, three phases have been delineated (Scarry 1994b:162): Lake Jackson (A.D. 1100–1500), Velda (A.D. 1500–1633), and San Luis (A.D. 1633–1704). It can be argued that the San Luis phase should not be included in the Fort Walton period but in a separate Mission period, since European control over the area ended Apalachee dominance. The precontact and postcontact Apalachee will only be synopsized here (for greater detail, see Hann 1988, Milanich 1994).

The Lake Jackson phase is the prehistoric part of the Fort Walton period in the Apalachee territory. The phase name is derived from the Lake Jackson site, on the north edge of present-day Tallahassee. This ceremonial mound center served as the paramount Apalachee village during this first phase. The Lake Jackson phase has been characterized as the first recognizable Apalachee manifestation. In that part of the Fort Walton period, the settlement pattern was a hierarchy of ceremonial centers, villages, hamlets, and farmsteads. Fort Walton–period political centers were marked by pyramidal earthen mounds. The Apalachee shared an artistic tradition with other Mississippian chiefdoms (e.g., distinctive decorative motifs on shell and copper items identified with the Southeastern Ceremonial Complex [Southern Cult]) and perhaps an ideology as well. Its ceramic complex resembled those of other Mississippian societies and incorporated design elements and vessel forms common in Mississippian societies to the north and west of Apalachee Province. Maize agriculture together with beans and squash probably formed the basis of the Apalachee economy during the Lake Jackson phase, with hunting and gathering of wild plants still important to the subsistence base (Scarry 1994b:160-61).

Even before European contact the Apalachee were undergoing major changes. The beginning of the Velda phase (A.D. 1500–1633) was a period of significant demographic shifts. The major mound center at Lake Jackson was abandoned, and the political center shifted to Anhaica Apalachee (the Governor Martin site). Mound building, in general, was discontinued, and there was a decline in the abundance of vessel forms and decorative motifs that previously had linked the Apalachee with other Mississippian polities to the north and west (Scarry 1994b:170). The impetus for these changes is not well understood but may have had to do with prehistoric politics (chiefly succession) or ecological reasons (deforestation, soil fertility).

In other areas such as the economic and technological bases, there was a great deal of continuity. Scarry (1994b) sees the cessation of mound building as a change in the symbolic representation of chiefly authority and the allocation of social surplus labor. Apalachee society, however, remained a complex chiefdom of social stratification and a hierarchically arranged settlement pattern.

Apalachee Province was located within the vague confines of what the Spaniards called *La Florida* (the southeastern United States). The reception received by the first two Spanish expeditions to the territory of the Apalachee gives some idea of the character of these native peoples. In 1528 the expedition of Pánfilo de Narváez landed on Florida's west coast. Early in the expedition the Spaniards learned of the Apalachee. They showed a captured native some gold and asked where more could be found. The reply was "that there was none in that land [the area around Tampa Bay], but only far from there, in the province that they call Apalache, in which there was much gold in great quantity according to what they gave [us] to understand by their signs. And everything whatsoever that they showed to those Indians that it seemed to them [the Indians] that the Christians held in value, they said that there was much of that in

Apalache" (Hann 1996:13). Having learned this, the Narváez expedition quickly moved north toward this fabled land of riches.

The Spaniards of the Narváez expedition reached Apalachee Province on June 25. They were tired and hungry, not having encountered much maize on their journey up the peninsular coast. Upon reaching a settlement of 40 houses, the Spaniards fell upon it, capturing stores of corn and many women and children. The men were elsewhere when the army arrived. Cabeza de Vaca, the chronicler of the expedition, spoke of many fields of maize in the region (Hann 1996).

The Apalachee did not meekly submit to the Spanish invasion. Two large forces of Indians attacked the Spanish camp on successive days and succeeded in setting fire to the village before they were driven off. This prompted the Spaniards to move to the village of Aute, nearer to the coast. The decision to go to Aute turned out to be ill advised. The army was repeatedly ambushed and suffered from illness during its nine-day journey. Upon arriving at Aute, they found that the Apalachee had burned the village and the surrounding maize fields. A desperate decision was then made to press on to the coast and build boats to take them back to their outposts in New Spain (Mexico). Eight years later, four survivors were rescued by a mounted patrol in northern Mexico.

In May 1539 Hernando de Soto arrived on the west coast of Florida in a more ambitious attempt to win *La Florida*. By October 1, de Soto was at the Aucilla River, which marked the eastern boundary of the Apalachee Province. He met some resistance there, but when the Apalachee saw that they could not prevent the Spanish crossing, they fell back. The Spaniards advanced and found the town of Ivitachuco in flames. Pressing on, they reached the principal village of the Apalachee Province, Anhaica Apalache, on October 6.

The village had been abandoned but not burned. Thus, according to the Gentleman of Elvas, a Portuguese knight accompanying the expedition, "the field master, whose duty it [is] to assign and provide lodging, lodged everyone round about this settlement" (see chap. 8). Garcilaso de la Vega describes the village as consisting "of two hundred and fifty large and good houses." De Soto himself moved into the cacique's residences "that were to one side of the village and, as houses of the lord, surpassed all the rest" (see chap. 11).

It was at this point that de Soto decided that his army needed to stop, reconsolidate its forces, and plan its future movements. Again, Garcilaso de la Vega describes the events that took place. "With these intentions he ordered the collecting of all the provisions that should be possible. He ordered the building of many houses in addition to those that the village had so that it would have suitable lodging for all his soldiers. He had the site fortified, which seemed to him appropriate for the security of his people" (chap. 11). De Soto and his men hoped to rest and recover their strength before pressing on after the mineral riches they were certain awaited them.

The rest and recovery sought at the winter encampment proved elusive. In fact, for nearly five months the army was literally besieged at Anhaica. Infuriated over the loss of their village, the Apalachee harassed the Spaniards at every opportunity. According to de Soto's private secretary, Rodrigo Ranjel, "And they [the Spaniards] wintered there [Anhaica] and remained until the fourth of March of the year 1540, in which time many notable things happened with the Indians, who are the bravest of men. And from what will be said now the discerning reader will be able to conjecture their great spirit and daring. Two Indians challenged eight horsemen and they burned the settlement on two occasions and they killed many Christians with ambushes on some occasions. And although the Spaniards pursued them and burned them, they never showed any desire to come to peace" (chap. 9). In short, no one left the camp alone or unarmed, and even then the Spaniards lost several soldiers to native attacks. The first Christmas Mass celebrated in *La Florida* could not have been very festive.

By the following spring, the Spaniards were ready to resume their quest. A captured native's stories of gold smelting in Yupaha, to the north of Apalachee, gave the expedition both a reason and a direction in which to travel. The Gentleman of Elvas describes the departure of the army and the consequences for the Indians of its having encamped there. "On Wednesday, the third of March of 1540, the governor set out from Anhaica Apalache in search of Yupaha. He ordered that all his [men] should be provided with maize for sixty leagues of uninhabited territory. The horsemen carried their maize on their horses and those on foot on their backs, because [of] the Indians that there were for work, most had died with the hard life that they had endured that winter, naked in chains" (chap. 8).

When de Soto's army decamped, the Apalachee returned to reoccupy their violated homes, while the Spaniards marched to their fate. One wonders what life was like for those Indians who had been overrun by an enemy of whose very existence they had been unaware only a short time before.

Nearly a century passed before the Spaniards ventured once more into the Apalachee Province, but this time at the request of the Apalachee themselves. Though the Spaniards began establishing missions in *La Flor-ida* during the latter part of the 1560s, it was not until the first half of the seventeenth century that the mission effort reached Apalachee Province. The Franciscan mission system resulted in significant material and demo-graphic changes in the province (see McEwan 1993) during the seven-teenth century. The dawn of the eighteenth century witnessed the destruc-tion of the mission system and Apalachee Province at the hands of the Carolina militia and their Native American allies.

PART I

The Search and Rescue Mission

Charles R. Ewen

1 · Looking for De Soto

Anhaica Apalachee did not simply cease to exist when de Soto's army decamped in March of 1540. The archaeological evidence indicates that the Apalachee returned to reoccupy their violated homes, while the expedition marched to its fate (see part 2). When the Spaniards returned nearly a century later (this time in the guise of Franciscan missionaries), they encountered a society probably similar to the one that saw de Soto. The village of Anhaica apparently remained a community of such importance that in 1633 one of the first missions in Apalachee, San Luis de Xinyaca, was established in its midst (Hann 1990:485–486). In 1656, this mission was relocated to the west to a more defensible position, and the original village of Anhaica faded from memory.

The route of the de Soto *entrada* and the site of his first winter encampment have been sought by cartographers, historians, and archaeologists for three centuries. The pioneering attempts of Guillaume de l'Isle in 1718 began the serious pursuit, scholarly and popular, that has produced a variety of alternatives for the expedition's route. One of the earliest studies was undertaken by Spain during the eighteenth century to show its prior claim to territory held by the English (Swanton 1985:14).

The narratives of the expedition are the primary source of information about the route. Four accounts of de Soto's foray are known to exist. Luis de Biedma, the king's factor, Rodrigo Ranjel, de Soto's personal secretary, and an anonymous Portuguese knight, the Gentleman of Elvas, all left first-hand accounts of their experiences on the trek. Twenty-five years after the expedition's demise, Garcilaso de la Vega (known as The Inca because he was the offspring of a Spanish adventurer and a Peruvian noblewoman) interviewed survivors of the entrada and wrote a detailed account of the adventure.

The accuracy of these narratives, especially that of Garcilaso, has been the subject of much debate. *The Florida of the Inca* relates the events occurring on the expedition in the greatest detail, but because it is a secondary source penned by a popular author it is the most suspect. Some scholars claim that the style of Garcilaso's account resembles the historical fiction of the time. All agree that his narrative is based on fact, but the details that set it apart from the other accounts may not be reliable. Recently the reliability of some of the other accounts has come under scrutiny as well. Thus, the reader should not invoke any of these documents uncritically. Rather, we have used them as a guide to direct the archaeological research.

The nineteenth century marked the onset of scholarly efforts to track the expedition. The earlier of these studies (McCulloh 1829, Irving 1835, Williams 1837) based much of their route reconstruction on the similarities between place-names on historic maps and those mentioned in the narratives of the expedition. This kind of reasoning is suspect, primarily because many "Indian" place-names in Florida derive from the Creek and Seminole population, which did not enter the state until the eighteenth century. Later nineteenth-century route reconstructions depended more heavily upon geographic descriptions and distances traveled as reported in the narratives but did not wholly ignore the work of their predecessors. These scholars (Pickett 1896, Milburn 1850, Rye 1851, C. C. Jones 1880, J. F. H. Clairborne 1880, and Shipp 1881) for the most part agree that the expedition landed at Tampa Bay and spent the first winter in the vicinity of Tallahassee. Two notable dissenters during this period were John Wescott and Edward Gaylord Bourne. Wescott has the army traveling straight north from Tampa and spending the winter "near the site of General Jackson's residence in Hamilton County" (on the Suwannee, three counties east of Tallahassee's Leon County) (Swanton 1985:32). Bourne, on the other hand, puts Anhaica on the opposite side of Tallahassee. Citing General Thomas Woodward, he locates the site on the Apalachicola River at a place known to the Creeks as Spanish Walka (Spanish Camp) (Swanton 1985:35).

These exceptions aside, the winter camp's location in the vicinity of Tallahassee was well established to the point where John R. Swanton, who was appointed as chair of the United States De Soto Expedition Commission in 1935, referred to the area as one of the route's "datum points." Based on a suite of data (that is, the limited archaeological evidence, the geographic descriptions of Apalachee in the de Soto narratives, and the distances that the Spaniards reported traveling from place to place), Swanton confidently placed the location of Anhaica in the Tallahassee area:

> The position of Iniahica [Anhaica] is fixed with reasonable accuracy by estimating the distance from the Aucilla River probably covered in two days' march. We should expect this to be not less than 20 nor more than 40 miles, and the distance from the Aucilla River to Tallahassee is, in fact, about 31 miles, which is not much greater than the distance in leagues given by Garcilaso, about 11 leagues or 28.6

miles. The country around Tallahassee is indicated clearly though the exact spot may have been on the site of Tallahassee itself, at the site of the later mission of San Luis de Talimali slightly west of Tallahassee or the mound group on Lake Jackson somewhat to the north. Judging by the distance to the sea . . . one of the first two sites is the most likely, and Tallahassee has more remains of the aborigines while the location of San Luis suggests that it was selected by the Spaniards with an eye to its defense. (Swanton 1985:158)

Despite the convictions of most researchers that the first winter encampment was located in Tallahassee, as of the 1980s no trace of the site had ever been found, despite over a century of development and land clearing in the region.

The next systematic attempt to locate Anhaica was made by Louis Tesar during an archaeological survey of Leon County that was carried out as an American Bicentennial activity. Building on Swanton's rather vague parameters and the data accumulated since the De Soto's Commission's report, Tesar reexamined the documentary and cartographic evidence and attempted to reconcile this information with known archaeological sites. Tesar (1980:301–4) rejected the suggestion that the Lake Jackson mound group was the site of de Soto's camp in Apalachee Province, noting that the chroniclers' diaries mention neither the mounds nor the large lake in their description of the village. He also recognized that excavations at Lake Jackson had produced no sixteenth-century Spanish artifacts. He rejected the San Luis mission site west of Tallahassee and a number of other known village sites (for example, 8Le484) on the same grounds. Of Swanton's earlier candidates, this left the city of Tallahassee itself, where Tesar attempted to define the possibilities more closely. Tesar was the first to set explicit criteria for what an archaeological site must contain or not contain to be considered the sixteenth-century village of Anhaica. One of his criteria is that the village resemble the one described in the narratives. A possible problem here is his heavy reliance on Garcilaso, whom most scholars consider the least reliable of the de Soto chroniclers. In any event, Tesar emphasizes two observations: "(1) there is no mention of earthen temple mounds at this site or any of the other Apalachee sites, although they are mentioned elsewhere in the documents; (2) the Apalachee villages do not appear to have been pallisaded" (Tesar 1980:343). He also would expect that Anhaica, unlike other contemporary Apalachee villages, would show evidence of Spanish buildings and fortifications since these are discussed in the Garcilaso narrative. The village should show evidence of burning as the result of the Indian raid mentioned in the Elvas account.

Spanish and Portuguese material culture dating to the sixteenth century is expected at Anhaica, but Tesar urges caution when considering such pieces of evidence, as "they might be derived from shipwreck material being traded northward from the Florida Keys or have been obtained from later explorers just after the middle of the sixteenth century. Finally, while the object or objects found may have indeed derived from the de Soto expedition, they may have been carried over such distances from the de Soto expedition route before reaching their final resting place that they no longer indicate their site of origin. (1980:342)

Another important factor that may have misled previous researchers was a description of how the site of Anhaica should appear in the archaeological record. Tesar presumed, based on the documentary record, that "division of the village into identifiable sections is characteristic of large Apalachee villages. . . . In this respect, it is noted that the results of the Leon County Survey indicated that possible simultaneous occupation of several adjacent finger ridges [occurred] in the Tallahassee Red Clay Hills area in the northern half of the county. If such an interpretation is correct, then the dwelling sites on these ridges should be considered as part of a single dispersed village with each ridge serving to divide the whole into apparent parts" (1980:303).

This distinction is important since separate, but adjacent, ridgetops are usually assigned separate site numbers. Such assignments would make the recognition of a single, large site such as Anhaica nearly impossible. At the time he wrote, Tesar knew of no site that fit the criteria for Anhaica. He believed, however, that he could narrow the area where the site was likely to be.

In delineating a likely survey area, Tesar first computed the distance from Anhaica to various other features (river crossings, distance to the ocean, for example) mentioned in the narratives. These were triangulated and plotted onto a topographic map. Next he examined historic maps of the area for possible additional information such as the locations of trails or roadways. Historic trails were considered important since it is assumed that de Soto's army did not wander across a trackless wilderness but followed established pathways. Such trails, Tesar reasoned, would continue to be used well into the historic period.

Tesar then took all of this disparate information and correlated it with Late Fort Walton site distribution data onto a single map that defined an 80-square-mile rectangular area in which he thought the archaeological search would prove most fruitful. Based on de Soto chroniclers' narratives and location of known historic trails, Tesar felt that "the most likely area for the de Soto wintering site was in the area north of Lake

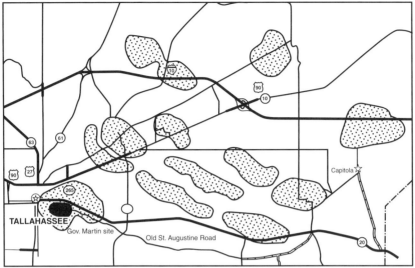

1.1. Tesar's revised map of the de Soto search area (after Tesar and Jones 1989).

Lafayette, east of Lake Jackson, and south of Lake Iamonia" (1980: 345–46). In fact, this area is close to where the Governor Martin site was later discovered.

Following the discovery of the Governor Martin site and its early recognition as an Anhaica candidate, Tesar reexamined the documentary evidence, physiographic data and historic trail locations (Tesar and Jones 1989). He was able to redefine and expand his original study area to the west so that it included the Governor Martin site. (fig. 1.1). The point of this reexamination was not to pinpoint the site's location (since presumably the discovery of the Governor Martin site had done just that); rather, it defined an area where the rest of the village was likely to be located, as well as the surrounding hamlets mentioned in the narratives.

Jeffrey Brain of the Peabody Museum, in his preface to the reprinted *Final Report of the United States De Soto Commission*, also examined the evidence that had accumulated up to 1981 and tentatively placed the site near Lake Lafayette. He was fairly optimistic that Anhaica could be found archaeologically:

Although archaeology has yet to make a positive contribution to the location of de Soto in the Apalachee region, it has there one of the best opportunities of the entire entrada to pin down the elusive army. The possibilities are fairly well circumscribed and within the scope of a realistic program of archaeological research. Furthermore, the stay was a lengthy one by the entire army, and many buildings and fortifications were constructed that should be manifest in architectural features contrasting with native constructions. Finally, only in its first year, the army was still well accoutered and recently resupplied from its base camp at the landing. It might be expected that discarded artifacts would be relatively abundant compared to subsequent stages of the journey. The caveat issued earlier, however, remains in force: archaeologists must look for, and find, an indubitable European encampment. Artifacts in native sites so close to the coast could have many origins. (Brain in Swanton 1985:xxiii)

Such was the state of the search for Anhaica in the middle of the 1980s. The parameters of the search were well defined, as well as the criteria against which all claimants would be judged.

Tesar, from his examination of the documentary evidence, constructed the following set of criteria for the site of Anhaica: "(1) the site is large (250 dwellings before the Spanish additions); (2) may be divided into parts or areas; (3) has structures of both Apalachee (generally oval or round) and Spanish (most likely rectangular with possibly some metal fastenings); (4) probably had an earthen or wooden breastwork of Spanish construction for fortification; and, (5) the cacique's dwellings were distinct or at least better than those in the rest of the town" (Tesar 1980: 350).

Milanich and Hudson (1993:224) expect that, since Anhaica was the site of a military encampment, findings should include discarded Apalachee artifacts (from the fleeing Indians); trade goods (beads) such as those found at the Ruth Smith Mound, Tatham Mound, and other de Soto contact sites; hardware and Spanish ceramic sherds; and perhaps some nonnative faunal remains (horse and pig). With search area and identification criteria so well established, one would expect that the eventual discovery of the site would be the result of an intentional search. Ironically, the discovery was serendipitous.

2 · A Sensational Discovery

Serendipity

When one thinks of Spanish missions, the images that spring to mind are of romantic, crumbling adobe-walled buildings in places like San Antonio or Santa Fe. They come to mind because the eighteenth-century presence of Spain in the American Southwest is still very visible. Not so for the earliest Spanish missions in North America: the seventeenth-century missions of *La Florida*. B. Calvin Jones, an archaeologist with the Florida Division of Archaeological Research, has been trying to change that perception for the past three decades.

Jones began his archaeological career in Texas, not far from some of those later missions. After completing his studies at the University of Oklahoma, he went east to Florida to pursue his interests in archaeology. These interests, coupled with his employment at the Florida Bureau of Historic Sites and Properties (now Bureau of Archaeological Research), naturally led Jones to undertake research on the Franciscan missions of the seventeenth century. During the sixteenth and seventeenth centuries, Spanish Florida possessed over 200 sites that had been either *doctrinas* (mission centers), *visitas* (out-villages), or European settlements frequented by the natives for religious purposes (Hann 1990:2–3; Jesús 1630:100). Jones had discovered the sites of nine of these mission centers in northwest Florida (Jones and Shapiro 1990). On March 11, 1987, he thought he had another to add to the list.

Nuestra Señora de la Candelaria de Tama, also referred to as La Purificación de Tama in the historical documents, was a Franciscan mission founded in Apalachee Province in 1675. It was actually inhabited not by the Apalachee but by Tama-Yamassee Indians from La Tama, an Indian province in the Georgia piedmont. At the mission both groups lived side by side but in separate settlements. Based on distances mentioned in the historic documents, Jones had suspected for some time that this mission had existed on a ridge nearly a mile east of Florida's state capitol building. A dozen years earlier he had reported that this mission site was likely to be located "along the east edge of the Capitol Center Planning area [roughly in the area of the Governor Martin site]. The exact location of this site has not been discovered, although a nineteenth century historical note made by Governor Duval, as well as finds of Spanish artifactual remains, strongly indicate that the location is within two known sites, 8Le137 or 8Le282" (Jones 1975:14). Others felt that the location was closer to Myers Park or Lake Ella (cf. Eubanks 1990:34, Hann 1988:85).

But because the property that interested Jones was in a sleepy, residential neighborhood, there seemed little opportunity to test his hypothesis. Still, Jones felt that "the more I observed the Martin property [the ridgetop] the more I sensed the realization that Spanish and Indians had shared their lives there. Along the top of the road embankment dark organic earth could be seen. On a meditative occasion, the hazy images of these forebears and the totality of their time at this site flashed through my mind. The aura of the de Soto site evoked these impressions in me although I did not know the identity of the Spaniards and exact time of their occupancy" (1988:403).

Like much of Florida in 1987, Tallahassee was experiencing rapid commercial and residential development. Noticing that an office complex was being planned for the very ridge in which he had been interested, Jones seized the opportunity to investigate. Chuck Mitchell, president of Mad Dog Design and Construction Company, which was developing the property, recalled being uneasy when he encountered Calvin at the construction site, but after Jones explained what he was after, agreed to let him "poke around for just a day or two" (Mitchell 1989:1). Thus given his lead, Jones began putting shovel tests in the ridgetop.

The first pit of the six he dug that day revealed sherds of Spanish Olive Jar and burned clay daub, both characteristic of mission sites. Olive Jar is a type of Spanish pottery that takes the form of large jugs (not unlike Roman amphorae). Used to transport a variety of commodities, from wine to olive oil, it is ubiquitous to Spanish sites in Florida and the Caribbean. Daub, on the other hand, is a ceramic remainder of the burned walls of houses (see chap. 5). The structures had a clay covering that was fired into a hard ceramic when they burned down. Often the impressions of house poles or roof thatching can be observed in the daub. Thus Jones first concluded that he had indeed found the mission site he sought.

Paradoxically, this exciting discovery created the first of a series of dilemmas. There was no money in the budget of the Bureau of Archaeological Research to mount a large, unanticipated field project. Further, the site was threatened with imminent destruction through development activity. Negotiations with the developers by Jones and Jim Miller (the state archaeologist and chief of the Bureau of Archaeological Research) brought a two-week delay in construction that allowed Jones to conduct further tests in order to get an idea of the site layout and to collect more artifacts diagnostic of the mission period.

In the two weeks that followed, however, Jones was unable to locate any of the other expected mission structures. The model for mission site layout in use at that time (Jones and Shapiro 1990) specified that the site have at least three distinct areas: church, convent, and cemetery. A *cocina,* or kitchen building, was also often present at these mission sites.

The material assemblage Jones was finding was puzzling as well. The Indian ceramics recovered consisted mainly of incised, late Fort Walton–period varieties that tended to predate the seventeenth century, rather than the stamped Jefferson series ceramics usually found on mission sites. The tin-glazed Spanish polychrome majolicas that characterize Spanish missions in northwest Florida were largely missing from the collection. Instead a few fragments of an unusual yellow-glazed European ceramic turned up. It would later be identified as Melado ware, a sixteenth-century Spanish type (see chap. 5). On March 23, Jones reported to Miller that he did not know the identity of the site (Jones 1988:403).

INITIAL INVESTIGATIONS

Faced with these questions and running out of time, Jones enlisted the aid of his wife and several avocational archaeologists (see acknowledgments) to expose more of the site quickly. Mobilizing these volunteers, Jones was able to open several units and recover an impressive array of artifacts. The developers had indicated to Jones that the first construction activity planned for the site was the entrance drive. Focusing his efforts on this threatened area, Jones established a transect down the middle of the planned drive and placed test pits along it at random intervals. The transect (fig. 2.1) ran north-south between the Governor Martin mansion and East Lafayette Street and then followed the proposed drive in a curve around the eastern side of the house. A short east-west transect was also established running along East Lafayette Street west of the drive. Fourteen test pits were placed along these transects, and all yielded some evidence of past occupation.

It became necessary to narrow the search area further in the limited time available. Earl Van Atta, a retired soil scientist, employed a metal detector to locate metal artifacts. Areas with metal hardware might mark the locations of Spanish buildings, and excavation in those areas would prove most profitable in determining the nature of the European occupation. The wrought nails recovered in this manner were not unexpected, but the small rings of rusted iron wire that turned up defied initial identification. An area roughly equidistant between the mansion and the street was deter-

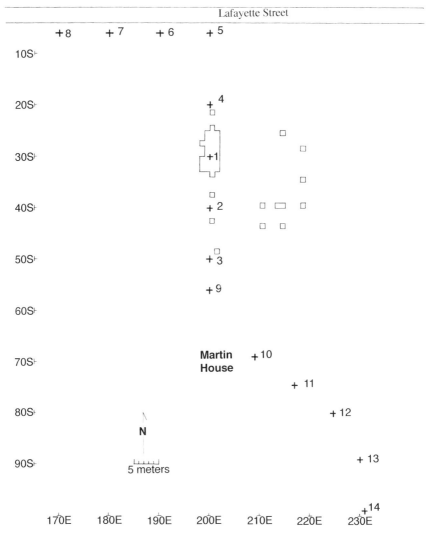

2.1. Original transect of test pits.

mined to contain the most artifacts as well as architectural evidence (such as daub fragments), so the crew opened a block excavation there. The area indeed proved fruitful, and by March 26 it had become apparent that the site contained evidence of a Spanish occupation *prior* to the seventeenth century and the time of the missions.

The rusted fragments of iron wire were pivotal in the identification of the site. Jones (1988:403) had at first thought that they might be the remains of curry combs, cot springs, or spiral notebook bindings, since there was a fair amount of twentieth-century debris on the surface of the site. Yet the iron ring fragments (measuring from 5 to 8 mm in diameter) were found in the deeper levels of the site, in association with the early European and Indian artifacts. It occurred to Jones that these rings might represent chain mail armor of the type mentioned in the de Soto narratives. From that point on, his working hypothesis was that the Governor Martin site corresponded to Anhaica Apalachee and that the Spanish artifacts were from the de Soto winter encampment of 1539–1540.

In the Tallahassee area, pre-mission period (before 1633) Spanish artifacts tentatively can be associated with the de Soto expedition because there had been few Spaniards in the area between 1540 and 1633. This is certainly what came to Jones's mind, and he proposed this hypothesis to his superiors at the end of March, after three weeks of digging. By this time, 21 features (evidence of discrete past activity such as postmolds or trash pits) had been found. Most of these features were associated with the initially discovered wattle-and-daub structure. However, as Tesar (1980: 342) had earlier cautioned, neither the earlier expedition of Pánfilo de Narváez nor salvaged shipwreck material could be ruled out. Jones dismissed the Narváez alternative on the basis that "he didn't come this far inland. Also there is too much broken pottery for his short 25 day stay" (1988:404). The shipwreck alternative could presumably be ruled out on the basis of the quantities and types of Spanish material being recovered as well. Though far from conclusive, the evidence was compelling that the site had been associated with de Soto, prompting the state to commit more resources to salvage excavations.

The Investigation Intensifies

The possibility that the Martin site might be associated with de Soto caused the Bureau of Archaeological Research to reassess the situation. The first requirement was confirmation of the site's significance before announcing the discovery of the long-sought location of Hernando de Soto's first winter camp. To this end, the professional archaeological crew then working at the nearby San Luis Archaeological and Historic Site was brought over to assist with the excavations. Under the supervision of Richard Vernon and Gary Shapiro, the crew worked for nearly three weeks and established exacting field controls while recovering a substantial body of data. The volunteers continued to render invaluable assistance, working side by side with the professional archaeologists and running the water-screening station.

After the addition of a professionally trained archaeological crew, the frantic pace slowed a bit, and it was possible to examine other areas of the site besides those threatened with immediate destruction. The backdirt produced by the initial salvage effort was fine-screened to recover small artifacts that might have been overlooked during the search for architectural evidence. A grid was established over the site, and previous excavations were tied to the grid for mapping purposes. Previous sketch maps were redrafted into detailed measured drawings (fig. 2.2).

The San Luis crew also started a reconnaissance program at the Governor Martin site to determine the limits of the occupation. They employed a technique that had proved highly effective at their own site: an auger survey. Rather than relying on judgmental sampling, the auger survey was conducted in a systematic fashion using the recently established site grid. This technique first placed a 2-foot x 2-foot open-top box on a designated grid point. The bottom of the box had a hole 10 inches in diameter, through which an 8-inch power auger bit was drilled into the earth. The resulting spoil was caught within the box and could be quickly sifted to recover any artifacts in the soil matrix. The auger holes were drilled at 10-meter intervals. By noting the presence or absence of chronologically diagnostic artifacts in the core samples, the survey was able quickly to determine the extent of the deposits for further excavation. The results of the survey were encouraging: "Of the 211 auger holes, about one third (72) contained no artifacts. These are rather regularly spread across the tract. About 60% of the holes (126) contained Indian artifacts, and these were also distributed across most of the tract. Artifacts from these holes could be from the time of de Soto or earlier. Eleven holes (5%) contained artifacts from the de Soto encampment. These are concentrated on the front half of the tract and suggest four different areas where Spanish artifacts might be more common" (Miller 1987).

Meanwhile, Jones and his volunteers focused on the two-acre tract, north of the Martin house, slated for initial development. This work uncovered several postholes and pieces of daub that were interpreted as the remains of a large, rectangular structure (a conclusion later subject to reinterpretation; see chap. 5). The postmolds associated with this structure had flat bottoms, suggesting that the posts had been cut with a saw, which would be indicative of European construction. Thin-walled Olive Jar sherds, chain mail, and chevron and blown glass beads were among the most exciting artifacts recovered by this crew. Wrought iron nails, interpreted as horseshoe nails (again, later subject to reinterpretation; see chap. 5), rounded out the evidence suggesting de Soto had been there.

Toward the end of April, the bureau managed to acquire limited funding to support the project (see chap. 3), and a new team of archaeologists was

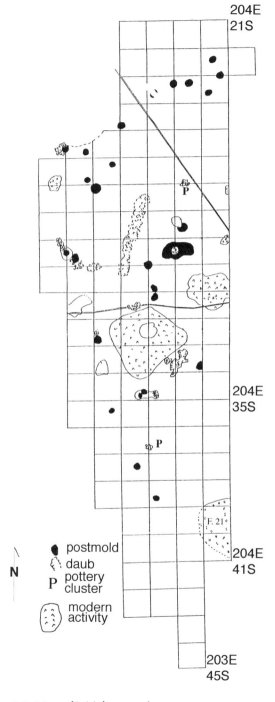

204E
21S

204E
35S

204E
41S

F. 21

● postmold
〈 daub
P pottery
cluster
modern
activity

N

203E
45S

2.2. Map of initial excavations.

hired in May. The San Luis crew returned to their own mission site, but continued to lend support in the form of facilities, equipment, and advice.

I became part of the project on May 5, an association as serendipitous as the discovery of the site itself. I had just received my Ph.D. from the University of Florida, graduating on May 2, when I received a call from the state archaeologist's office. Much of the effort to preserve the Governor Martin site hinged on its association with the de Soto winter encampment. However, since no one had ever seen a de Soto site, it was difficult to determine what one would look like. My dissertation work had been done on a sixteenth-century Spanish site in Haiti (Ewen 1987, 1991), so I was at least familiar with the artifacts of the time period. Thus I was offered the opportunity to codirect the project with Jones.

In the movie *The Wizard of Oz,* the magician told Dorothy that he had come to be wizard after his balloon had blown off course over Kansas and he had ended up in Oz. "The people mistook me for a powerful magician and proclaimed me first Wizard of Oz. Times being what they were, I took the job." This quote seemed apropos as I had had no serious job prospects after having finished a long graduate study program. A national conference I attended immediately after accepting the position with the de Soto dig confirmed the dismal employment outlook in academia. Thus what seemed like tremendously bad timing in terms of entering the job market actually allowed me to work on the most interesting site of my career.

KNEE-DEEP IN THE HOOPLA

Rumors of the site's possible association with de Soto had been rampant throughout the state's archaeological community since shortly after Jones had reported his suspicions to his colleagues at the end of March. In Gainesville, at the University of Florida, we had heard about the alleged chain mail links, the beads, and other sixteenth-century Spanish artifacts in association with Late Fort Walton–period Indian pottery. It sounded intriguing but hardly conclusive. The Florida Department of State, in which the state archaeologist's office is located, was also skeptical and wanted confirmation before the news of such an important discovery was released to the general public. It was a good idea, anyway.

The primary goal of the dig became testing the de Soto hypothesis. I was admonished to not talk to the press until we could conclusively identify the site. Thus, I departed for the Society for American Archaeology meetings, prior to starting work in Tallahassee, blissfully unaware that the dig had become front-page news in the local newspaper.

As early as April 21, the *Tallahassee Democrat* had broken the news that de Soto had camped out near the state capitol building, complete with a map showing the exact location. Public response was immediate and immense, as the *Tallahassee Democrat* reported three days later: "curious adults as well as children on Spring break have showed up to soak up the palpable feel of sixteenth-century Florida." Visitation had become such a problem that the April 24 story was headlined "Give de Soto diggers a break by staying away, officials urge." The paper did nothing to dissuade public interest, however, and on Sunday April 26 it featured the de Soto dig on the front page, complete with site map and preliminary archaeological interpretations. The Tallahassee newspaper would continue to run periodic updates for the duration of the dig.

The caution that I, and other archaeologists, gave to the local press, that there were other possible explanations for the presence of sixteenth-century Spanish artifacts, never saw print. Local television coverage, which was extensive, similarly edited interviews to push the de Soto hypothesis. I was barraged by phone calls from my colleagues wondering how I could make such bold claims based on the available evidence, at the same time being upbraided by exasperated reporters wondering how I could remain so skeptical given the available evidence.

Local coverage alerted the general public to the discovery of the site and the plight of the archaeologists, but it was the *New York Times* that made the state legislature sit up and take notice. On May 19, the *Times* ran a story about the site in its Science section, discussing the de Soto expedition and the alleged discovery of the first winter encampment. It also played up the significance of the find: "The discovery, if confirmed by further excavation and research, would be the crowning achievement of recent scholarly efforts to determine more precisely the route of the de Soto expedition from 1539 to 1543. The work has already resulted in many revisions in the course as it has been outlined in history books." With that, the Governor Martin site hit the big time. News of the site was carried throughout the nation on the wire services. The *Orlando Sentinel, Tampa Tribune,* and *Miami Herald,* to mention only a few of the larger in-state papers, sent reporters to interview archaeologists at the dig.

Joining the press in covering the excavations, several of the local television stations sent reporters to the site every month the dig was in the field. Radio coverage was equally generous; the site was highlighted in several local public radio broadcasts and appeared in a feature segment of National Public Radio's *All Things Considered.* Most people, however, probably learned of the site when it was mentioned on *Paul Harvey's News at Noon—Page 2.* The coverage targeted all adult audiences and even younger readers, for whom Calvin Jones was profiled in the *Weekly Reader.*

The extensive news coverage attracted a crush of visitors to the site. Tour buses made regular stops, and dozens of school groups visited on field trips. Jones and I were in great demand as speakers for civic and educational organizations. The archaeologists at work were distracted by visitors' constant questions, and while answering the questions was recognized as important, it did slow work considerably. A public relations specialist was eventually hired, and the Museum of Florida History provided volunteer docents to act as tour guides during the week so that the trained crew could keep doing what they were hired to do: dig. Security became a concern to both the archaeologists and the developers, who were also working at the site. A security guard was hired to patrol the area at night, and a crew had to be kept in the field seven days a week, not only to keep the work apace but also to oversee the site on weekends, when crowds visited.

For all its negative aspects, the publicity proved absolutely crucial to the project. It was its high visibility that prompted the state of Florida to explore the possibility of acquiring all or part of the site. The extensive news coverage was used to the archaeologists' advantage in fund raising from private sources. The negotiations between the landowners, developers, city officials, and state bureaucracy produced a variety of acquisition scenarios that changed almost daily.

The story of the battle to preserve the site is nearly as interesting as the history and archaeology. The story of the de Soto expedition's struggle with native peoples and de Soto's political intrigues at the Spanish court were part of the news in Tallahassee nearly 500 years later. To understand and appreciate the archaeologists' strategies and their ability to continue work at the site for nearly two years, it is necessary to know something of the struggle that kept them in the field.

3 · The Struggle to Preserve the Site
Timing Is Everything

It was the best of times and the worst of times. Depending upon your perspective, the archaeological site on Lafayette Street represented an exciting opportunity or a major headache. Often it represented both at the same time for all parties concerned.

From the public perspective, the discovery of the early Spanish artifacts at the Governor Martin site was an extremely timely find. The 450th anniversary of de Soto's wintering at Anhaica was coming in 1989 and the Columbian Quincentennial was not far behind. Many activities were being planned for the Quincentennial, and the discovery of the early Spanish contact site gave Tallahassee a natural tie-in.

The odds against the discovery were enormous. If Calvin Jones hadn't believed that the Tama mission was located on the ridge east of the state capitol building, and if he hadn't taken note of the development activities before any serious construction began, and if he hadn't been bold enough to ask for permission to put in test pits, and if the developer hadn't been enlightened enough to grant that permission, then it is likely that the location of de Soto's winter encampment would still be lost to us today.

These coincidences might sound amazing, but if Jones hadn't been able to follow up on his inklings about the site, wouldn't one of the construction workers have spoken up when they began to unearth those remarkable artifacts? In this case, probably not. Not for the stereotypical reason that construction workers are ignorant or dishonest. Or even for the reason that the developers would have bulldozed a major archaeological site rather than jeopardize a lucrative commercial venture. Rather it was because the artifacts were *not* remarkable to the untrained eye (as explained in chap. 5).

The small glass beads, rings of iron mail, and drab fragments of Spanish Olive jar would probably have escaped the notice of all but the keenest-eyed worker. Even if the construction workers had noticed and reported these artifacts, what then? The *National Geographic* sent a photographer after the site's identity had been established but didn't print any of the pictures because the finds weren't particularly impressive. Jones tested the site and studied the artifacts for three weeks before the true significance of the assemblage became apparent to him. No, the discovery could have occurred only through the combination of the right man being in the right place at the right time. On the other hand, the timing couldn't have been worse.

Tallahassee is home to a large university as well as being the seat of the Florida state government. It is a growing town, with new housing construction and commercial developments a common sight. For developers and contractors to make money in this intensely competitive environment, they need to stay within their budgets. Anything that throws them off schedule and idles their crews, even for a couple of weeks, can spell financial ruin for a construction project.

The potential for fiscal disaster is why it is so remarkable that Chuck Mitchell, of Mad Dog Design and Construction, permitted archaeological testing on a site and that Steve Allen, of Tallahassee Development Corporation, allowed excavations to continue. At best they could have hoped that Jones would not discover anything and so would only slightly delay their work. At worst they could have expected what eventually happened: a full-blown archaeological project and thousands of visitors at the site. Mitchell's initial decision was not made on a whim or out of ignorance. He recalled receiving phone calls from two other developers who told him that he was crazy and that they had bulldozed cemeteries rather than let an archaeologist on their sites. However, Mitchell, who had majored in history in college, wanted to "do the right thing."

For many developers, doing the right thing means complying with the law. Section 106 of the National Historic Preservation Act states that "any proposed Federal or federally assisted undertaking in any State . . . shall prior to approval of the expenditure of any Federal funds on the undertaking or prior to the issuance of any license, as the case may be, take into account the effect of the undertaking on any district, site, building, structure, or object that is included in or eligible for inclusion in the National Register." Clearly, the site of de Soto's first winter encampment would qualify as significant and eligible for the National Register. However, since the development had no federal involvement, Mitchell was under no legal obligation to do anything to protect the site. In fact, as there were no relevant state laws or local ordinances in effect at that time, the archaeological discovery had no legal protection whatsoever. Lacking a legal imperative, the best the archaeologists and state and local agencies could do was to prevail upon the good will of the developers. Fortunately, this was enough, at least initially.

However, as is the case with most construction projects, time is money, and there was no money available to pursue the archaeological research, let alone to compensate the developers for the delays that they were experiencing.

FUNDING

Finding a way to pay for the archaeology was a problem even before the site was thought to be associated with de Soto. The reason that Jones assembled a group of amateur volunteers to assist with the initial archaeological testing of the site was that there simply was no other option if he wanted to get the job done. This was, in part, how Jones had come to work with amateurs in the first place. State funds are dedicated primarily to inventorying and managing archaeological properties on state-owned lands. Occasionally, money would be budgeted for archaeological investigations at some of these sites. However, there was typically very little additional funding, beyond Jones's salary, to conduct excavations, especially on private property. On the occasions when additional funds could be made available, a year or more would elapse between the request for funding and the availability of dollars for any further investigations.

By involving amateurs in his projects, Jones was able to move a lot more dirt than he could move by himself. It also gave him many more eyes around the state to help locate sites. Though Jones employed amateurs long before most of his contemporaries did, many archaeologists these days are finding their work greatly enhanced by properly trained volunteers. State archaeological societies and other organizations, such as Earthwatch, now offer many opportunities for the interested lay person to participate in an archaeological dig.

Volunteers are great for short projects but usually cannot be relied on for work of more than a couple of weeks' duration. They allow themselves to be distracted by such small matters as earning a living or spending time with their families. The volunteers that Jones was able to assemble were remarkable in both their previous training and their ability to devote far more time than usual, due partly to the importance of the site and partly to Jones's charismatic qualities. Still, once the true nature of the site was suspected, it became imperative to field a crew of professional excavators to conduct a sustained project.

The Bureau of Archaeological Research (BAR) was already supporting a group of highly trained excavators at the San Luis Archaeological and Historic Site on the other side of town. Transferring the San Luis field crew to the Governor Martin site could only be a temporary solution, but even a short stint by the San Luis crew was invaluable. It allowed Jones the luxury of time to sit down and think about the project while a supervised professional crew established a grid, helped coordinate the volunteers, and took care of the endless details that plague the director of a large and complex project. It also bought the BAR some time to search for a more permanent solution.

The solution, and indeed the cobbled-together approach should be called that, was a combination of private and public funding. Bill Thomas, owner of a local Chevrolet dealership who had read about the archaeologists' dilemma in the newspaper, stepped in with a $10,000 donation. This essentially paid the interest on the developers' loans, giving the archaeologists a window of opportunity to continue their excavations. The funding for the archaeologists' work came from the Institute for Early Contact Period Studies at the University of Florida–Gainesville. Through the institute, Michael Gannon and Jerald Milanich had contracted with the Florida Park Service to search for de Soto sites in Florida. Since the Governor Martin site appeared to be exactly the kind of archaeological target they sought, it was a logical step to expend some of the grant on the verification of its identification. The $13,000 dollars from their grant hired me and a half dozen other field crew for at least a month. At this early stage of the project, Jim Miller estimated that the cost of the digging and analysis of recovered materials would probably be less than $20,000. As it turned out, this would be just a down payment.

Even though definitive proof was lacking (and would not come until months later), many archaeologists and most of the general public believed the site represented contact with de Soto. Although the archaeology was geared to testing this hypothesis, fund raising proceeded as if it were an established fact. Given the assumptions concerning the site, the bureau's efforts diverged into two related but separate lines. One set of negotiations was concerned with modifying the commercial development plan to allow the acquisition and preservation of a portion of the site. The other fund-raising activities were focused on keeping the archaeologists in the field, excavating the areas subject to immediate development.

Fund raising is never easy, even when the cause is a popular one. The de Soto project was hampered by the public's perception that it was a state-supported endeavor. And so it was, but only in part. State institutions, such as the University of Florida, the Florida Department of State, and the Department of Natural Resources were able to provide some emergency funds for hiring a professional crew. As development continued and the critical importance of the site became fully realized, it became apparent that the original estimate of $20,000 would prove wholly inadequate. The more the archaeologists dug, the more they found—and the more money needed to keep them digging.

Because of the volatile financial situation, the crew waxed and waned according to available funding. Crew size varied from twelve to three paid members depending on what the payroll could support. Fortunately, the strong volunteer effort, which included experienced professional archaeologists, buoyed the crew numbers. I was particularly pleased when two of my colleagues, Larry Conrad, of Western Illinois University, and Russ Skowronek, of Santa Clara University, volunteered to spend their summer vacations working at the site. Their association with a project that I was helping to direct was especially gratifying since Conrad had directed my first dig in 1973—the Orendorf Village site, from the middle Mississippian period—on which Skowronek was a fellow crew member.

Though the public entities were anxious to help, the reality was that the Bureau of Archaeological Research did not have the funding in its annual budget to cover the costs of an unanticipated large-scale project. Other state agencies such as the Department of Natural Resources, the Florida Museum of Natural History, and the University of Florida's Institute for Early Contact Period Studies were able to cover the costs of the dig in its early months. Even so, by July these funds were nearly exhausted, and the crew had been notified to finish up what they could as the project's end was in sight. Then came a remarkable find.

On July 2, a copper coin was found during a metal detector search of the northwest quadrant of the site. The coin turned out to be a four-maravedi piece, one of the first coins to be used in the New World (see chap. 5). This exciting discovery made the front page of the *Tallahassee Democrat* and was picked up by the wire services and flashed across the country. Accompanying this story was the news that the dig would be closing up due to lack of funding. The emotional appeal struck a chord with the public, and by the end of July several private donors had given money specifically for the archaeology. In addition, the Historic Tallahassee Preservation Board spearheaded the formation of a private fund-raising committee.

The Florida Trust for Historic Preservation established the Florida Trust De Soto Account to handle private donations, which eventually accounted for nearly $20,000. T-shirts commemorating the site that were printed and sold for $10 apiece proved highly popular and actually generated enough money to cover the purchase of field equipment and many incidental expenses. Local businesses donated money and in-kind services. A local pizza parlor and sandwich shop made sure the volunteers and crew never went hungry. Even the clients whose offices had been slated for the buildings being erected on the site lent their support.

The Trust for Public Land, which eventually wound up purchasing the site for later sale to the state, put out brochures urging public support for the archaeological work. They went to bat for the project at other funding agencies as well. The trust's support was, in part, responsible for the un-precedented $25,000 emergency grant from the Elizabeth Ordway Dunn Foundation. This last grant kept the crew in the field until mid-December, when the final negotiations for the land had been completed and the area to be disturbed by construction had been thoroughly investigated by the archaeologists.

Thus the fieldwork expanded from a two-week crash salvage effort to a ten-month professionally staffed project. But a major part of the project still remained: the analysis of the finds. It had been difficult to raise enough money to keep a crew in the field. It was impossible to repeat the same feat for a lab crew. When a well-respected international journal was approached concerning funding for laboratory analysis, their reply was that they primarily supported fieldwork and funded analysis "only when it was crucial to the project." This response illustrates the low appeal of the less glamorous aspects of archaeology, since it is difficult to imagine a case when analysis would not be crucial to a project.

Even though funding was a problem, the basic processing and analysis of the artifact assemblage was in fact carried out concurrently with the fieldwork. During the course of the project there were many rainy days that would halt fieldwork. The crew would then adjourn to the onsite lab to process, or clean and sort, the recovered artifacts. Volunteers were cru-cial in this effort also, and "lab days" were scheduled for weekends and holidays to take better advantage of their availability.

Many of the specialized analyses were performed by a separate grant or by the personal favors of professional colleagues. The analysis of the beads found at the site was done at a bargain rate by Marvin Smith under a grant from the Bead Society of America. Analysis of the human remains was conducted at no cost by Rebecca Storey and Randolph Widmer, both of Houston University, with additional commentary by David Dickel, of the Florida Bureau of Archaeological Research, and the late William Maples, of the University of Florida. Specialized ceramic analyses were undertaken by Emlen Myers, of the Smithsonian Institution, and Stephen Mitchell, of California State College–Bakersfield. The extraordinary dedi-cation of the paid crew, who donated uncounted hours of overtime for analysis and supervision of the volunteer labor, kept the project going through uncertain times. These and other donations of time and money, along with modest funding from the BAR, enabled the basic analyses of the recovered material to be completed.

The conclusion of the funding struggle was the eventual triumph of the De Soto/Apalachee Project. This addendum to the original de Soto project represented a $71,600 grant from the National Endowment for the Humanities to determine the true extent of the de Soto winter encampment. Much of the original de Soto crew was retained for this auger survey of the surrounding neighborhood. Part of the purpose of this project was to identify areas that the state's Conservation and Recreation Lands Program might want to acquire as part of a proposed interpretive park.

NEGOTIATIONS

The discovery of the early Spanish presence at the Governor Martin site was exciting to the state's historic preservation program. It was also something of a dilemma—and not just from the standpoint of how the archaeological work would be supported. If this was indeed the de Soto winter encampment, what would become of the site itself? It was clear that excavation of the threatened remains was the highest priority, followed by the acquisition of the undeveloped areas of the site. There was little agreement, however, on how the property should be used once in public ownership. Possibilities ranged from a simple memorial to an interpretive historic park that would include an ongoing archaeological project.

As early as April 1987, meetings were occurring among the various state, county, and city agencies, the Historic Tallahassee Preservation Board, and the commercial developers to determine what, if anything, could be done to preserve the site. Several suggestions were put forth, including purchasing the entire 6.1 acres from the developers, swapping other county land for the Governor Martin site, or simply condemning the land by right of eminent domain.

The fundamental problem with these scenarios was that the commercial developers had already sold two of the six lots to be developed. The prospective tenants, while sympathetic to the situation and the need to preserve sites significant to the heritage of the United States, were nevertheless adamant about moving into their buildings on the dates they had been promised.

Nothing less than condemnation would have recovered the entire parcel, and the state of Florida was reluctant to invoke this option as long as several questions remained unanswered. Was this truly the site of de Soto's first winter encampment? If so, how big was the site, and would it be contained within the property held by the developers? It didn't make sense to contemplate something as publicly distasteful as land condemnation if even that act would not secure the entire site. Condemnation, it was widely agreed, would send a message to landowners that their land would be taken if it contained significant archaeological sites. Since the contracted tenants of the prospective buildings were not budging and immediate public acquisition was not possible, the developers prepared to start construction on the two lots in question. However, they gave archaeologists the opportunity to dig in the areas threatened with immediate construction. The developers even assisted with heavy equipment to remove some of the soil overlying the site.

As the archaeologists labored in front of the bulldozers and it became clear that the whole parcel was not going to be acquired, the preservation question was reduced to "How much of the site can be preserved?" To answer this question, an auger survey of the development tract was undertaken. The results of this testing indicated the area with the heaviest concentrations of artifacts. Later, a survey of the surrounding neighborhoods would provide similar data for a much larger area (the NEH-funded De Soto/Apalachee Project). However, during the course of the Governor Martin site excavations, it was known with certainty only that the site extended over the entire 6.1 acres held by the developers. Negotiations focused on whether the remaining undeveloped 4.8 acres of the tract should be purchased or only a representative acre.

This question appeared moot, since the state could not move quickly enough to acquire the undeveloped portion of the site before the interest payments on loans used to purchase the property ruined the developers. State land acquisition procedures are strictly regulated by law and require surveys, appraisals, and other evaluations before any negotiations can begin. A year would be required before the state could make a purchase, and this was out of the question for the developers. Efforts were focused on finding another agency that could quickly purchase the property.

Several agencies were approached concerning the site, and while all were sympathetic, none could offer any help. The prospects for the preservation of any portion of the site looked grim when another player appeared in the nick of time—the Trust for Public Land, a private nonprofit corporation that works nationally to preserve open spaces for the use and the benefit of the public. Like the Nature Conservancy or National Trust for Historic Preservation, the Trust for Public Land acquires significant properties that are threatened and holds them until a long-term owner, such as a state or local government, can purchase the property from it. Though its usual focus was on environmentally sensitive properties, the trust decided that the Governor Martin site held such historically significant value that it should act.

In June, the Florida governor and cabinet passed a resolution requesting the Trust for Public Land to act as their broker and purchase the remaining 4.8 acres of the planned development. The state planned to purchase the site from TPL at some point through its Conservation and Recreation Lands (CARL) program. To acquire the land, TPL had to take out

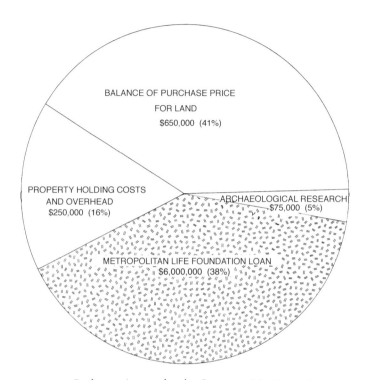

COST TO PROTECT DE SOTO-APALACHEE SITE
$1,575,000

BALANCE OF PURCHASE PRICE
FOR LAND
$650,000 (41%)

PROPERTY HOLDING COSTS
AND OVERHEAD
$250,000 (16%)

ARCHAEOLOGICAL RESEARCH
$75,000 (5%)

METROPOLITAN LIFE FOUNDATION LOAN
$6,000,000 (38%)

3.1. Budget estimates for the Governor Martin project.

$600,000 in loans to cover the $1.25 million purchase price. When combined with the property holding costs, overhead, and the costs for the archaeological research, the total for protecting the de Soto–Apalachee village site amounted to $1,575,000 (fig. 3.1).

To cover the costs of the loans, the Trust for Public Land started a fund-raising campaign of its own. The archaeologists assisted by giving lectures around the state and in Washington, D.C. Brochures explaining their dilemma were distributed at the site and at other high-visibility locations such as highway rest areas. These fund-raising efforts were successful, and the TPL secured loans from the Metropolitan Life Foundation, the National Trust for Historic Preservation, the Elizabeth Ordway Dunn Foundation, and First Florida Bank. Thus it appeared that 4.8 acres of the site and the Governor Martin mansion would be preserved and the archaeology on the other 2.3 acres would be completed when a last-minute complication threatened to invalidate the whole arrangement.

In June 1988, the archaeologists' excavations of the Governor Martin site had been finished for six months, and they were busily working on the analysis of the artifacts and the survey of adjacent properties. The governor and cabinet unanimously approved the purchase of the site from the Trust for Public Land. The trust, euphoric after its long battle to preserve the site, arranged for an elaborate closing ceremony to be held at the site on August 11 and invited many state and local dignitaries. It was then that the state's land acquisition agency discovered an outstanding lawsuit against the property.

Unbeknownst to TPL, the original developers and the city of Tallahassee had been sued by one of the neighbors of the site over the storm-water runoff that would be generated by paving much of the property for driveways and parking lots. Adjustments had since been made to handle the runoff, and the developers had assumed that the issue had been resolved. Yet the lawsuit, though dormant for many months, had never been officially settled. The state would not purchase the site unless TPL agreed to buy it back if the lawsuit was decided in the neighbor's favor. All parties convened for an eleventh-hour negotiation, which finally secured this last loose end. The property was conveyed to the state a couple of months later than originally planned, which made little difference in the end.

FUTURE INTERPRETATIVE PLANS

After the successful acquisition of the property, activity on it slowed considerably. The long-term plans for the site at the time of purchase were never well defined, but initial thoughts were to develop a small park, with the Governor Martin house as its centerpiece. It was to anchor the Florida portion of the proposed De Soto National Historic Trail.

Following the end of the fieldwork at the site, a small caretaker's cottage on the rear of the property served as a lab and artifact storage facility. The Trust for Public Land graciously allowed the building to be used by the state even before the sale was finalized, in part to maintain a visible presence on the site while negotiations progressed. This arrangement was wholeheartedly endorsed by the archaeologists since it eliminated the planned commuting between the site and Bureau of Archaeological Research's lab facilities, over a mile away. The analysis of the artifacts took place in the cottage, which also served as a base for the archaeological survey of the surrounding neighborhood.

The most ambitious plans for the site called for a continued archaeological presence. Small field projects would be conducted each year on the remaining acreage and perhaps at other promising off-property portions of the site, such as nearby Myers Park and Capitol City Country Club. In this, the Governor Martin site would very much resemble the nearby San Luis Archaeological and Historic Site across town, and perhaps that was its undoing.

As can be seen by the struggle to acquire the property, single-event state funding is difficult to obtain. A continuing commitment of funding such as would be necessary to staff and maintain a park represents another order of magnitude of difficulty. It would have been unrealistic to make such a request during a time when many state park systems across the country, including those in Florida, were facing the possibility of closing parks to stay within budget. The proposition of opening a new archaeological park when another such park existed in the same town was a negative factor for a system trying to spread its limited resources across a large state.

Yet another disappointment was the Columbus Quincentennial. The colossal 500th Columbus anniversary hoopla that the state hoped to plug into with its de Soto connection was as big a letdown as the less than spectacular reappearance of Halley's comet. Most of the Columbian Jubilee activities were a bust. The final blow for the site came when the National Park Service recommended against establishing a De Soto National Historic Trail.

Still, the battle to preserve the site was successful. The site *has* been protected, and much was learned from the excavation of the Governor Martin site (see part 2 of this book). We now know where the de Soto encampment took place, and at least a portion of what remains will be safeguarded for A.D. 2039–40, when the de Soto Quincentennial rolls around.

PART II

The Archaeology of
the Governor Martin Site

Charles R. Ewen

4 · Testing the Hypothesis
Excavations at the Governor Martin Site

The ideal archaeological project begins with a well-thought-out research design to guide the collection and examination of data from a particular site or collection of sites. It is rare that an archaeologist has the time or money to address every aspect of a site, so there is a need to set priorities as to which data are most important. A good set of research questions does just that: it establishes priorities that direct the excavation and analysis of the data from an archaeological site. More often than not in a salvage situation, however, the archaeologist does not have the luxury of formulating a research design in advance.

The excavation plan at the Governor Martin site was influenced more by the exigencies of the developers' construction schedule than by a formal research design. It was not that research was in any way an afterthought. Rather, the research questions had to be worked within the parameters established by the owners of the property.

Apart from the constraints imposed by the construction activities, the political manueverings of the state over the acquisition of the property, and the economic realities of the small funding base, the research design also had to cope with the accumulation of data. With each passing day, at least in the beginning, the newly discovered artifacts and features changed the archaeologists' perception of the site. Each new insight affected the subsequent research priorities. The archaeologists had to factor their evolving interpretation into the mix of theoretical possibilities and pragmatic realities and adjust the field strategy accordingly.

When Calvin Jones turned over his first shovelful of earth, his goal was to determine whether a seventeenth-century Spanish mission had been located on the property. His initial recovery of Spanish Olive Jar and daub fragments appeared to confirm his expectations and called for a new goal. The new goal involved mapping out the mission compound and recovering artifacts diagnostic of that time period. Work toward this second goal eventually overturned the initial hypothesis.

The more Jones tried to fit the site into his archaeological model for mission sites (Jones and Shapiro 1990), the less like a mission it seemed. Eventually, the artifact assemblage diverged so far from the pattern established for north Florida missions that it belied the idea that the Governor Martin site could be the Tama mission. The third research goal was to discover what sort of Spanish presence was represented at the Governor Martin site. The ultimate goal of the project became defined after Jones arrived at the conclusion that the Spanish artifacts had been left by de Soto's army and that the site was part of the 1539–40 winter encampment. Testing the hypothesis that the site was indeed that of Anhaica Apalachee served as the primary research question for the remaining eight months of the excavation.

I've said elsewhere (Ewen 1991:44) that doing archaeology is like trying to work a jigsaw puzzle without having all the pieces. Nor is there is a picture on the box to let you know what the puzzle is supposed to look like when assembled. Determining how past activity is likely to be manifest in the archaeological record is perhaps the most difficult task confronting the archaeologist.

In keeping with the puzzle analogy, the archaeologist's hypothesis becomes, in effect, the picture on the box, and the data represent the puzzle pieces. The test implications for the hypothesis can be thought of as how the pieces of the puzzle fit together. This is what rigorous test implications do for a hypothesis. They simply ask, "What data should be found at the archaeological site if your hypothesis is true?"

The first chapter of this book discussed the question of what we should have expected to find at de Soto's winter encampment. Once the dig was underway at the Governor Martin site, the test implications for this hypothesis became paramount. The public readily accepted the hypothesis as fact; after all, it was printed in the newspaper, backed up with "expert" testimony. The scholarly community was a harder sell.

The stumbling block was that, in the absence of a "Welcome to DeSoto-land, population 622" sign, there is no single definitive archaeological marker for such a site. Early in the dig, one of the volunteers presented Jones with a hubcap from a 1957 De Soto, claiming it was the proof that was sought. However, only a collage of various archaeological, geographic, and documentary evidence would satisfy the scholarly community.

The site would have to conform to, or at least not contradict, the information contained within the narratives associated with the de Soto expedition. The geographical description of the area, taking into account modern alterations, should generally describe the area around the Governor Martin site. The location should lie within the parameters set out in the narratives, although there is a lot of latitude in this case, as interpretations of distances traveled and correlations with modern features vary widely.

Finally, as far as the historical record is concerned, the site should show an admixture of aboriginal and European traits, since Anhaica was an aboriginal village that was usurped by an invading army for nearly half a year.

Archaeologically, the site should primarily represent a large, Velda-phase aboriginal occupation. Although European influence should be present, the site appeared to be the principal village of the Apalachee both before and after the de Soto occupation. European influences should be seen in the architecture through the use of European hardware (iron nails, sawn timbers) and distinctive design elements (rectangular floor plan with interior partitions). The artifact assemblage should contain European artifacts, including types not normally associated with trade objects, in quantities that suggest onsite use. The faunal assemblage should include non-native animals such as horses and pigs, which were known to have been part of the de Soto expedition.

Meeting the above criteria would not prove that the Governor Martin site was Anhaica. However, it would make Governor Martin the leading contender in the absence of another site meeting the same criteria. Failing to disprove the hypothesis would allow its continued use to guide future research in the area.

METHODOLOGY

Like the research design, the field methods evolved during the life span of the project. Initial testing by Jones, when it appeared that he would have only a day or two to complete his work, employed a judgmental sampling strategy. That is, shovel tests were dug in areas that he thought likely to produce artifacts. Jones's uncanny knack for finding significant artifacts made this initial strategy highly effective and demonstrated the need for the subsequent archaeological project.

Once the importance of the site had been demonstrated and more time allocated for the excavations, Jones was able to establish a north-south baseline 200 meters east of an arbitrary datum. The datum was established to the north and west of the limits of the planned office development. All subsequent measurements for mapping features and excavation units were done in meters east and south of this datum point. The location of each excavation unit was designated by the grid coordinates of the unit's northeast corner.

As mentioned in chapter 2, early excavations were performed using volunteer labor under the supervision of Calvin Jones. While the job could not have been done without these volunteers, there were scheduling and placement difficulties because some volunteers could be onsite for only part of the day, and others had little archaeological training and so were limited in where they could work on the site. These conditions made supervision and record keeping difficult. The situation was exacerbated by the constant demands on Jones's time for meetings with state officials, developers, and the many other visitors to the site.

Excavations were at first conducted in 1 x 1-meter units that were excavated to sterile subsoil. Excavated soil was not screened during this initial salvage phase as time was of the essence. Artifacts found in situ during the excavation phase were noted in Jones's fieldbook and placed in bags labeled with the excavation unit's provenience.

In April, when the crew from the nearby San Luis archaeological site was sent to assist in the excavations, the surveyed baseline established by Jones was expanded to a full grid system that covered the entire property. Excavation units were enlarged to 2 x 2 meters to better accommodate multiple excavators and provide more ground surface open to observation at the same time. The east-west grid baseline was aligned perpendicular to Lafayette Street (12° 30' east of magnetic north). A transit station was established to ensure vertical control over the units. An iron pipe on the east side of the property served as a benchmark, since it had a known elevation: 60.42 meters (198.17 feet) above mean sea level.

Most archaeologists prefer to dig within the natural soil strata of a site, since they often represent discrete deposition episodes. Unfortunately, the layers at the Governor Martin site were ambiguous and could often be distinguished only after the unit had been dug, by examining the unit's profile. This being the case, excavations were performed in arbitrary levels of 10 centimeters (4 inches). By excavating in 10-centimeter increments, it was possible to differentiate between the various components at the site on the basis of datable artifacts. The floor of each unit was mapped after every completed level, and photographs (color transparencies and black and white prints) were taken if intrusions (for example, filled-in trashpits) or other unusual soil conditions were observed.

An intrusion is defined as any disturbance, natural or cultural, of the soil matrix of the site. These were handled by prescribed methods during the course of the excavation. Disturbances due to natural phenomena (for example, rodent burrows or tree roots) were labeled as such and removed separately so as not to contaminate the proveniences into which they intruded. The same procedure was applied to modern disturbances such as pipe trenches and driveway fill.

Of more interest were intrusions that resulted from long past human activity. These were labeled as either features, areas, or possible postmolds (ppm). A *feature* was defined as tangible remains of discrete human behavior. This behavior is manifest in such phenomena as trash and storage pits, hearths, postmolds, pottery clusters, and such. *Area* was a more or less temporary designation given to a disturbance resulting from an unspecified human activity. Areas were numbered consecutively within an excavation unit and were often redesignated as either features or natural disturbances once their true nature became known. *Possible postmold*, as the term implies, was a holding designation for a postmold-like intrusion until it could be profiled and its function recognized.

The cataloging system established by the San Luis crew was retained for the duration of the project. All archaeological proveniences except features (that is, excavation unit levels, areas, possible postmolds, and so on) were numbered consecutively within each excavation unit. Features were numbered consecutively on a site-wide basis, regardless of unit location. Each provenience was assigned a unique field specimen (FS) number on a consecutive basis. By the end of the project 1,998 field specimen lots had been collected.

Archaeological excavation destroys sites more completely than any development project ever could. The difference between the archaeologist and the developer is the manner in which they excavate. It is the responsibility of the archaeologist to ensure that the excavated data are meticulously recorded so that the site can be reconstructed on paper.

At the Martin site, field records were recorded by both Jones and Ewen in a series of three notebooks. These data were later entered into a computerized database. In addition to the field notebooks, an FS catalog was kept. This log contained data on the horizontal and vertical location of each provenience, the date excavated, the excavator, the type of sample recovered (general excavation, flotation, charcoal), and number of bags used for each particular FS. The FS catalog also kept track of which provenience samples had been washed and analyzed. Information concerning each feature (location, FS number, map number, photo number, observations, and interpretations) was recorded on separate forms and maintained in a feature log. Separate logs also recorded the photographs taken and the fine-screen samples processed. A map log containing the plan and profile maps of the individual excavation units filled three notebooks. Last but not least, a provenience guide was developed to assign each provenience to a chronological period. Time periods were designated on the basis of artifacts contained within each provenience and their stratigraphic position relative to one another. That is, a particular provenience may have contained artifacts dating no later than A.D. 1600. However, if it overlaid a deposit with artifacts dating to A.D. 1700, then both proveniences were dated at A.D. 1700.

Volunteers water-screened all excavated soil through 1/8-inch hardware cloth. Although many archaeologists typically employ 1/4-inch mesh, the finer mesh was considered essential for recovering small beads and links of chain mail armor. Mechanical sifters were later employed to sift most of the soil through 1/8-inch mesh in an effort to speed up the screening process. The residue of the clayey soil that remained after mechanically sifting was then water-screened to recover the individual artifacts. In addition, soil samples were taken from all discrete areas and features and bagged separately. These soil samples underwent a flotation process that recovered extremely small artifacts as well as floral and faunal remains, which would have passed through even 1/8-inch mesh screens.

The flotation system at the Martin site separated artifacts and faunal and floral remains from the surrounding matrix using a gentle water current action. The flotation device consisted of a 55-gallon barrel with a water sprayer attachment at the base of the barrel though which water entered the system. A screen insert with an overflow funnel fit into the upper portion of the barrel. The barrel was then filled to capacity with water and the sprayer allowed to continue to run, inducing a light turbulence in the barrel. Samples to be processed (usually 1-liter samples) were poured into the screen insert in the barrel. The heavy fraction of the sample sank to the bottom of the insert where it became separated from the soil matrix, which, having been reduced to sediment, passed through the screen. The lighter fraction was borne out of the barrel by means of the water current, where it was collected in a cheesecloth mesh located at the end of the overflow funnel. Overall the mechanics of the excavation were the same straightforward procedures routinely followed on all archaeological projects undertaken by the Bureau of Archaeological Research.

Randolf Widmer and Jean Wilson conducted an experiment designed to test the effectiveness of the data recovery methods of the 1987 excavations. They removed a small (10-cm x 10-cm) column sample from each unit and sifted this soil through window screen. The intent was to determine whether the 1/8-inch mesh used at the water screens was effectively recovering most of the artifacts. No appreciable difference was noted in the artifacts collected by the two methods. Smaller fragments of some classes of artifacts turned up in the window screen, but the test did not reveal new classes of artifacts that the 1/8-inch screen had missed. Differences between the two screen sizes in the quantity of artifacts recovered were negligible.

LABORATORY STRATEGY

Analysis of recovered materials also followed standard procedures suggested for all projects undertaken by the Bureau of Archaeological Research in the late 1980s. Most of the initial processing of the recovered material was performed by the dozens of volunteers who had been so helpful during the course of the excavations. This processing consisted of washing the artifacts and roughly sorting them into groups (ceramics, glass, iron, and so on) to facilitate formal analysis.

Lab technicians trained in the identification of historic and prehistoric artifacts performed the formal analysis. Artifacts were identified, coded (for subsequent entry into a computerized database), counted, weighed, and in some cases measured and sketched. All observations were then recorded on preprinted analysis sheets in coded form.

The data recording system used for this project, first developed at the San Luis Archaeological and Historic site, was modified as necessary to accommodate the unique artifacts recovered from the Governor Martin site. As for the details, a good idea of the basic procedures can be gained by consulting the description in Shapiro (1987:54–58). Separate files were created for provenience information (unit location, type of provenience, center coordinates, unit size, screen size) and artifact data (artifact code, form modifiers, condition modifier, color modifier, measurement, count, and weight). These two files were linked in the relational database program according to FS number. This information was compiled using Ashton Tate's dBase II database management software running on an 8088-based personal computer.

Once the data had been entered, they were manipulated and printed out in tabular form using the BAR program developed by John Scarry of the Bureau of Archaeological Research. This menu-driven program was used to extract data from the master data file according to a number of different criteria. For example, it was possible for the program to list all the FS numbers for all the beads recovered at the Martin site, as well as the provenience data and descriptive information associated with them. Similarly it was possible to produce files of artifacts for every level and feature. The output from the program was in the form of a text file, which was converted to a tabular format using Borland's Reflex database management software and Microsoft Word 1.0 word processing program.

It is interesting to note that this was considered cutting-edge technology at the time. Queries of the database required three hours of running time, and the printers were subject to frequent paper jams. Still, the system was a considerable improvement over punch cards and typewriters.

Table. 4.1. Artifact functional categories.

Group #	Artifact category
1	Majolica
2	European utilitarian ceramics
3	Non-majolica European tablewares
4	Aboriginal ceramics
5	Kitchen artifacts
6	Architectual
7	Weaponry and armor
8	Clothing and sewing items
9	Personal items and jewelry
10	Activity-related items
11	Unidentified metal objects
12	Masonry construction items
13	Furniture hardware
14	Tools
15	Toys and games
16	Harness and tack
17	Religious items
18	Miscellaneous
19	Unaffiliated/disturbed objects

The organization of the data for the Governor Martin site served as a pilot program for a new system devised for all Bureau of Archaeological Research projects. Instead of categorizing artifacts by composition, as had been done on previous projects, artifacts are organized into functionally specific groups for analytic and comparative purposes (see table 4.1). The purpose of these groups is to provide a meaningful organization of the artifact assemblage in terms of human behavior. Once adopted by the BAR for other projects, it could be used as a basis for intersite as well as intrasite comparison. Particular attention was given to the ceramic assemblage, since work in St. Augustine has demonstrated its utility in providing a chronological framework for assessing change.

The actual quantification of the data was no small task since the material assemblage included more than 80,000 artifacts. A series of summary tables in the following chapter make the data more easily accessible.

5 · The Data

The preservation efforts discussed in the first part of this book establish the milieu in which the archaeology was conducted. Without this background of external constraints, it would be easy to wonder why certain procedures were not followed in the field or why certain specialized analyses were not performed. Still, even given the imposed limitations, an impressive amount of data was recovered by the archaeologists.

The purpose of this chapter is to describe and quantify these data. The following chapter offers my analysis and overall site interpretations, but here the artifacts and features are presented with only limited interpretation. The idea is not so much to let the data speak for themselves as to allow the reader to see upon what the interpretations are based.

The chapter begins by examining the stratigraphy of the site and how it has been interpreted according to the material found within these layers of soil. The various features of the site, both natural and cultural, are then discussed, along with suggested identifications of their age and functions. Finally the artifacts themselves are described, and their numbers and distribution are both quantified in tabular form and presented graphically.

GENERAL STRATIGRAPHY

The Martin tract is pleasantly situated atop a ridge in the fertile Tallahassee Red Hills amidst abundant water sources. It is located on a former portion of Old St. Augustine Road, which in the seventeenth century was part of the mission trail leading from St. Augustine to the mission of San Luis and beyond (Hann 1988:149–51). The mission trail, in turn, followed previously existing native trails in the area. Given its location close to water and a major transportation route, the Martin site has been prime real estate for a long time.

The Governor Martin site is not a deeply stratified archaeological site. Although it was occupied intermittently for nearly 2000 years, it was only in the last 500 years that more intensive occupation took place. Unfortunately for the archaeologists, the entire archaeological record of the site—all two millennia—is contained, for the most part, within the top foot of soil. Teasing apart the various occupations was a tremendous challenge.

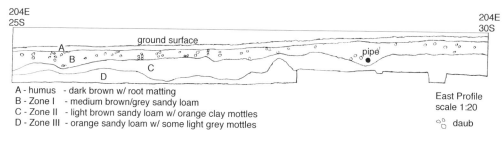

5.1. General stratigraphy of the Governor Martin site.

As mentioned in the previous chapter, profiles were drawn for every unit after it had been completely excavated. While each unit had its unique aspects, some general statements can be made about the stratigraphy at the Governor Martin site. The general stratigraphy is typified in a 5-meter profile (fig. 5.1) of all levels. A subtle stratigraphy could be discerned after the unit profile walls had been scraped clean and sprayed with a light mist of water. The strata could be divided into four designated zones that varied only in their thickness across the site. All four zones were represented in each unit that was excavated to sterile subsoil. Additional zones were not present in any of the units except as feature fill or other intrusions (discussed later), and these were designated separately.

The uppermost level was a layer of dark-brown humus and root matting and was not given a zone designation. This level varied from 5 to 10 cm in depth and generally contained only modern artifacts. Due to the shallow nature of the deposits, older artifacts were occasionally found near the surface. However, time constraints precluded the careful screening of this disturbed layer. Below the humus layer, three artifact-bearing zones could be distinguished in the excavation unit profiles above the culturally sterile clayey subsoil (which was designated zone 4).

Zone 1 consisted of a medium brown-gray sandy loam. This zone, 5 to 15 cm thick, generally comprised all of arbitrary level 2 and the upper half of arbitrary level 3, from 10 to 25 cm below the ground surface (cmbs). The first arbitrary level (0–10 cmbs) contained a general hash of nineteenth- and twentieth-century material. At the base of this level, especially along the western edge of the site, Seminole material began to appear. The Seminole material continued to dominate the second arbitrary level in that part of the site. Elsewhere on the site, Mission-period material was found in the upper portion of the second arbitrary level, although this presence was ephemeral and quickly gave way to a sixteenth-century Apalachee Indian occupation.

Zone 2 was characterized by light-brown sandy loam with orange clay mottling. It varied between 5 and 15 cm in depth. This zone generally included the bottom half of arbitrary level 3 and part of arbitrary level 4. The third and most of the fourth arbitrary levels were solidly sixteenth century in their constituent artifacts.

Zone 3 was the last zone before sterile orange clay. It was defined by orange sandy loam with some light-gray mottling. This zone was usually not more than 10 cm thick and comprised the bottom of arbitrary level 4 and below. At the base of the fourth arbitrary level (which was generally the last level excavated), some scattered remains of pre-Apalachee occupation were present.

Zone 4, the last, was comprised of culturally sterile orange clay subsoil. There was no reason to dig any farther except for the cultural features that intruded into this zone. It should be noted that variations and disturbances between the natural zones and arbitrary levels was quite common. However the deposits do, in general, reflect a logical occupational sequence that is consistent with the known history of the area.

FEATURES

There were 192 features recorded at the Governor Martin site. Since this book focuses on the sixteenth-century occupation, only the major Apalachee-Spanish features will be discussed here (fig. 5.2). Although many features were investigated, very few of them, with the exception of the obvious twentieth-century intrusions, could be confidently assigned to other time periods. This was due largely to the wide chronological range of many of the artifacts and the disturbed nature of many of the deposits. Fortunately, there were a few relatively undisturbed features that could be assigned to the sixteenth century. They are described here, along with tentative interpretations as to their function.

The identification of structures was an early goal of the project. One of the test implications concerning the winter encampment is that structures would reflect either European design elements, such as rectangular floor plan and interior partitions like those found at the Spanish mission of San Luis (McEwan 1993:299–301), or the use of European hardware (iron nails, saws) in their construction.

Like many prehistoric sites in north Florida, the Governor Martin site boasted a plethora of postmolds. Interpreting their arrangement involves more than simply playing dot-to-dot since a prolonged occupation with extensive building and rebuilding is represented in the archaeological record. These caveats may help to explain some of the disagreements concerning the interpretation of the structures defined at the site that still exist among the archaeologists involved in their excavation.

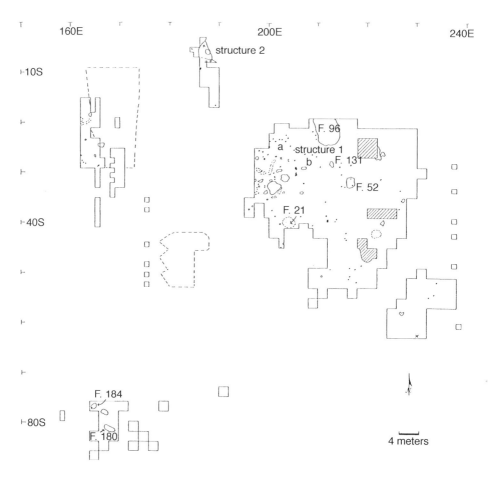

160E   200E   240E

-10S

structure 2

F. 96

a structure 1
b   F. 131

F. 52

F. 21

-40S

F. 184

-80S

F. 180

4 meters

5.2. Major features at the Governor Martin site.

Structure 1

This feature is actually a very complex arrangement of posts and associated features that appear to describe two separate structures (fig. 5.3). The total extent of the structures lies within a 25 x 15-meter block bounded by 187E-212E and 20S-35S. A major portion of this area was impacted by the placement of a water main early in the fieldwork. Fortunately, this area was excavated before the water main was emplaced. However, because of the construction, the entire structure complex was never totally exposed at the same time and had to be reconstructed on paper. Three separate crews and supervisors excavated different portions of the area, further complicating its interpretation.

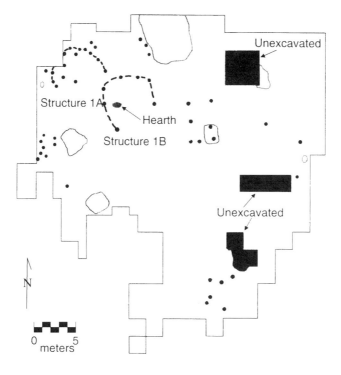

5.3. Structure 1.

Initially the feature was interpreted as a rectangular wattle-and-daub structure oriented roughly southwest-northeast (see *Tallahassee Democrat* April 7, 1987, 1A, and Paisley 1989:19). The southwest corner was interpreted as being feature 12, the northwest corner as feature 10, making the west wall approximately 8 meters wide. The east-west extent could not be determined during the early weeks of the project, and subsequent excavation radically altered the interpretation of the postmold pattern.

I believe that the posts actually describe two noncontemporaneous, circular wattle-and-daub structures. The later house (here designated structure 1B) may be a rebuilding of the initial edifice. Structure 1B is defined by features (postmolds) 75, 88, 89, 86, 95, 107, 105, and 124. These posts form a circular arrangement just over 5 meters in diameter. The posts are widely spaced (in some cases over 1 meter apart); Scarry and McEwan (1995:485) report that the structures uncovered at the contemporary Velda site are similar in size and have similar spacing between wall posts. Located just to the west of the center of structure 1B is a hearth (feature 93). The posts previously mentioned can be differentiated from the other

5.4. Daub with palmetto frond impression (Florida Department of State).

posts in the area on the basis of their point of initiation in the stratigraphic record. The posts associated with structure 1B all initiated above 58.85 meters above mean sea level (mmsl). The posts associated with structure 1A were not encountered until the excavations penetrated below 58.70 mmsl.

Structure 1A is extremely difficult to define precisely because of the modern intrusions disturbing the southern portion of the structure. However, it does appear that it too is a circular building approximately 5 meters in diameter, formed by features (posts) 6, 18, 19, 20, 22, 24, 34, 35, 36, 73, and 80. Again, the southern portion of the structure appears to have been disturbed by recent activity in the area, indicated by features 8 and 27, which are twentieth-century trash pits.

The lower points of initiation for the posts of structure 1A suggest that it predates structure 1B. The proximity of the two structures (actually overlapping on one edge) indicates that they did not exist at the same time. A possible scenario is that structure 1A was built first, then burned. Evidence of burning was found—charcoal and burned clay in the postmolds, as well as a great deal of burned clay daub in the surrounding fill. Some of the daub bore the impressions of twigs used as wattles and palmetto fronds employed as roof thatch (fig. 5.4). At some later time structure 1B was built, and later it also burned.

Structure 2

This structure was located and excavated when the developer put in an entrance drive to the office complex from Lafayette Street. The western edge of the driveway exposed in profile a portion of burned clay floor (feature 183). Subsequent excavation was hampered by the close proximity of office construction work, inclement weather, and the impending close of the field season. As a result, only a limited area could be opened and the interpretations offered here are somewhat speculative (see fig. 5.2).

The most prominent feature of the second structure was the prepared clay floor. This surface, which measured approximately 3.7 meters in diameter, was composed primarily of yellow clay that had been fired to a deep red color along the eastern margin of the exposed portion. A nearly complete, reconstructable Carrabelle Punctated *var.* Meginnis bowl was recovered from the floor of the structure.

On the southern edge of the clay floor were two small pits (features 185 and 186), which were filled with burned pine cones. The exact function of these pits is not certain; however, pits of similar size filled with burned corncobs have been found at other sites in Apalachee Province (San Luis, Patale). Milanich found similar small pits filled with corncobs inside a house structure at the Richardson site in Alachua County under what were probably sleeping beds. He interpreted them as smudge pits. He suggests, based on a 1564 description by the French explorer Laudonniere, that these "smudge pits were necessary in summer to keep the bugs, especially mosquitoes, away from the sleepers" (Milanich 1972:42). Binford proposes an alternative function. Based on ethnographic analogy, he feels that smudge pits were primarily used in smoking hides, to give them color. He also notes that pine cones were sometimes used instead of corncobs to produce the smoke (Binford 1972:33–51).

There are two posts (features 192 and 193) outside the clay floor, but they cannot definitely be linked to the structure. They are widely spaced and nearly 2 meters from the clay floor. It is possible that structure 2 is an open structure, like a Seminole chickee, rather than a closed-wall house. Again, the area opened was insufficient for positive identification, but clearly a structural feature of indeterminate form is indicated by the exposed evidence.

Borrow Pit

Defined by a large, roughly circular stain of medium-brown sandy loam with orange clay mottling, feature 96 was one of the most extensive intrusions excavated at the site (fig. 5.5). It was located within the bounds of 19S-25S and 209E-215E. The long axis of the excavated pit was 6 meters and oriented roughly north-south. The feature initiated at the base of level 4 (40 cm below the ground surface) and extended to a depth of 84 cm. The profile revealed several lenses of water-washed silt at the base of the feature underlying a mixed clay-loam backfill.

5.5. Clay mine, feature 96.

Artifacts recovered from the fill dated to the late Fort Walton period. A few fragments of glass and a cut nail fragment were recovered from the uppermost levels of the feature and represent a minor, nineteenth-century intrusion into this otherwise intact late Fort Walton deposit. Of the diagnostic ceramics, Fort Walton Incised and Carrabelle Punctated *var.* Meginnis are the most prevalent. Spanish artifacts consist of a small fragment of white majolica and two links of mail. Also present were some fragmentary faunal remains and burned corn kernels (table 5.1).

Feature 96 is interpreted as a clay mine or borrow pit. Structures 1A and 1B appear to have been made of wattle frames covered with clay daub. Since the pit is within 10 meters of structures 1A and 1B, it may have served as the clay source for the daub covering those structures. The water-washed silt at the bottom of the feature indicates that it remained open for a period of time before it was filled. It also apparently served later as a refuse pit, as evidenced by the broken pottery, faunal, and floral remains in the feature fill. The Spanish artifacts in the fill suggest that the feature was being filled during de Soto's stay at Anhaica.

Human Cremation

Feature 131 was one of the most hotly debated features uncovered at the Governor Martin site. Located entirely within 214E/27S, feature 131 was an irregular ovoid area of burned clay mixed with small fragments of

Table 5.1. Artifacts from feature 96

Group	Artifact	Count	Weight (g)
Majolica	uid white	1	.1
Utilitarian	Olive Jar	1	1.9
Aboriginal ceramics	Plain	478	4003.1
	uid aboriginal	38	685.4
	Ft. Walton Incised	9	92.8
	Ft. Walton Incised *var.* Englewood	1	21.5
	Ft. Walton Incised *var.* Ft. Walton	1	104
	uid Incised	5	43
	uid pinched/punctated	11	139.3
	uid punctated	1	7.2
	uid stamped	1	13.4
	Leon Check Stamped	1	11.8
Kitchen	Faunal remains	0	8.4
Architectural	Brass rivet	1	.5
	Iron spike	1	15.8
Weaponry	Chain mail	2	.3
Construction	Burned clay (daub)	0	6438.5
Tools	Utilized chert flake	1	2.7
	Ground sandstone	1	16.7
	Ground steatite	1	59.1
Miscellaneous	Charcoal	0	69.3
	Corn (carbonized)	0	1.3
	uid marine shell	0	.1
Disturbed object	Glass fragment	7	3

highly charred bone (see fig. 5.2). The area of burned clay measured 130 cm x 78 cm, with the long axis oriented north-south. An assessment was made in the field that feature 131 represented a human cremation. At the time this determination was made, that part of the site was in imminent danger of destruction. To ensure that the feature would receive proper treatment, it was encased in a plaster jacket and shipped to the physical anthropology laboratory at the University of Houston.

Once the encased feature arrived at the Houston lab, it was excavated by Randolph Widmer, and the bone was analyzed by Rebecca Storey. Because of the fragmentary nature of the evidence and the volatile nature of the interpretations, the final report (Storey and Widmer 1988) was reviewed by David Dickel (Florida Bureau of Archaeological Research),

William Maples (Florida Museum of Natural History), and Clark Larsen (University of North Carolina–Chapel Hill). All agreed that the bone was human. After that agreement ended, especially in regard to the scenario of deposition.

According to Storey and Widmer (1988:31–38), feature 131 represents the remains of an Apalachee male burned at the stake in retaliation for the deaths and harassment suffered by the Spaniards during their winter encampment of 1539–1540. The impetus for this interpretation appears to have come from the Ranjel narrative: "And although the Spaniards pursued them [the Apalachee] and burned them, they never showed any desire to come to peace" (chap. 9 of this book). Evidence for this reconstruction is the presence of a possible postmold next to the bone scatter; the arrangement of the bones, suggesting that the individual had been bound to this post; and the dissimilarity of feature 131 and other aboriginal cremations. "The feature does not provide definite proof of this reconstruction, as it was too fragmentary to provide all the evidence necessary to support the reconstruction, but provides only circumstantial evidence. Thus feature 131 of site 8LE853 may be early archaeological evidence in North America of the hostile interactions of the Spaniards and native Americans which heretofore has only been known from historical documents" (Storey and Widmer 1988:38).

Dickel (1988, personal communication), Maples (1989), and Larsen (1990) do not directly dispute the execution scenario, but they feel there is insufficient evidence to reconstruct the events leading to the deposition of the burned bone. It should be noted that there is a distinct lack of pre–Mission period burial data from Apalachee Province that would justify any statements as to burial customs of the Apalachee. At this point, it seems prudent to interpret feature 131 as a human cremation and refrain from speculation about the circumstances surrounding its deposition.

Cooking Pit

Located in the area bounded by 216–218E/31–32S, feature 52 consisted of a rectangular area of medium- to dark-brown sandy loam with burned clay and heavy charcoal inclusions (see fig. 5.2). Mixed in with the fill were a large number of aboriginal sherds. Possibly associated with this feature were seven postmolds (features 44, 65, 67, 68, 134, 135, and 137).

Feature 52 is interpreted here as an outdoor cooking pit. Some of the associated posts (features 44, 134, 135, and 137) may be from an open chickee-like canopy built over the cooking pit to shelter it from the elements. The other posts (features 67 and 68), since they are located adjacent to feature 52, may be associated with cooking activities. The artifacts found in the feature fill (primarily Carrabelle Punctated *var.* Meginnis and Fort Walton Incised ceramics) place the feature in the late Fort Walton period. However, most of the aboriginal sherds that were found came from plain vessels, consistent with the interpretation of the feature as a cooking pit. Plain vessels were most often employed in utilitarian activities, such as cooking, while highly decorated ceramics were usually associated with less mundane activities. The presence of a single wrought nail suggests that the feature was in use during de Soto's encampment.

An alternative function for this feature has recently been proposed by Scarry and McEwan. They hypothesize that the feature's location near the first structure indicated that it represents an auxiliary structure. "The additional postmolds near the circular structures mark small rectangular features that measure roughly 2.5 m x 3.75 m [fig. 5.6] and may be the remains of *garitas*, or elevated storage facilities" (Scarry and McEwan 1995:485). These elevated food storage structures are mentioned in historic accounts (see Hann 1988:208–9) as being located to one side of dwellings. However, the presence of a charcoal and potsherd-filled pit in

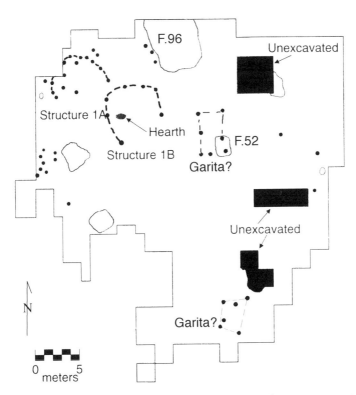

5.6. Scarry and McEwan's *garitas* (after Scarry and McEwan 1995).

5.7. Pat Jones and feature 21 (Florida Department of State).

the midst of the post configuration would seem to argue against this alternative explanation of the feature's function.

Feature 21

Found early in the field season and excavated by volunteer Pat Jones, this feature yielded the first solid evidence of sixteenth-century Spanish contact. Located in 204E–205E/38S–40S, it was described as a large oval stain containing tan or brown sandy loam with charcoal flecks and numerous artifacts (fig. 5.7). This feature was very indistinct and defined mainly by the presence of clustered artifacts. Though there had been some modern disturbance, the feature was largely intact, and the majority of the artifacts dated to the late Fort Walton period. The Spanish artifacts included early style Olive Jar, mail, and a chevron bead.

This feature also played a significant role in the genesis of the de Soto project itself. It was one of the first sixteenth-century features recognized as such on the site. The artifacts recovered from it were responsible for stimulating the early scholarly and public interest in the site. The high visibility of the site in both the electronic and print media that was aroused by the artifacts from this feature literally allowed the archaeologists to continue digging at the site.

The Data · 71

Child Burial

Feature 180 was located within the area bounded by 166E–170E/80S–82S and is described as an oblong-shaped stain of light-brown sandy clay fill (see fig. 5.2). The feature, measuring 156 x 69 cm, was located directly beneath feature 179, a large, roughly circular intrusion of medium-brown sandy loam. The two features were distinguishable from one another but definitely related.

Discovered toward the end of the field portion of the project, feature 180 was a burial pit dating to the time of the de Soto encampment. The presence of an early Spanish majolica type (Caparra Blue), mail, and Carrabelle Punctated *var.* Meginnis in the strata where the feature initiated, as well as in the feature itself, places the feature chronologically in the sixteenth century. The narrow, oblong shape of the feature and the five human deciduous enamel tooth crowns recovered from the fill indicate that the feature was a burial pit.

The teeth are all molars and were unerupted, so that the tooth roots never formed (Glen Doran: 1988, personal communication). This indicates that the individual was a subadult and probably quite young. The acidic nature of the soil dissolved the bones of the child, leaving only the more impervious tooth enamel to mark the remains with the pit. No other burials were detected in the area, though only limited excavation could be performed during the time remaining in the field season.

Cistern

Feature 184, roughly circular, was located in 166E/76S (see fig. 5.2). It began in level 3 (30 cm below the surface) and extended to a depth of 1.82 meters, making it the deepest feature on the site. Most of it was carved out of the surrounding sterile orange clay matrix. The feature fill initially consisted of a sandy brown loam with some orange mottling. In the lowest 17 cm of the feature, the fill became a tan-gray clay with charcoal flecking. A postmold (feature 191) was discovered along the western edge of the feature.

Only some charcoal and a little burned clay were found in the feature itself. However, in area 2, which overlay the feature and extended to the east of it, many diagnostic artifacts were recovered. These included such Contact-period Indian ceramics as Point Washington Incised and Carrabelle Punctated *var.* Meginnis. Early-style Olive Jar fragments, a sherd of Green-glazed earthenware (a Spanish utilitarian ware; see South et al. 1988:254), and a horse tooth associated the feature with the de Soto encampment. An interesting but enigmatic artifact was a hand-sized piece of pumice that had been worn perfectly smooth on two surfaces. A suggestion was made that this had been used to polish the Spaniards' steel armor, but no reference to such a usage could be uncovered in the literature.

This feature has been very tentatively identified as a cistern. Its water retention capabilities were amply displayed after every rain during its excavation. The documented guerrilla tactics of the Apalachee (see part 3 of this book) graphically illustrate the need for water sources within the fortified village. The post in the side of this feature may represent some sort of aid for the removal of water from the feature, be it a handhold or bucket support. No similar features have been reported in the Apalachee area. It is tempting to think of this as a Spanish construction, a stopgap measure in lieu of the barrel wells that they would have built in a more permanent settlement.

There were, of course, numerous other features that could be associated with de Soto's occupation of the site, mainly isolated postmolds, artifact concentrations, and intrusions whose function could not be determined. The discussed features were the least disturbed and most diagnostic of the de Soto occupation. All of these features were associated with sixteenth-century artifacts, which aided in their chronological placement. The description of the artifacts themselves is important for demonstrating the affiliation of the site with the de Soto expedition.

Artifacts

The burden of proof as to whether the Governor Martin site can be equated with Anhaica Apalachee rests on the artifact assemblage. None of the previously discussed features, by itself, can be interpreted as anything other than a part of a late Fort Walton–period Apalachee village. However, the association of sixteenth-century European artifacts with these same features casts a brighter interpretive light on the site. The historic artifacts, especially the ceramics and coins, can tightly date a site; their distribution across the site also can suggest the nature of its occupants.

The following descriptions are not intended to cover all the artifacts or even all the classes of artifacts recovered from the Governor Martin site. Such a task would duplicate much of the information already found elsewhere (see Scarry 1985; Shapiro 1987). To reduce the redundancy, the only artifacts described in this chapter will be the Spanish ceramics and pre-nineteenth century metal artifacts. The pertinent aboriginal ceramics and beads will be briefly discussed here.

Spanish Ceramics

The Spanish ceramics at the Governor Martin site accounted for less than 5 percent of the total ceramic assemblage. Nevertheless, this is an impres-

Table 5.2. Spanish ceramics

Category	Ceramic Type	Count	Weight	% by weight
Majolica	Columbia Plain, green variant	8	6.7	.09
	Columbia Plain	4	5	.07
	Caparra Blue	4	2.6	.03
	Aranama Polychrome	3	1.7	.02
	Blue on White majolica	5	3.1	.04
	Polychrome majolica	49	51.1	.67
	Plain majolica	34	26.9	.35
Utilitarian	Olive Jar, glazed	412	1859.1	24.48
	Olive Jar, unglazed	1952	5513.3	72.60
	Bisque	1	2.3	.03
	Lead-glazed coarse earthenware	55	92.7	1.22
	Unglazed coarse earthenware	6	10.4	.14
Tableware	Cologne stoneware	1	4	.05
	Melado	5	15	.20
	Black lead-glazed coarse earthenware	1	.1	.00
Total		2540	7594.9	100.00

sive amount for a sixteenth-century Florida site. It would suggest a source other than trade or shipwreck salvage, given the number (over 2500 fragments) and variety of early types (see table 5.2).

Most of the Spanish ceramic assemblage is Olive Jar fragments. Ubiquitous to Spanish sites in Florida and the Caribbean, the utilitarian Olive Jar can be dated to three general periods on the basis of rim type and body form (fig. 5.8). The chronologically identifiable fragments from the Governor Martin site can be classified as the early type. Also recovered were such sixteenth-century majolica ceramic types as Columbia Plain and Caparra Blue. The date ranges assigned to these types are based on their appearance at sites in the New World where the span of occupation is well documented.

Bisque or *Bizcocho* is essentially an unglazed majolica. Specifically, it is a thin-walled, intentionally unglazed, decorative ware in the form of vases, pitchers, and plates. Though specimens have been found at sixteenth-century Spanish sites in the Caribbean, it has not been reported from sites postdating 1550. Fragments recovered from the Martin site, though closely resembling the published descriptions of Bizcocho, may represent majolica fragments that have lost their glaze (Deagan 1987:43; Ewen 1991:60–62).

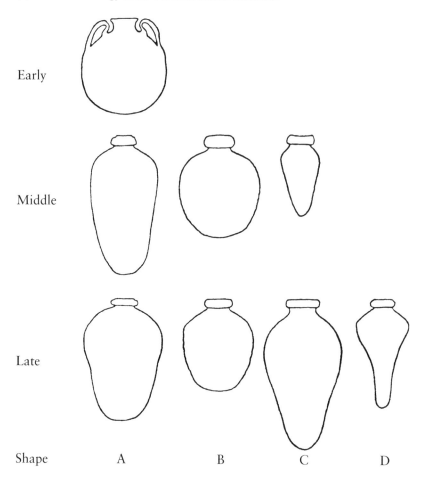

Early

Middle

Late

| Shape | A | B | C | D |

5.8. Olive Jar types (after Goggin 1960).

Caparra Blue, named for the site of Caparra, Puerto Rico, is a distinctive sixteenth-century type. The exterior is a solid blue enamel while the interior is white or grayish white. Some of the specimens recovered from Puerto Real have a slight greenish cast to the interior white enamel. Kathleen Deagan (1987:63) suggests a chronological range in the New World of 1492 to about 1600 and notes that specimens from pre-1550 contexts are likely to be of Italian manufacture. This type is known only in the *albarelo* (drug jar) form (Goggin 1968:134–35).

Columbia Plain is one of the most numerous and variable sixteenth-century majolicas found in the New World. Only small fragments were recovered from the Martin site. The paste is uniformly chalky in consistency but varies in color from pink to cream. The glazes range from a thick, glossy, opaque white to a thin matte white. The fragments were too small to reveal much about vessel shapes, though a foot ring and pieces from a small cup or bowl were noted. Several fragments have been identified as a Columbia Plain variant known as Columbia Plain Green. This variety is a Columbia Plain vessel that has been partially covered with a clear green glaze. It is an early variety that dates primarily to the first half of the sixteenth century, though some specimens have been recovered from post-1565 St. Augustine (Chaney 1987). The extremely fragmentary nature of the specimens has made their identification tentative and the determination of vessel form impossible (Deagan 1987:56–57; Ewen 1991:62–65; Goggin 1968:118–19).

Melado has been called Honey-colored/Seville ware (Willis 1984) and Honey-colored ware (Goggin 1968; McEwan 1983). Deagan (1987:48) describes it as having "a cream to terra-cotta colored paste, similar to majolica paste with a honey colored, opaque lead glaze resulting from the inclusion of an iron oxide, which is one of the main mineral resources of southeastern Andalusia" (see also Lister and Lister 1982). Specimens from the Martin site have a cream-colored paste. Goggin (1968:227) places the chronological range of this ceramic between 1493 and 1550.

Unidentified polychrome majolica was represented at the Martin site by a number of very small fragments. The thin-walled (3–5 mm) ware is characterized by a buff-colored majolica paste covered with a thin green and/or maroon glaze. The small size of the fragments recovered made it impossible to identify any pattern in the distribution of glaze colors. Vessel forms appear to be small bowls or cups. This may be an opaque lead-glazed ware rather than a true majolica.

Unidentified lead-glazed coarse earthenware appears to date to the sixteenth century (Kathleen Deagan 1987, personal communication). It has a relatively light-bodied (5–6.2 mm) red, sandy paste, and the interior is covered with a brown-green lead glaze. Vessel forms appear to be small bowls and plates (Deagan 1987:53).

Olive Jar was the most numerous Spanish ceramic recovered at the Martin site. The majority of the Olive Jar sherds that could be classified were early style, defined by Goggin (1960:8–11) as having a distinctly shaped globular body, a raised, everted mouth, and attached handles. The exterior surface was often covered by a white slip and the interior often glazed in some shade of green. Goggin dates this style from A.D. 1493 to approximately 1575. Deagan (1987:33) puts the end date at about 1570.

Vessel wall thickness has been used to distinguish Olive Jars chronologically (Goggin 1960). There is a tendency for the walls to become thicker through time. Deagan (1987:33) states that the early style measured approximately 7 mm in thickness. The Olive Jar from the Martin site ranged from 2.8 mm to 11.4 mm, averaging 6.4 cm. This agrees well with the reported thickness of early style.

Distinguishing between early- and middle-style Olive Jar body sherds on the basis of thickness alone is at best tentative. Range of sherd thickness overlaps between styles. Moreover, wall thickness varies according to location on the vessel. In an effort to create a new criterion for discriminating between the styles, a petrographic analysis was performed by Steven Mitchell, a geologist at the University of California at Bakersfield. Analyzing the mineralogical composition of the Olive Jar paste can identify the source of the clay used. Early-style Olive Jar should be of Old World manufacture, while middle-style Olive Jars found in Florida were most likely made in the New World. The results of Mitchell's analysis suggest that the Olive Jar fragments recovered from the Martin site were manufactured in the province of Andalucia, Spain.

Rim shape is a more diagnostic style trait than vessel thickness. All rims recovered at the site were the flaring early style. Middle-style rims are very different, looking more like doughnuts than spouts. None of these was found at the Martin site. Most conclusive were a couple of handle fragments excavated at the site. Handles occur only on early-style Olive Jars.

Aboriginal Ceramics

Aboriginal ceramics account for 90 percent of the total artifact assemblage. The majority of the ceramics recovered (over 60 percent) are Fort Walton–period types (A.D. 1450–1633), including Lake Jackson Plain, several varieties of Fort Walton Incised, and a late variety of Carrabelle Punctated, which is characteristic of the site. The aboriginal ceramic assemblage (table 5.3) is consistent with the identification of the site as part of Anhaica.

The investigations at the Governor Martin site provide important data for the construction of a ceramic chronology for Apalachee Province. They provide information on both marker types and temporal trends (in comparison with data from other sites). Carrabelle Punctated *var.* Meginnis (fig. 5.9) appears to be a good marker type ceramic at the Governor Martin site. This type, which is rarely found in the precontact Fort Walton, dominates the aboriginal ceramic assemblage and tapers off in Mission-period sites. This predictable pattern of initiation, fluorescence, and decline makes this ceramic type a useful chronological tool.

Additional research on this marker type may further refine its spatial or chronological placement. At the early sixteenth-century Governor Martin

Table 5.3. Aboriginal ceramics

Period	Ceramic type	Weight (g)	Percentage	Group %
Late Archaic	Fiber-tempered	31.1	.18	.18
Weeden Island	Wakulla Check Stamped	122.2	.71	.79
	Wakulla Check Stamped *var*. Wakulla	13.3	.08	
Fort Walton	Cool Branch Incised	43.3	.25	60.01
	Cool Branch Incised *var*. Cool Branch	21.7	.13	
	Cool Branch Incised *var*. Ft. Gaines	22.1	.13	
	Ft. Walton Incised	3465.9	20.10	
	Ft. Walton Incised *var*. Blalock	54.0	.31	
	Ft. Walton Incised *var*. Cayson	8.9	.05	
	Ft. Walton Incised *var*. Crowder	103.3	.60	
	Ft. Walton Incised *var*. Englewood	19.5	.11	
	Ft. Walton Incised *var*. Ft. Walton	176.7	1.02	
	Ft. Walton Incised *var*. Safety Harbor	20.0	.12	
	Lake Jackson Incised	253.9	1.47	
	Carrabelle Punctated *var*. Meginnis	6159.3	35.72	
Transitional	Lamar Bold Incised	29.3	.17	20.96
	Lamar Complicated Stamped *var*. Early	265.7	1.54	
	Leon Check Stamped	3040.9	17.63	
	Marsh Island Incised	32.7	.19	
	Marsh Island Incised *var*. Columbia	20.4	.12	
	Marsh Island Incised *var*. Marsh Island	4.1	.02	
	Point Washington Incised	191.3	1.11	
	Point Washington Incised *var*. Nunnaly	30.6	.18	
Mission	Lamar Complicated Stamped	14.6	.08	.57
	Lamar Comp. Stamped *var*. Curvilinear	41.5	.24	
	Lamar Comp. Stamped *var*. Jefferson	3.8	.02	
	Lamar Comp. Stamped *var*. Rectilinear	17.5	.10	
	Ocmulgee Fields Incised	5.4	.03	
	Copy wares	14.8	.09	
Other	Alachua Cob-marked	50.7	.29	17.50
	Chattahoochee Brushed	2966.9	17.20	
Total		17245.4	100.00	100.00

5.9. Carabelle Punctated *var.* Meginnis.

site, a multiple-rowed punctated subvariety of Carrabelle Punctated is most common, whereas at the late sixteenth-century Velda site (8LE44) a single-row punctated variety predominates.

The European artifacts are what captured the public's imagination, but it may be the aboriginal assemblage that will prove most interesting to archaeologists working in north Florida. Still, the European artifacts are crucial to establishing the site's identity and occupational span.

Metal Artifacts

Mail, often referred to as chain mail, is a type of armor that was popular from the second to the seventeenth century. The term is derived from the Latin *macula,* meaning the mesh of a net. Over 2000 links of iron mail were recovered from the Martin site, as well as 20 links of what is being interpreted as brass mail. Mail links identical to those found at the Martin site have been reported from Martin's Hundred, where they are believed to have been deposited in 1631 (Noel Hume 1983:30–31). Other reports of this type of armor on archaeological sites are rare, although some has also been reported from the Tatham Mound in Citrus County, Florida, a possible contact site (Jeffrey Mitchem 1988, personal communication). It is possible that the badly corroded individual links were not recognized as mail by their excavators at other sites. This is hardly surprising since they were not recognized initially at the Governor Martin site.

Mail was a type of personal body armor that provided an effective defense against the blows of edged weapons such as swords. A method for the manufacture of mail is described by Ffoulkes (1967:44–45): "when the wire was obtained, either hammered out or drawn, it was probably twisted spirally around a rod the diameter of the required ring. It was then cut off into rings, with the ends overlapping. The two ends were flattened and punched or bored with holes through the flat portion. A small rivet, and in some cases two, was then inserted, and this was burred over with a hammer or with punches. . . . Before the rings were joined up they were interlaced one with another, each ring passing through four others."

Mail from the Martin site appears to have been made by this method, except that each link appears to have been joined to six others, forming a much tighter weave (fig. 5.10). The links vary in diameter from 5 mm to 8 mm, the size varying in accordance with its location on the mailed garment. The links of brass mail, which were 9 mm in diameter, may have served a decorative function since, being softer than iron, brass mail would have provided less protection. Unlike the iron mail, the brass links were pinched closed rather than riveted. An illustration in Wilkinson (1970: fig. 31) shows a fine coat of mail with the neck, sleeves, and hem edged with a row of brass rings. Olds (1976:99–100) also reports brass mail from sixteenth-century shipwreck materials recovered from the Texas tidelands.

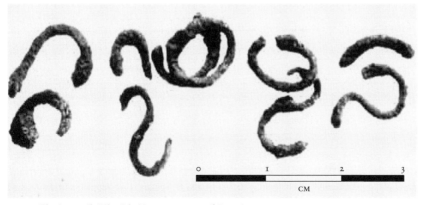

5.10. Chain mail (Florida Department of State).

5.11. Crossbow quarrel (Florida Department of State).

Crossbow quarrel, an iron bolt point, is the only Spanish offensive weaponry that can be assigned with any certainty to the de Soto expedition. The piece measures just over 4 cm and weighs 5.7 grams (fig. 5.11). The point has a circular, socketed base that tapers to a square pyramidal head. Similar points were recovered from sixteenth-century Santa Elena, a Spanish site in South Carolina (South et al. 1988:103–7). Like the points from Santa Elena, the Governor Martin site quarrel appears to be a type 3, or armor-piercing point, as illustrated in Payne-Gallwey (1958:18).

The crossbow was essentially a bow-and-arrow gun. The iron bow and cocking mechanism gave the average archer far greater range and accuracy than could be achieved with a hand bow. Though invented in the first millennium B.C., it achieved its greatest popularity in Europe between the eleventh and the sixteenth century (Foley et al. 1985:104). The chroniclers of the de Soto entrada list it as the principal weapon of the expedition although arquebuses were carried as well. This artifact helped distinguish the encampment from a mission site, since during the mission period muskets had replaced crossbows as the weapon of the Spanish foot soldier.

Coins were perhaps the most sensational of all the artifacts recovered. Of the five copper coins, two were Spanish maravedis, and the other three appear to be Portuguese ceitils. The true value of these artifacts lies in their use as chronological markers. While no specific dates appear on the coins, numismatic records indicate when they were minted and their average circulation span.

The first coin recovered (FS no. 685; fig. 5.12) was in the best condition of the five and was thus the most readily identifiable. It is a copper 4-maravedi coin minted in Burgos, Spain, for use in the New World. This coin, worth little to the Spaniards, dates from 1505 to 1517 (Ortega 1982:141; Vicenti 1978:21). The identification was confirmed by William Bischoff, curator at the American Numismatic Society, in correspondence with K. C. Smith of the De Soto/Apalachee Project. The next coin (FS no. 889), found in the water screen by a volunteer, is a 1-maravedi coin dating to the same time period.

The other three coins (fig. 5.13) are badly corroded but are definitely Portuguese. Pushing the identification further was difficult. In the opinion of Alan M. Stahl, curator of medieval coins at the American Numismatic Society, FS no. 1218 is from the reign of Alfonso V (1438–1481) and FS no. 1065 is from the reign of either João II (1481–1495), Manuel (1495–1521), or João III (1521–1557). Coins from these three reigns are difficult to tell apart, even in the best of condition. The last coin, FS no. 1534, appears to be from the reign of João III, but again a positive identification is difficult.

Wrought nails were recovered from the Governor Martin site in a variety of types (fig. 5.14). The term *wrought nail* refers to iron nails forged by hand—as opposed to machine-cut or wire nails—which were widely used in the New World until well into the nineteenth century (Noel Hume 1978:252). Given their long period of use, they are not good chronological indicators (see Nelson 1968). At the sixteenth-century site of Santa

5.12. Four-maravedi coin (Florida Department of State).

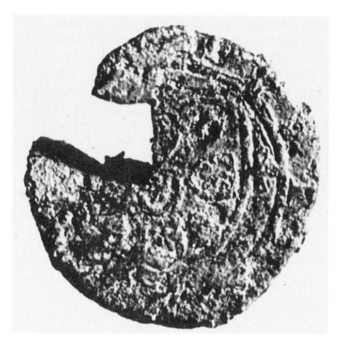

5.13. Portuguese ceitil (Florida Department of State).

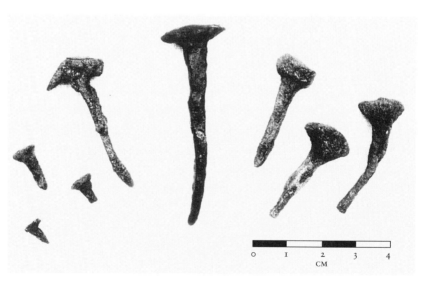

5.14. Wrought nails (Florida Department of State).

Elena in South Carolina, nail types were described according to head type and nail length (South et al. 1988:33–57). This system was used as a starting point for the classification of nails at the Governor Martin site.

Six types of nail heads were distinguished at the Governor Martin site.

Rose heads, which are dome-shaped, "generally had five hammered facets spreading out and down from a central point" (Noel Hume 1978:252). The least common type recovered (numbering only six), they ranged from 30 to 85 mm in length, with an average of 55 mm.

Flat heads, round in shape, are included by South et al. (1988:40) in the same classification as the domed rose-head nails. Twenty-eight flat-head nails were found, ranging in length from 25 to 56 mm, with an average of 36 mm.

L-heads were simply formed by hammering the end of the nail perpendicular to the shaft. Willis (1984:96) and South et al. (1988:40) suggest that these were finishing nails, perhaps used for flooring. Given the temporary nature of the de Soto encampment, flooring seems an unlikely function if these nails can indeed be linked to that time period. Fourteen L-head nails were recovered at the Martin site, 31 to 59 mm long and averaging 45 mm.

T-heads differ from those defined by Noel Hume (1978:252) but correspond to the description offered by South et al. (1988:50): "characterized by having the crossbar of the 'T' flush with the width of the shank of the nail." The T-head is also interpreted as a finishing nail by Noel Hume (1978:252) and South et al. (1988:41). Forty-nine of this type were unearthed at the Martin site. The nail length ranged from 25 to 52 mm and averaged 36 mm.

The following two types are variants of the T-head nail.

Thickened heads, a blocky type, are essentially T-heads in which the crossbar is usually as thick as it is long. Twenty thickened-head nails were recovered, 22 mm to 49 mm long and averaging 33 mm. These nails resemble the horseshoe nails illustrated in Simmons and Turley (1980:62, 65) and may have served that function.

∧-heads, an unusual type, also appear to be T-heads modified by hammering the arms of the "T" into an inverted "V." Easily the most numerous nail-head type, 146 specimens were recovered at the Martin site. They ranged in length from 24 to 46 mm, averaging 37 mm.

The function of this last type is problematic. During the Martin excavation it was suggested that they were horseshoe nails. Examination of references on the subject (Douglas 1873; Lungwitz and Adams 1913; Simmons and Turley 1980) failed to locate any nails identical to the ∧-head nails. Similar nails were recovered from a site in New Mexico (LA54147) that has been assigned to the sixteenth century and is possibly associated with the Coronado expedition (Vierra 1989). Bradley Vierra (1988, personal communication) does not concur with the horseshoe nail identification, citing the lack of characteristic wear on the specimens that he has examined. He also notes that this nail type is different from known horseshoe nail types that have been recovered from sixteenth-century contexts. Vierra suggests that these nails were used as fasteners on tool or weapon handles or on saddles.

The length of all the nails falls in the range of small joining nails (*barrotes*, *media barrotes*, and *tillados*) as outlined by Lyon (1979:3). These types of nails would not be used for joining heavy timbers, but for finish work such as flooring or any other tasks requiring relatively little strength or length (South et al. 1988:40). Nails of this length may have been used in crates or for some light framing in house building.

Rear gunsight, a diagnostic artifact from the Seminole period, was recovered from the western portion of the site. It was identified by James Levy of the Conservation Lab at the Florida Division of Historic Resources as a rear sight from an eighteenth-century English trade gun (FS no. 575). This artifact is a grooved piece of cast brass that dovetails onto the rear of the barrel of a Hamilton type G trade gun. It is illustrated in two of Hamilton's publications (1980:72, fig. J, and 1968:15, fig. 16). Hamilton (1980:13) places this particular gun part in the time span 1725–1770, which falls nicely within the Seminole occupation of the site.

Two *brass buckles* were recovered that may date to the sixteenth century. The smaller of the two is a complete rectangular specimen measuring 17 x 11 mm. It is similar to specimens found at the sixteenth-century site of Puerto Real, Haiti, which have been tentatively identified as harness buckles (Ewen 1991:83, 97). The larger specimen is a fragment of a more ornate buckle frame, possibly a shoe buckle. It also resembles specimens recovered from Puerto Real (Ewen 1991:83–84). Unfortunately, both buckles were recovered from disturbed contexts.

Two *brass fastener pieces* were recovered from early proveniences at the Governor Martin site (fig. 5.21). The larger and more ornate of the two had apparently been fastened to a leather strap by an iron rivet. It measured 37 mm in length and had a curved hook at one end. The other fastener was quite a bit shorter (18 mm) and had been fastened to leather or wood by two brass tacks. Similar fasteners or clasps at Puerto Real have been tentatively identified as book hardware (Ewen 1991:90–91).

Two fragments of *silver earrings* were recovered from controlled backhoe scrapings along the western edge of the site. They are the pendant parts of the earring, minus the wire loop that pierces the earlobe. The

5.15. Beads. *Left to right:* seed beads; Cornaline d'Aleppo; faceted chevron; Nueva Cadiz; faceted amber; blown glass (Florida Department of State).

pendants are hollow cones, closed at the base. Similar artifacts have been found at San Luis, but the context in which they were found at the Martin site suggests that they date to the Seminole period.

Beads

Beads of European manufacture have been one of the primary tools for tracking the route of de Soto through the Southeast. Several clear blown glass beads, a faceted amber bead, a dozen chevron beads, and a single Nueva Cadiz bead were recovered at the Governor Martin site (fig. 5.15). These are considered good sixteenth-century marker artifacts (see Smith and Good 1982). All of these types of beads have been found at other sites associated with the de Soto expedition (see Mitchem 1989, Skowronek 1991).

The early discovery of the faceted chevron beads (fig. 5.16) was an initial indicator that the site predated the Mission period. Following the recovery of one of the chevron beads, I was quoted in the *New York Times* (May 19, 1987) as saying, "We were all dancing for awhile yesterday. So far in Florida, this type of bead is only found associated with de Soto."

5.16. Chevron beads (Florida Department of State).

5.17. Blown-glass
beads (Florida
Department of State).

Chevron beads may be the "margaridetas" referred to in the Elvas narrative (chap. 8 of this book; see also Deagan 1987:190).

The blown-glass beads (fig. 5.17) are more problematic, having all been recovered from disturbed contexts. A bead of smaller size, but possibly similar manufacture, was found at the Poarch Farm site in northern Georgia, which is also associated with the de Soto expedition. Although these beads may in the end prove to be relatively modern, they were of value in directing attention to the site when the status of the archaeological investigation was in doubt.

Marvin T. Smith described and analyzed the beads from the Martin site. He reports that, while many beads that date to the mid-sixteenth century were recovered, the majority of the beads date to the late eighteenth or early nineteenth century. There is also evidence of a seventeenth-century Mission-period occupation, and a late nineteenth-, early twentieth-century occupation.

Artifact Distribution

The horizontal distribution of artifacts, after analysis in the lab, corresponded very closely to what was observed in the field. Patterns in the artifact distribution are illustrated by a series of maps prepared using the SURFER program (a Golden Graphics product that plots artifact location and generates contour maps of distribution density). The maps reinforce some of the archaeological interpretations.

The maps show that the artifacts associated with the Seminole occupation were clustered, as observed in the field, along the western edge of the

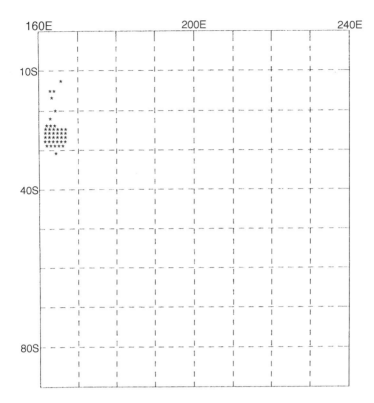

5.18. Distribution of Cornaline d'Aleppo beads.

site. Cornaline d'Aleppo beads (fig. 5.18) and brushed pottery are most frequent in the areas bounded by 160-170E and 20-30S. Curiously, the distinctive ∧-head wrought nails discussed earlier are most common in that area (fig. 5.19). They occur all across the site, but there is a concentration in the middle of the Seminole area, suggesting that these nails may not be associated with the de Soto occupation.

In the field we observed the artifacts associated with the de Soto occupation clustering around the first structure. Again, the distribution maps bear this out. Olive Jar and mail (figs. 5.20 and 5.21) are all most concentrated in the area bounded by 200–210E and 20–40S. Structure 1B is in this area. It is suggested here that structure 1B was occupied by de Soto's troops and may have been destroyed by fire, perhaps as the result of one of the documented Apalachee raids against the camp. The concentration of burned clay in this area attests to the burning of the structure.

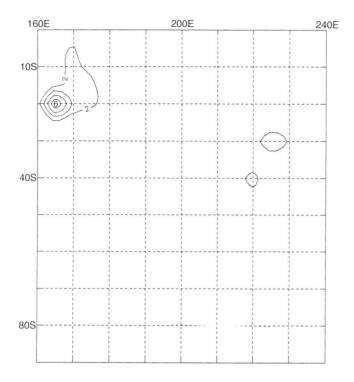

5.19. Distribution of ∧-head wrought nails.

One of the most valuable traits of the Governor Martin site is the known date of Spanish occupation, 1539–1540. With this time anchor, it is possible to tune more precisely the ceramic seriation for Apalachee Province (see next chapter). It has been debated whether or not the appearance of stamped ceramics preceded the Mission period. Scarry (1985:221–23) argues for the appearance of some varieties of Lamar Complicated Stamped (*vars.* Bull Creek and Early) in pre-Mission contexts. Lamar Complicated Stamped ceramics were recovered from the Martin site, and they were clustered in the same general area as the other de Soto–period artifacts. This would seem to indicate that, while not abundant, Lamar Complicated Stamped ceramics may predate the Mission period in northwest Florida.

The case with Leon Check Stamped is less certain. Suggestions that this type predates the Mission period are only tentative. This type does occur at the Martin site, and it is spread across the site. However, a distribution density map (fig. 5.22) shows this type clustering in the southwest corner of the site. It should be noted that the auger survey of adjacent properties

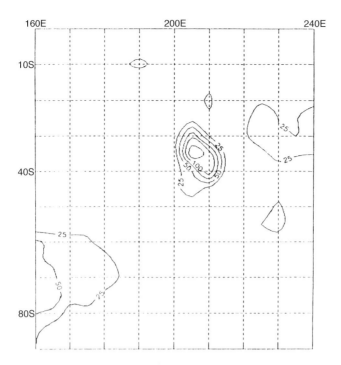

5.20. Distribution of Olive Jar sherds.

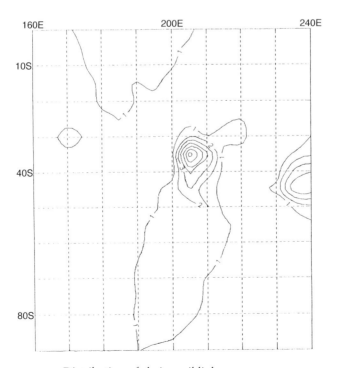

5.21. Distribution of chain mail links.

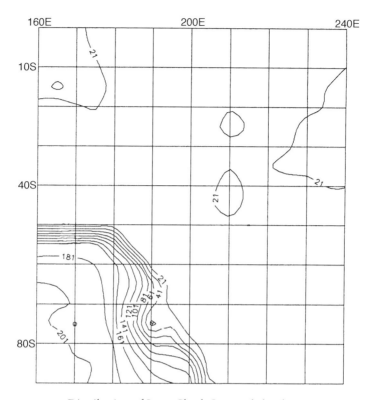

5.22. Distribution of Leon Check Stamped sherds.

during the De Soto/Apalachee Project found evidence of a later Spanish mission to the southwest of the site. Based on the evidence from the Governor Martin site, it is not possible to state that the type Leon Check Stamped predates the Mission period.

FAUNA AND FLORA

Faunal preservation at the Martin site was remarkably poor, primarily because of the acidic soils that characterize the Tallahassee Red Hills. For the most part, very little bone remained in identifiable condition. A notable exception were pig and horse bones.

In a good sixteenth-century context, the shattered but identifiable fragments of the right maxilla of a pig (*Sus scrofa*) were recovered. Included with the maxilla fragments were four teeth. Two of them were worn but complete molars. There was also a complete crown of molar (no roots) and a fragment of a molar crown. The crowns show evidence of having been burned. The size and wear exhibited by these teeth indicate a fairly old animal. A horse tooth was identified in association with sixteenth-century Spanish ceramics and Contact-period Indian pottery as well.

Very few other bones (apart from the human burials mentioned earlier) could be identified in a secure context. During the course of excavation, the remains of deer, turtle, dog, and unidentified birds were noted but not in any unambiguously datable contexts. The faunal remains have been weighed but not specifically identified.

A large amount of carbonized seed and other plant material was recovered during the course of the 1987 excavations. Soil samples from all the features have been processed using a water flotation system, which produced a good sample of the material for floral analysis. Unfortunately, funding was not available to engage an ethnobotanical specialist. However, during the process of flotation, an ethnobotantist who visited the site noted the presence of corn, persimmon, and hickory nuts (Margaret Scarry, personal communication). There were also two smudge pits filled with charred corncobs on the west side of the site (features 84 and 111) and two pits filled with charred pine cones (features 185 and 186) associated with structure 2. As with the faunal assemblage, the floral samples await a more thorough examination.

THE DE SOTO/APALACHEE PROJECT

The army of Hernando de Soto occupied the principal village of the Apalachee for five months. The 1987 excavations covered only 1 1/2 acres and raised the question "Where was the rest of the village?" It was expected that the survey would reveal that the Martin site was part of a large late Fort Walton–period (A.D. 1450–1600) Apalachee village. It was further hoped that the survey might be able to delineate the boundaries of the village. If the extent of the site were known, steps could be taken before new development impacted more of the de Soto encampment.

The basic objective of the De Soto/Apalachee Project was to determine the extent of the site by means of a subsurface archaeological reconnaissance. This was accomplished through the recovery of subsurface artifactual remains, and detection of their distributional pattern, by means of a systematic auger survey and test excavation within 1 square kilometer of the Governor Martin site (see fig. 5.23). The research design was predicated on two assumptions. The first was that the de Soto encampment could be distinguished by the presence or absence of diagnostic artifacts in the archaeological assemblage. The second assumption was that the techniques employed in the survey would be adequate to assess subsurface

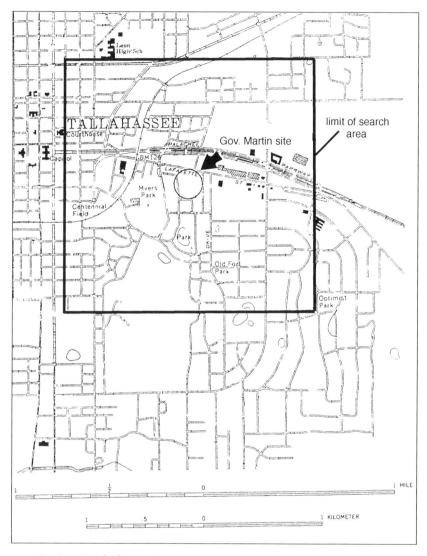

5.23. De Soto/Apalachee project area.

patterning and reveal site location. The results of previous surveys have demonstrated that such sampling procedures do indeed reflect subsurface archaeological patterning (Deagan et al. 1976; Deagan 1981; Shapiro 1987).

Research in the Florida Master Site File revealed that the area of the proposed survey had not been previously surveyed in a systematic fashion, although sites had been recorded in the area. An informal monitoring of the survey area by B. Calvin Jones indicated that it was rich in aboriginal artifacts. An auger survey of the Martin site suggested that the site continued onto adjacent properties in all directions. On the basis of this evidence, the Institute for Early Contact Period Studies of the University of Florida obtained funding from the National Endowment for the Humanities to survey these properties for evidence of Anhaica.

The De Soto/Apalachee Project, as it came to be called, was based primarily on the techniques successfully employed in St. Augustine, Florida, and at the mission site of San Luis in Tallahassee, Florida. The following description of these techniques is drawn largely from the St. Augustine project reports (Deagan et al. 1976; Deagan 1981) and the San Luis report (Shapiro 1987), with some modification.

The stratified systematic sampling strategy (cf. Mueller 1974) used auger tests at 10-meter intervals throughout most of the survey area. Much of this area had been extensively developed and was covered with asphalt, concrete, and standing structures or was landscaped so as to destroy underlying archaeological deposits. These areas were not tested.

The goal in this project was to indicate, by presence or absence of materials diagnostic of the sixteenth century, the extent of the de Soto encampment. Vertical placement and quantification of the recovered materials was not crucial to the survey phase of this project. This conclusion is based on experience in St. Augustine, where "although many of the auger tests yielded numerous datable artifacts, these were in every instance of several different diagnostic types. Very rarely did multiple instances of a single type occur in any one test, and in no case were more than two items of the same type recovered from a single hole. In the analysis and map plotting procedures, therefore, each instance of a particular diagnostic *type* was plotted, rather than each item itself" (Deagan et al. 1976:14). It will remain for future test excavations to determine artifact density and reveal specific activity areas.

Before the survey began, permission was secured from all property owners in the survey area. City property tax records were consulted to obtain information concerning lot ownership within the survey area. Upon obtaining names and addresses, a mass mailing of permission forms was undertaken. These forms explained the nature and purpose of the survey. Appearances at neighborhood association meetings and personal contacts answered many of the questions that landowners had concerning the survey.

At first, landowners were reluctant to have us test their property. Visions of backhoes devastating their carefully manicured lawns lay at the root of their trepidation. However, these attitudes changed when it became apparent that the auger testing would have no lasting adverse effects on their property. More than 80 percent of the responses received from the mass mailing were positive, and many of the negative responses changed after the benign nature of the survey had been demonstrated. It soon became something of a status symbol to have the archaeologists seen in the homeowners' front yards. By the end of the project, the problem was that more people wanted their yards tested than our funding would cover.

The survey strategy used two 5 1/2-horsepower earth augers, each operated by a two-person team. The auger was fitted with an 8-inch bit 36 inches in length. Excavations in the area have indicated that this length was sufficient to penetrate culturally sterile subsoil. When deeper penetration was called for, bit extensions were employed.

Given the presence of roads, structures, and landscaping in the survey area, an overall grid for the area was not practical. Instead, individual lots were gridded using street corners or other permanent features as datums. Test borings were put in at 10-meter intervals. Each auger hole had a unique designation relative to its particular lot grid. Each boring was marked on a map prepared for that lot.

The actual augering procedure was simple and systematic so as to minimize confusion and maximize data recovery. After a lot grid had been established, the locations of test bores were marked with flagging tape upon which the coordinates had been marked. The soil brought up by the auger was bagged and transported back to the lab, where it was water-screened through 1/8-inch mesh because the clay soil did not pass easily through a dry screen onsite. However, under an efficient rotation system, augered soil was taken to the lab and exchanged for sterile soil to backfill the holes. Volunteer labor handled the screening process.

The project was successful in its primary goal. The survey recovered evidence suggesting that the Governor Martin site was part of a larger aboriginal site (fig. 5.24). More specifically, the distribution of sixteenth-century Spanish material (fig. 5.25) and of Fort Walton–period ceramics (fig. 5.26) demonstrated that the Apalachee village that de Soto visited extended as far west as Myers Park, north of the Apalachee Parkway, east to Magnolia Drive, and south into the Capitol City Country Club.

It was not possible to determine the total extent of the Apalachee village. Part of the reason was that time and funding constraints limited the area that could be tested. Artifacts were found at the limits of the survey area, but the density of the concentration of finds dropped dramatically toward the fringes of the surveyed area.

Another consideration was the feasibility of such an undertaking. In other words, it may be unrealistic to expect that the village of Anhaica had

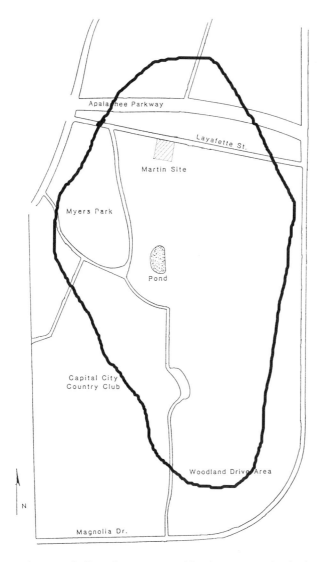

5.24. Distribution of all artifacts recovered by the De Soto/Apalachee project.

definable limits. The Apalachee appear to have had a hierarchically arranged settlement pattern in which great towns, like Anhaica, were surrounded by smaller hamlets and farmsteads (Scarry 1994b). If the village was not palisaded, as Anhaica apparently was not, it would be difficult to determine this boundary archaeologically.

Seventeenth-century artifacts (middle-style Olive Jar, majolica, and Mission-period aboriginal ceramics) were recovered on the eastern edge of the Capitol City Country Club golf course. It is suggested here that this is

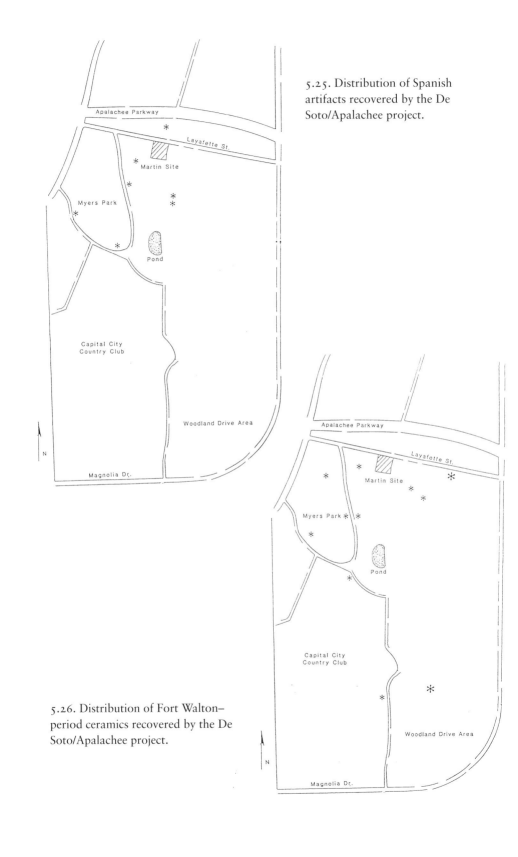

5.25. Distribution of Spanish artifacts recovered by the De Soto/Apalachee project.

5.26. Distribution of Fort Walton–period ceramics recovered by the De Soto/Apalachee project.

the first location of the San Luis mission, San Luis de Xinyaca (Anhaica). John Hann, historian for the Bureau of Archaeological Research, places this mission one league (ca. three miles) east-southeast of the present site of San Luis de Talimali (fig. 5.27). Hann (1988:78–79) suggests that Capitol Hill or the Governor Martin site is a likely candidate for the location of this early mission. No evidence of a mission has been recovered on Capitol

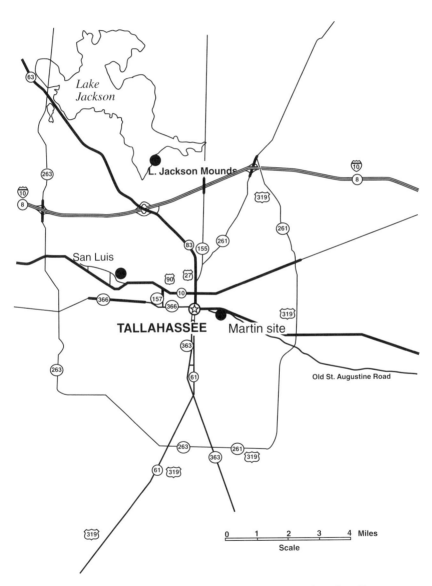

5.27. Location of Governor Martin site vis-à-vis San Luis de Talimali.

Hill to date. Given the close proximity and continuous distribution of aboriginal artifacts, it appears that, though representing two different phases of occupation, the Martin site and material from the Capitol City Country Club can be considered part of the same site: the principal Apalachee village of Anhaica.

Archaeology in general and archaeology in north Florida in particular have benefited from the information provided by the DeSoto/Apalachee Project. The early sixteenth-century Apalachee village associated with the de Soto encampment and the early seventeenth-century mission discovered by the survey represent important phases in the history of Apalachee Province. When the Martin site is combined with the Lake Jackson site, which predates it, and with the site of San Luis de Talimali (1656–1704), the chronological sequence of the province is unbroken. Thus Apalachee Province becomes an archaeological laboratory for the study of the rise and fall of an aboriginal chiefdom, as explored in the next chapter.

6 · The Governor Martin Site and Apalachee Province

The natural environment is an important element in understanding where individuals have settled, during both prehistoric and colonial times. Access to water and food resources play important roles throughout the human history of any given area. This is well illustrated in Apalachee Province.

The most notable topographic feature in Apalachee Province is the Cody Scarp. This land form divides the province into two distinct areas: the northern highlands, known as the Tallahassee Red Hills, consisting generally of rolling, fertile lands with a clayey subsoil; and the southern portion, the Coastal Lowlands, which are relatively flat and very sandy. The Cody Scarp was associated with the road that connected the Apalachee missions during the seventeenth century. According to Shapiro, "beginning at the Aucilla River and continuing west, the mission road followed close to the Cody Scarp until it reached the St. Marks valley. The St. Marks valley probably did not form a complete barrier to travel, but its swampy terrain could be avoided by skirting around the drainage to the north. The Patale mission was located at the very headwaters of the St. Marks drainage, and from here the mission road split into a northern and southern circuit from which the missions in the western highlands of Apalachee could be reached" (1987:16).

It is known that Old St. Augustine Road roughly follows the mission road, which in turn followed aboriginal trails. That the Governor Martin site is situated on Lafayette Street, which is an extension of Old St. Augustine Road, suggests that Anhaica was on the major east-west trail across north Florida.

The Governor Martin site occupies the western slope of a ridgeline located approximately three quarters of a mile east of the state capitol building. As the site has been part of a plantation and then a housing development, the vegetation surrounding it has been altered through time. However, aerial photos from 1941 show that the Martin tract itself has changed little in the last fifty years. Presently it is landscaped with a mixture of hardwoods and pine, with little understory apart from some ornamental shrubbery.

Located 180 feet above sea level, the site presides over well-drained fertile soils, which until the late nineteenth century were under cultivation. Fresh water is readily available from several nearby sources. Two small ponds (formerly known as Houston's First and Second) are a brief walk south of the site, while to the west a small creek runs through Myers Park. There is an active springhead just north of the Apalachee Parkway, and local residents speak of additional springs that have been filled in by recent developments.

An archaeological survey of the surrounding area recovered evidence that the village extended over an area much larger than the Martin tract. Hann (1990) suggests that the main portion of the village may have been on Capitol Hill, since this is one of the highest points in the area, with a commanding view in all directions. However, excavations around the Capitol Hill area have failed to turn up any evidence of a large Apalachee village.

OCCUPATIONAL SEQUENCE

Hernando de Soto and his army spent five months in the chiefdom of Apalachee. While recognized as a significant historical event, this was by no means the only important event to occur in Apalachee. The territory between the Aucilla and the Ochlockonee Rivers has a long history of human occupation.

The span of time people have lived there has been broken up into several distinct cultural periods by researchers. Many of these occupational episodes are represented at the Governor Martin site. The events that occurred before, during, and after the de Soto encampment are all represented in the archaeological record and required the archaeologist's attention. A brief sketch of the chronological sequence of cultures in Apalachee Province will account for the range of artifacts recovered during the excavations and show more clearly how the Governor Martin site fits into the larger historical landscape.

The Archaic period (7500 B.C. to 1000 B.C.) is the earliest culture represented at the Governor Martin site. The populations were semisedentary, subsisting on small game such as deer and raccoon, aquatic resources, and wild plants. Small bands moved around the area on a seasonal basis, exploiting various resources as they became available. At the close of this period, the population became more sedentary and began manufacturing such labor-intensive items as ground stone tools and crude, hand-molded pottery. Plant fibers were used to temper these crude pots, the earliest known in the United States. The presence of Kirk Serrated points and fiber-tempered pottery suggest a Late Archaic presence at the Governor

Martin site, although the nature of this ephemeral occupation could not be determined from the scant evidence recovered.

The Fort Walton period in Florida (A.D. 1000–1704) can be roughly equated with the Mississippian period in the eastern United States. The Fort Walton period, at least in the area between the Ochlockonee and Aucilla Rivers, also corresponds to the tenure of the Apalachee chiefdom. John Scarry (1994b) has identified three phases for the Fort Walton in the Tallahassee Red Hills: Lake Jackson (A.D. 1100–1500), Velda (A.D. 1500–1633), and San Luis (A.D. 1633–1704). It can be argued that the San Luis phase should not be included in the Fort Walton but in a separate Mission period instead. The transitions between phases are marked by changes in the ceramic assemblages and by periods of sociopolitical change and instability.

The first major occupation of the Governor Martin site occurred immediately after the Lake Jackson phase of the Fort Walton period (ca. 1400). The Lake Jackson phase (1100–1500) is the prehistoric phase of the Fort Walton period in the Apalachee territory. The phase name is derived from the Lake Jackson site, a ceremonial mound center that served as the paramount Apalachee village during this first phase. Mississippian in character, the Lake Jackson phase has been characterized by Scarry as "the earliest recognizable Apalachee polity. There is no evidence of contact between Lake Jackson-phase Apalachee and Europeans. . . . The late Lake Jackson-phase polity was a complex chiefdom with two administrative units above the local community. There are four classes of Lake Jackson-phase settlements—homestead, hamlet, single mound center, and multimound centers. . . . And status differentiation and political (or religious) offices are evident in mortuary patterning" (1994b:162).

Maize agriculture probably formed the basis of the Apalachee subsistence during the Lake Jackson phase, though hunting and gathering of wild plants were no doubt still important. Maize has been recovered from excavations at the Lake Jackson, Winewood, and Bear Grass sites (Scarry 1988:13). Tesar (1980:169) adds that beans and squash were also important cultigens.

The hierarchical settlement pattern and stratified social system has been commented on by numerous researchers (Fryman 1971; Jones 1982; Payne 1981, 1982; Scarry 1984, 1994b; and Tesar 1980). The major social division of this complex chiefdom was between elites and commoners, and elites were probably subdivided into various ranks of higher and lower status. The settlement pattern reflects the hierarchical social structure of the Apalachee. At the top of the pyramidal pattern is the multimound paramount ceremonial center, Lake Jackson in this case. Below the major center were smaller, single-mound centers. Next were hamlets of five to ten houses, followed by farmsteads of one or two structures (Scarry 1988:14). This hierarchy may have collapsed to a simpler form in the succeeding Velda phase.

Even before European contact, the Apalachee underwent major changes. According to Smith and Scarry (1987), the beginning of the Velda phase (1500–1633) was a period of significant demographic shifts. Mound building in general was discontinued, and vessel forms and decorative motifs that previously had linked the Apalachee with other Mississippian polities to the north and west declined in abundance (Scarry 1994b). The impetus for these changes is not known.

In other areas there was a great deal of continuity. The subsistence base remained unchanged. Scarry (1994b) sees the cessation of mound building as a change in the symbolic representation of chiefly authority and the allocation of social surplus labor. Apalachee society, however, remained a complex chiefdom, with social stratification and a hierarchically arranged settlement pattern.

Scarry (1994b) suggested that when the Lake Jackson site was abandoned, Anhaica became the principal Apalachee village. The ceramic assemblage, discussed later, places the major occupation of the Martin site during the Velda phase of the Fort Walton period. It was during this period that Europeans arrived in Apalachee Province.

It has been hypothesized that Spanish incursions into Apalachee Province had profound consequences for the native population. The immediate social and demographic impacts due to trade and battle may have paled in comparison with the long-term effects of the introduction of European diseases. Contagious diseases such as typhoid fever, measles, and influenza are thought to have had devastating effects on the native inhabitants of *La Florida*. Having no natural immunities to these pathogens, the Apalachee may have suffered great population losses. The extent and chronology of these losses is not known, though Dobyns (1983:52n) has suggested that half of the Apalachee succumbed to typhus introduced by the 1528 Narváez expedition.

However, recent research suggests, at least at the Governor Martin site, that there was more continuity than change in Apalachee Province following sixteenth-century Spanish contact. Although change did occur as a result of the invasion of the Spaniards, it was not the disease-induced, catastrophic cultural changes proposed by some scholars (Dobyns 1983; Crosby 1994; M. T. Smith 1994). Those changes would come about a century later as part of the evolution of the Florida mission system.

After de Soto and his men left Anhaica and Apalachee Province, the

Apalachee appear to have reoccupied their village. They were apparently still there when the Spanish returned to stay in the Florida panhandle in 1633 (indeed, Inihaica was mentioned when Apalachee was visited by Spanish friars in 1608), this time at the request of the Apalachee themselves. Though the Spaniards began establishing missions in *La Florida* during the latter part of the 1560s, it was not until 1633 that the formal mission effort reached Apalachee Province.

One of the first and certainly the most strategically important of perhaps as many as fifteen missions was the mission of San Luis (Hann 1988). It supported a garrison of soldiers and served as the western anchor for the north Florida chain of missions. Founded shortly after 1633, the mission moved once before being abandoned in 1704. According to Hann, "the site to which San Luis relocated in 1656 is evidently the one currently identified with that mission which is being explored under the auspices of Florida's Bureau of Archaeological Research under the direction of the Secretary of State. Comparison of data from the 1655 mission list with that from the two 1675 sources for the location of the missions vis-à-vis one another indicates that prior to 1656 San Luis was one league [2.6 miles] east-southeast of today's San Luis. Tallahassee's Capitol Hill or the de Soto encampment site are likely candidates for the earlier site of the mission" (1990:486).

While there is only scant evidence of any seventeenth-century material at the Martin site proper, a survey of adjacent properties turned up Mission-period artifacts on the nearby Capitol City Country Club. As mentioned earlier, it is tempting to call this evidence of the first location of the San Luis mission, San Luis de Xinyaca (Anhaica). Given the close proximity and continuous distribution of aboriginal artifacts, the Martin site and the material on the Capitol City Country Club can be considered part of the same site, the principal village of Anhaica.

In 1656 the village moved to the present location of San Luis de Talimali in order to be closer to the garrison of soldiers (Hann 1990:486). It appears, again based on the ceramic assemblage, that the Governor Martin site was more or less abandoned at this time. The entire Apalachee Province was vacated after the devastating raids of Colonel James Moore and the Creeks in 1704.

The Tallahassee Red Hills were just too inviting a place to remain vacant for long, however. The Lower Creek of Alabama and Georgia had been using Apalachee Province as a hunting ground since the early 1720s and by 1755 had established several permanent towns in the area (Hudson 1976:464). Gradually, these immigrants grew apart from their Creek stock and formed distinct groups known as Seminoles and Mikasukis.

Little is known, archaeologically, about the Seminoles in northwest Florida. A survey conducted by Denise Breit, a graduate student at Florida State University, located fewer than two dozen Seminole sites, and even these were evanescent. The material assemblage of such sites consists primarily of Chattahoochee Brushed pottery and British trade goods. There were two large Seminole settlements, one on Lake Miccosukee and the other, Tallahassee Taloofa, near the ruins of San Luis in the old Apalachee Province. The Stuart Purcell map of 1778 refers to the abandoned cornfields of the Mission-period Apalachee, although the Apalachee themselves had long since disappeared.

The Seminole presence at the Governor Martin site is revealed by the significant amounts of Chattahoochee Brushed pottery, an eighteenth-century brass musket sight, and numerous eighteenth-century beads. The large eighteenth-century material assemblage suggests a fairly sizable Seminole village site. The Seminole period in north Florida effectively ended with the dispersal of the Seminoles by Andrew Jackson in 1818, following the First Seminole War, although scattered bands remained in the area along the Apalachicola River until the 1830s (Ewen et al. 1988: 24–25).

Territorial Governor William Duval was the first recorded landowner in the area of the Martin site. In 1827 he purchased 160 acres in the northwest portion of section 6, township 1 South, range 1 East (Thompson 1986:13). Although the boundary descriptions are not clear, it seems likely that the Governor Martin site was included in this tract. Artifacts found in the area suggest that the Duval residence was located in the northern portion of Myers Park. The Duvals sold the property in 1836. It passed through several hands until becoming part of the Houston (pronounced *House-ton*) family holdings in 1853 (Thompson 1986:15–16).

The Houstons established a plantation on their property and raised cotton and rice as cash crops. After the Civil War the focus of the holding shifted to a more pastoral economy. Patrick Houston converted the plantation into a stock farm specializing in horses, mules, and dairy cattle (Thompson 1986:20). The property remained in the Houston family until the turn of the century. After passing from the Houstons, the property was subdivided by developers, a major part of it becoming Country Club Estates.

In the late 1920s the Martin tract (then 27 acres) was purchased by former Florida Governor John W. Martin. Hoping to be reelected, Martin built a large house on the tract in the early 1930s. Appropriately enough, this mansion was named Apalachee, though it is likely that Martin was unaware of the true significance of the name for his property. In any event, Martin was unsuccessful in his bid for governor and eventually sold the tract in 1941. All but six acres surrounding the mansion were developed into the Governor's Park subdivision.

The remaining six acres were sold first to the Stoutamire family, then to the Lewis family. During these years, the Martin house saw a number of uses. During World War II the house functioned as an officer's club known as the Forest Inn (Mrs. A. L. Stoutamire 1988, personal communication). The interior of the house was later renovated by Mr. Lewis to better serve as a private residence. A Florida governor returned to the mansion, which hosted one of Governor Bob Graham's first inaugural parties (Mrs. C. D. Lewis 1988, personal communication). In 1986, when the mansion had been abandoned and was in general disrepair, the six-acre tract was purchased by the Tallahassee Development Corporation for development into a modest office complex.

The modern (nineteenth- and twentieth-century) occupation is all too apparent to those interested in the earlier components of the site. The earlier deposits are often disturbed by later landscaping done by John Martin or the subsequent residents of the mansion. To the late-nineteenth and early-twentieth century antiquarian, the Governor Martin site offers an array of pharmaceutical bottles and reconstructable pearlware tablewares. Marbles, doll parts, and cap-guns attest to the presence of children on the site. Metal condom containers tell us that safe sex was an issue in the 1940s, when the Martin house functioned as an officer's club.

After analyzing the 80,000 artifacts recovered, it can truly be said that the history of the Tallahassee area can be read in the strata of the Martin site. However, it is the de Soto component that led to the furor surrounding the site's discovery and excavation.

EVIDENCE FOR DE SOTO

Spanish artifacts recovered from the Governor Martin site can be added to the sixteenth-century New World artifact database for comparative purposes by researchers elsewhere in the Southeast. A conference held in Bradenton, Florida, in January 1988 and a 1991 symposium in Cáceres, Spain, brought together de Soto researchers from around the world. Since the Governor Martin site was the only bona fide de Soto campsite known at either conference, the artifacts recovered from it became the standard for comparison. It is now virtually impossible to do any research on the de Soto entrada without referencing the Governor Martin site.

Yet the identification of the site as de Soto's winter encampment is still only a hypothesis. To test this hypothesis, it was first necessary to define what evidence would be needed. The significance of the data recovered from the site, described in chapter 5, is discussed here.

Artifacts are an important category of evidence, but like the documents associated with the expedition, they must be evaluated judiciously. The presence of sixteenth-century Spanish artifacts on the site does not necessarily mean that de Soto slept here. The European artifacts recovered from the Governor Martin site (beads, coins, mail, and such) could easily have been carried far from their original point of deposition. Similar items have been found in burial mounds and village sites in the Southeast, and no one is suggesting that de Soto made pilgrimages to all those sites.

A good indication of a Spanish encampment is large numbers of typical sixteenth-century trade goods, hardware, and utilitarian items found in contexts that suggest loss or disposal rather than exclusively the ritualistic burial of a prized item. Given the recorded presence of both pre– and post–de Soto Spaniards in Apalachee Province, artifacts indicative of a de Soto camp must either have a tightly dated terminus post quem or be peculiar to the de Soto expedition. The artifact assemblage should also be predominantly aboriginal in composition, and at least one component of the aboriginal assemblage should date to the early sixteenth century. The Spaniards spent less than six months in the Apalachee chief's village, so while they would have had an impact on the total artifact assemblage, it would not have been very great. Finally the site itself should be as described—a large village of over 250 houses that the Spaniards took for themselves (chap. 11 of this book).

The location of the Governor Martin site does not contradict any of the four narratives associated with the de Soto expedition. Prominent geographic features, such as mounds, rivers, or lakes, that might have occasioned comment but are not present in the narratives are not present at the site. As discussed in chapters 1 and 4, the Governor Martin site falls within the approximated distances from Anhaica to various other landmarks (the Aucilla River, the site of Ivitachuco, the Gulf of Mexico) as recorded in the accounts of the expedition. The site has evidence of burning (structure 1), as mentioned in the documents, and there is evidence of European improvement (sawn posts, wrought nails) of a structure as well. The site is also located on a major Indian trail, befitting its importance.

Aboriginal artifacts account for most of the material assemblage recovered from the Governor Martin site. The majority of the ceramics recovered are late Fort Walton types (A.D. 1450–1633) typical of the Contact period in north Florida. In other words, the aboriginal ceramic assemblage is consistent with the interpretation of the site as being part of a Velda-phase Apalachee settlement.

Spanish ceramics at the site consist mainly of Olive Jar fragments. Chronologically identifiable rim fragments from the Governor Martin site can be classified as the Early type with date ranges of A.D. 1490–1650. Also recovered were such sixteenth-century majolica types as Columbia Plain (1492–1650), including a pre-1550 green variant, and Caparra Blue (1492–1600).

Beads of European manufacture were a staple trade item for Spanish explorers and are recorded as being part of the inventory brought by de Soto. A faceted amber bead, a dozen faceted chevron beads, and a single Nueva Cadiz bead recovered at the Governor Martin site are good sixteenth-century marker artifacts and also have been found at other sites thought to be associated with the expedition. Wrought nails of various sizes and types are present in the material assemblage. Many of these are associated with a burned sixteenth-century structure on the site and may represent evidence of European modification of an aboriginal structure. A crossbow quarrel is the only example of sixteenth-century weaponry recovered. The crossbow was the principal weapon of de Soto's army but had become obsolete when Spain returned to the Panhandle in the seventeenth century and are not found on seventeenth-century Mission-period sites. Another example of military hardware that was obsolete by the Mission period is the many pieces of chain mail armor. Over 2000 links of iron mail were recovered, as well as 20 links of brass mail. This type of armor proved to be ineffective against Apalachee weaponry, and its use was discontinued during the army's winter encampment at Anhaica.

The most datable artifacts recovered were the five copper coins. They were found scattered across the site and not deposited in any ritualistic manner. They are badly corroded but appear to be Spanish maravedis and Portuguese ceitils dating to the late fifteenth and early sixteenth centuries.

All of these items place the site in the early sixteenth century but cannot distinguish between the expedition of Pánfilo de Narváez in 1528 and that of Hernando de Soto 11 years later. The documents associated with the expeditions place Narváez closer to the coast than Tallahassee (especially Garcilaso de la Vega; see chap. 11 of this book), but the descriptions in the Vega account are fairly general and are not considered to be totally reliable. Fortunately, just before the close of the 1987 field season, a burned maxilla fragment from a domestic pig (*Sus scrofa*) was unearthed during the excavation of a sixteenth-century structure. Artifacts in the same context include late Fort Walton ceramics and a Nueva Cadiz bead. The remains of the pig are significant because it is recorded that de Soto brought a herd of swine with him to avoid the same fate as the earlier Narváez expedition. Narváez and his men found little food in the southern reaches of Apalachee province and were eventually reduced to eating their horses to survive.

SIGNIFICANCE OF THE SITE

The discovery and excavation of the Martin site is an example of serendipity followed by herculean efforts on the part of many groups and individuals to preserve this tremendously significant site. Timing was everything. The site was found in time for the 450th anniversary of de Soto's trek through *La Florida*. It was found just before commercial development would have destroyed a major portion of it. Important artifact finds during the course of the excavations kept public interest piqued and kept additional funding flowing. However, luck alone did not save the Governor Martin site; it merely provided the opportunity.

The extraordinary cooperation among the land developers, state agencies, universities, private businesses, public organizations, and hundreds of individuals allowed over 80,000 artifacts to be recovered during 10 months of excavation at the site. Along with the artifacts from the de Soto expedition, evidence of a large Apalachee village, a later Spanish mission, and an eighteenth-century Seminole village were also uncovered.

A great deal of time and effort by a great many concerned people went into the work at the Governor Martin site. Time and materials donated by both professionals and amateurs alike far exceeded that actually paid for out of the project's meager budget. Was it all worth it? What qualities does this site possess that made its excavation and preservation so important?

POPULAR SIGNIFICANCE

The significance of the Governor Martin site has been widely recognized. A century of searching for the first winter encampment appears to have ended in success. The *New York Times* (May 19, 1987) referred to it as "the crowning achievement of recent scholarly efforts to determine more precisely the route of the de Soto expedition." The late Gary Shapiro, looking at the site from the perspective of a scholar, said that it "opened the door to a new understanding of the Apalachee and many other native cultures that have long since vanished" (1987). Actually, the Martin site is significant for both these and a number of other reasons.

The Governor Martin site has its share of historical firsts. One of them is likely to have occurred during de Soto's wintering in Apalachee Province: the first Christmas mass celebrated in the United States. It is known that twelve priests accompanied the expedition, eight regular and four secular clergy (Swanton 1985:86–87). The army remained in Anhaica from October 1539 to March 1540. Although not mentioned specifically in any of the narratives (which are all extremely sketchy concerning the in-camp events of that first winter), surely the priests conducted some sort of Christmas service for the men. It was, after all, the time of the Inquisition, and strict adherence to religious ceremony was observed by all Spaniards. Smith (1975:9) notes that Christmas fell on December 15 in 1539 rather than on December 25 since the change to the Gregorian calendar did not occur until 1582. There is no record of any Christian expedition, with the appropriate clergy, being in the territory of the United States at Christmas prior to the de Soto entrada. To commemorate the mass likely said at the camp, the Trust for Public Land sponsored a Christmas service at the site on December 20, 1987.

Of even greater significance to the general public were the educational benefits of the discovery and excavation of the Governor Martin site. It is a sad fact that Spain's role in the history of the United States has received such short shrift in contemporary history textbooks, even after the Columbian Quincentennial. Most elementary and secondary school texts devote no more than a few paragraphs to the nearly 500-year Spanish presence in the American Southeast. Hernando de Soto, when he is mentioned at all, is credited only for "discovering" the Mississippi River. The 450th anniversary of de Soto's landing in Florida has presented an opportunity to educate the general public about this turning point in American history.

Archaeology is not a high-profile activity that readily grabs the attention of most people, but the investigations at the Governor Martin site received broad exposure in both the electronic and the print media. The archaeologists who were interviewed by reporters and who delivered lectures to school and civic groups made a special effort to encourage a greater understanding of the role of Spain in the history of the United States. Neither did we neglect to point out the tragic consequences of European contact for the native inhabitants. It was for this reason that archaeologists chose to commemorate rather than celebrate events such as the 450th anniversary of de Soto's landing and the 500th anniversary of Columbus's discovery of the New World.

ARCHAEOLOGICAL SIGNIFICANCE

The academic community surpassed the general public in its enthusiasm over the discovery of the site. However, its interest in de Soto was somewhat peripheral. The Governor Martin site represented an excellent opportunity to establish a better understanding of the cultural evolution of the Apalachee and perhaps of native cultural response in general to the European invasion. The following section concerning ceramic chronologies is expanded from an outline by John Scarry based on his research and that of Claudine Payne and Marion Smith.

Time is a fundamental concept for the archaeologist. Chronological frameworks are tools used by archaeologists to organize sites in an understandable way. Sites where occupations can be tightly dated can be used to identify synchronic similarities and differences, identify diachronic stability and change, measure the duration of stability or change, measure the rates of change, indicate the directions of change, and identify the sources of influences for change.

From an archaeological perspective, the de Soto encampment site represents a solid chronological anchor for refining the local ceramic sequence (see chap. 5). As Shapiro (1987) points out, "excavations at this site tell us *for the first time* [emphasis his] what pottery styles were prevalent in Apalachee around the year 1539." This information can then be used to seriate other Apalachee sites with a precise date rather than an approximate, relative date.

The Governor Martin site is a solid reference in the construction of chronological trends. The known date of 1539–1540 for its de Soto component makes it the earliest well-dated site in Apalachee Province. Among other Apalachee sites are Velda (probably late sixteenth century), Patale (1633–1650), San Luis de Talimali (1656–1704), and Ocuya (?–1703). When the data from the Martin site are combined with data from Velda, Patale, and late seventeenth-century missions (San Luis, Scott Miller, and Ocuya), several trends are suggested: (1) Lamar Complicated Stamped increases in frequency through time, (2) rectilinear forms of Lamar Complicated Stamped motifs increase in frequency through time, (3) the ratio of Leon Check Stamped to Lamar Complicated Stamped decreases through time, and (4) the ratio of Lamar Complicated Stamped to Fort Walton Incised increases through time.

The results of this analysis are preliminary and may not be proven. However, these hypotheses are worthy of further testing. If these trends are shown to be valid, the chronology of the Early Contact period will be greatly refined. The presence of early varieties of Lamar Complicated Stamped and Carrabelle Punctated *var.* Meginnis at the Governor Martin site is helping area researchers span the time period between the occupation of the Lake Jackson and San Luis sites.

Apalachee Province has been the subject of archaeological investigation for over 50 years (for a summary of the archaeology of this region, see

Milanich 1994, 1995). Direct contact occurred early and was more sustained in Apalachee than in the interior chiefdoms of the Southeast, and changes due to contact should thus be most readily apparent in this region. Regional surveys (Tesar 1980; Bryne 1986; Smith and Scarry 1988) and synthetic studies (Scarry 1990, 1994b) permit a regional perspective and provide a provisional chronology for the province. The archaeological data are complemented by an extensive body of documentary materials pertaining to the sixteenth- and seventeenth-century Apalachee (see Hann 1988). This makes the Governor Martin site a particularly good locus for the study of the consequences of contact.

The prevailing catastrophic model of contact hypothesizes that the aboriginal cultures collapsed following contact with Europeans due to depopulation brought on by epidemic diseases. Such a catastrophe should be readily apparent in the archaeological record. The fall of native chiefdoms would be characterized by the end of public works such as mounds and palisades, the loss or at least simplification of a settlement hierarchy, the breakdown of status systems as reflected in grave goods, and the breakdown in organized, part-time craft specialization (M. T. Smith 1987:89).

Most of these changes do appear to have occurred in Apalachee Province. However, many seemingly occurred either earlier or later than the Contact period. The Velda phase, which began prior to European contact in Apalachee Province, was characterized by a cessation of mound building, changes in the ceramic assemblage, and a shift of the principal village from Lake Jackson to the Governor Martin site. Ceramic changes occurred before, during, and after the Contact period. The role of the Spaniards in these later changes is unclear. The bioarchaeological evidence from the Contact period is almost completely lacking. Only two burials were discovered at the Governor Martin site, an adult cremation and a subadult burial so poorly preserved that only the burial pit and tooth enamel remained.

Is disease the only or even the primary factor that could account for the changes that did occur in the Apalachee chiefdom? Perhaps some of the changes in the native societies were the result of cyclical political upheaval. Scarry characterizes chiefdoms as politically volatile, claiming "that there will be brief periods of breakdown every generation or so; successional disputes, minor rebellions, and small wars. Region-wide rebellions, civil wars, and the replacement of one chiefly line by another will occur less frequently. . . . These major breakdowns should be evident in the destruction or abandonment of great centers or by changes in traditional chiefly symbolism" (1990:178). The causes of these revolutions could certainly be brought on or worsened by population decline. However, even Lake Jackson appears to have been abandoned before the Spaniards came to the New World, let alone to Apalachee.

Clearly the Apalachee suffered at the hands of the Spaniards. But what were the long-term consequences of the encounter? Settlement patterns in the region do not appear to have been radically affected by the European presence prior to the late seventeenth and early eighteenth centuries. The archaeological survey of the Governor Martin site discovered an early mission established in the area, San Luis de Xinyaca. This was probably at the original village of Anhaica, hardly what one would expect if a plague had devastated the village.

This is not to say that European-introduced disease was not a factor in the cultural transformation of native societies in the Southeast or even in Apalachee Province, only that it may have been one of several factors, some having little to do with European contact. As can be shown in Apalachee Province, some changes may already have been underway prior to contact. Other social changes were engendered by the political response to the presence of the Europeans. Further research into the Contact period will clarify the role of European arrivals in the demise of the native polities.

As we study the expedition of Hernando de Soto through the southeastern United States, we should stop and reflect on the reasons why this event was important. Charles Hudson, Marvin Smith, and Chester de Pratter explain the real importance of research concerning the de Soto expedition: "an accurate reconstruction of the route will enable us to advance greatly our understanding of the aboriginal people of the Southeast. It will provide archaeologists with more chronological precision than they now possess, and this will allow them to do more precise descriptive and comparative work. . . . Moreover, by combining the information in the de Soto documents with archaeological information, we can gain at least some insight into the internal structure of the Southeastern chiefdoms, as well as some understanding of the kinds of relationships which existed between chiefdoms" (Hudson et al 1984:75). Thus, as in NASA's moon program, the destination is actually secondary to the trip itself. It's what is learned along the way that's really important. Unfortunately, many people have missed this central point.

What should scholars researching the Contact period be concerned with? Again, Hudson, Depratter and Smith (1984:75) make the point: "It is our hope that an accurate reconstruction of the de Soto route will enable us to draw a social map of the sixteenth-century Southeast. We would like to be able to locate specific, named societies and towns on specific rivers and creeks. Such a map could be used as a baseline from which to move both forward and backward in time. That is, it may become possible for scholars to reconstruct the prehistoric antecedents of the societies that de Soto visited, as well as to reconstruct the ways in which these societies were transformed into the far different societies that existed in the eighteenth century (Depratter 1983; M. T. Smith 1984). This would put the social history of the Southeast on a new footing." Indeed, it would be the beginning of the archaeogeography of the United States.

PART III

The Documents Relevant to the Governor Martin Site

John H. Hann

7 · Hernando de Soto in Apalachee Archaeology and History

Introduction to the Documentary Record

Recent discovery and exploration of the site of Hernando de Soto's winter camp in Apalachee created a need for translations of the accounts of the de Soto expedition's experiences in Apalachee tailored to the needs of archaeologists. A few comparisons of the Spanish and Portuguese texts with the more commonly used standard translations of those texts made it evident that most of the standard translations fell short on occasion in providing a precise and faithful rendition in matters of vital interest to archaeologists and anthropologists. Because translation involves a certain amount of interpretation, translators may disagree here and there on how best to render a phrase or word in a particular context, but the translations I found questionable involved more than simple differences of interpretation. When I prepared my own translations of each of these accounts, I did not expect to find that previous versions had taken such a magnitude of liberties with the Spanish and Portuguese texts. That exercise made it clear that the previous versions are relatively free translations that often lack an adequate warning to the reader about the degree of tampering with the original paragraph and sentence structure, syntax, choice of words, and so forth in rendering those accounts into readable English. The one exception I found was James Alexander Robertson's translation of the account of the Gentleman of Elvas.

The liberties in rendering the accounts into readable English encompass practices such as completely rewriting sentences, adding words, deleting words, splitting long sentences into a number of separate sentences, and (more questionably) joining together sentences that are distinct in the Spanish text or joining together in one sentence clauses that are parts of distinct sentences. On several occasions the result was a change in the meaning of the Spanish text when rendered in English. It is such liberties that probably gave rise to the Portuguese axiom that "to translate is to betray," playing on diverse meanings of the verb *traduzir.* That reality is reflected in the word's cognate "to traduce."

In none of the flawed translations did the translator make any attempt to alert the reader that some of the words or phrases rendered in one fashion might have been rendered as justifiably (or in some cases more justifiably) in one or more different ways that at times change the meaning significantly. An example is the rendering of the Spanish *monte* as "hill" or "mountain." In sixteenth- and seventeenth-century documents concerning Florida, *monte* most often means "woods." Rarely do any of the translators alert the reader to the original Spanish word in circumstances when the Spanish word itself might well be of interest to anthropologists, archaeologists, or ethnohistorians. For example, when Luís de Moscoso was preparing to leave Ocale to rejoin de Soto, the Gentleman of Elvas noted that Moscoso and his men buried hardware (*ferragem*) and other objects in Ocale. In addition to the general meaning of "hardware made of iron," *ferragem* has the specific meaning of "horseshoes," which might be of significance archaeologically. On a somewhat lesser scale of importance, scholars might be interested in the nuances, for example, of the precise Portuguese term that the Gentleman of Elvas used when he spoke of de Soto's order that his men gather in all the maize that was "ripe"; the term Elvas used was *seco,* which literally means "dry." Inclusion of the Portuguese term in parentheses can communicate something about the natives' harvesting practices not found in the English term "ripe" by itself.

Admittedly, there are few instances of such examples in any single run of the pages I have translated for this project. But if they occur with the same or greater frequency in the remainder of these narratives, the nuances and alternative meanings lost when no such information is available in footnotes could amount to a critical mass.

None of the editors or publishers of successive editions of some of these translations has corrected obvious errors in matters of importance that over the years must have caught the eye of scholars, who occasionally took the care to make the errors public after looking at the original or at an alternate or earlier translation of the passage in question. A glaring example is Buckingham Smith's rendition, in editions as recent as the one by Palmetto Books in 1968, of the Gentleman of Elvas's account of the distances from Anhaica Apalache to Ochete and to the sea. In the 1968 edition, the sea is "eight leagues distant" from Anhaica, while Ochete is described as "eight leagues on the way" to the sea from Anhaica. The contradiction between the two statements of distance should have made an editor or publisher investigate. In the original Portuguese and in Robertson's translation, Ochete is placed six leagues from Anhaica and the sea at 10 leagues from Anhaica.

None of the relatively modern translations—from Smith's mid-nineteenth-century pieces to those of Edward Gaylord Bourne and Fanny Bandelier at the beginning of the twentieth century to the more recent work of John and Jeannette Varner (1951) and Gerald Thiesen (1972)—was made with an eye to the needs of anthropologists, archaeologists, or ethnohistorians. They all fail to provide translations of the words in the order in which they flowed from the pen of the narrator, without rearranging, blanching, filtering, transmuting, "genericizing," or otherwise altering the words to suit the sensibilities or literary pretensions of the translator.

In this respect, perhaps the most surprising and disappointing translation is the Varners' *Florida of the Inca*. Because it was published by a prestigious university press, it might be expected that more attention would have been given to the needs of scholars in the manner described here or that a clearer warning might have been given by the translators or the editors about the nature of the changes introduced in the process of translating the work. The Varners observed about the nature of their translation, "Our text is complete and without alterations other than those required by the process of translation, for our sole purpose has been to present clearly and accurately the meaning and feeling the Inca was trying to convey. In the main we adhered fairly closely to the syntax of the original, but when such procedure resulted in cumbersomeness, grotesquerie or obscurity, we sought a form which would be agreeable and at the same time uninjurious to sense and tone" (Varner and Varner 1951:vi).

Excellent as the Varners' contribution is, it is my opinion, after translating the Apalachee portion of Garcilaso's narrative and comparing the Varners' translation of that portion with the Spanish text, that the Varners used the text's "cumbersomeness, grotesquerie or obscurity" as an excuse to edit the original text excessively—occasionally, albeit infrequently, in such a way as to violate their pledge to translate in a manner "uninjurious to sense and tone."

There is little correspondence between the division into paragraphs in the 1723 edition, which the Varners used in their translation, and that found in their version. The changes are not confined to dividing cumbersome, overlong paragraphs into several smaller, more cohesive ones. That would be understandable. The Varners exercised a similar license in dividing long sentences into several shorter ones and in combining in one sentence material found in distinct sentences in the 1723 edition, as well as in altering the structure of sentences and paragraphs. In this respect, the Varners have probably taken more liberties with the Spanish text than did any of the other translators whose work I examined while preparing my translations, with the exception of Fanny Bandelier. Bandelier at least told her readers clearly that she was "paraphrasing rather than translating." Although the Varners' translation is not as free as the one by Bandelier, the degree to which they have altered the Spanish text is not reflected adequately in their introductory caveat.

In the name of eliminating "cumbersomeness, grotesquerie or obscurity," the Varners did a massive rewrite of Garcilaso's work, syntactically, structurally, and stylistically. Cumbersome words, phrases, clauses, and those that are repetitious or overlapping have been deleted freely. Occasionally the deletions have eliminated details actually or potentially of interest to archaeologists, anthropologists, ethnohistorians, or historians in general. In the portion of Garcilaso's work that I have also translated, the most glaring example of this is the Varners' rendition of Garcilaso's description of the plaza at Osachile as typical of all the plazas of the native settlements of Florida.

The Varners rendered this passage thus: "In those areas at the foot of this hill, which may be either natural or artificial, they construct a plaza, around which. . . ." The following is my literal rendition of the same passage. "On the *level* area at the foot of the hill, either natural or artificial, they make a *squared* plaza in accord with the size of the Village that is to be settled and around it. . . ." In their editing of this passage, the Varners eliminated the important details that I have italicized in my rendition. They excised the information that the plaza was "squared" and built on "a level area" and proportioned to "accord with the size of the village" that was to be constructed around it. The omitted details also suggest an element of planning that would not be gleaned as easily and clearly from the Varners' truncated rendition of the Spanish text.

The Varners rendered the next sentence on the same page thus: "They make an effort not to be far distant from the site upon which the dwelling of their lord is located." My literal rendition of the same passage is "They try not to be distant from the *hill* where the house of the lord is, *instead they work to crowd about it with theirs.*" In this case the Varners traded Garcilaso's graphic and concrete "hill" for their bland and generic "site" and eliminated his words beginning with "instead" that I have italicized. The words they have eliminated here and elsewhere are, admittedly, generally repetitious ones, but the repetition often reinforces the image that Garcilaso meant to convey and adds nuances that are lost by such deletions. In John Varner's case, such editing of Garcilaso's text may well have been a reflex action arising from his training as a professor of English, possibly more interested in how things are said than in what is said, analogous to Professor Higgins's quip about the French in Lerner and Loewe's *My Fair Lady:* "The French don't care what they do actually as long as they pronounce it properly." But such cavalier treatment of so important a passage is no less damaging and regrettable.

In their rendering of graphic and concrete or specific terms, the Varners often manifest a penchant for the bland, imprecise, and generic term. Their rendition of Garcilaso's description of Osachile provides an example of their dilution of the precision of Garcilaso's Spanish term. In describing the log walls that lined the pathway that ascended the hill or mound on which the chief's house was located, Garcilaso noted (in my rendition) that "they drive thick logs . . . more than an estate (*estado*) into the earth." In the Varners' rendition, the "thick logs" become "thick pieces of wood . . . thrust side by side into the earth to a depth of more than the height of a man." In a sense, the Varners' rendition is here more graphic and communicative, but in the interest of precision they should have informed the reader in a footnote about the precision of the term *estado* used by Garcilaso: 2.17 yards.

In other instances, the Varners went in the opposite direction, rendering somewhat imprecise Spanish terms or phrases more precisely in their English rendition. Thus "*pasos*" or "paces" becomes "feet." In a subsequent passage telling of the distance covered on a particular day's march, Garcilaso said, literally, "On this day they traveled *more than* [italics mine] another thirteen leagues." The Varners rendered this as "another thirteen leagues," deleting Garcilaso's *mas de* or "more than."

The Varners commonly made other changes as well, including changes from singular to plural and plural to singular. And in order to present as quotations material that is not so presented in the Spanish text, the Varners changed the person of the verb from third to first.

In one respect the Varners have made Garcilaso's text more concrete than it is in the Spanish, by frequently inserting "cacique" or the person's name where the Spanish text had only "he." One would not fault them much for that. But the practice is more questionable when it involves interpretation, as it does in the first paragraph of chapter 10 of book 2, part 2 (p. 203) of the Varner text (see my rendition in chapter 11). What I rendered literally as "And in a few days *they* brought him a correct report," the Varners presented as "and in a few days received positive information from his *spies* to the effect . . . " (my emphasis).

Although the Varners have transformed the text with which they worked more than have the translators of the other de Soto accounts, none of the existing translations is entirely satisfactory, particularly with respect to the interests of archaeologists and anthropologists. There is need for new critical translations of all of the texts for both the de Soto and Narváez expeditions that would be guided by a sensitivity toward the interests of archaeologists, anthropologists, and ethnohistorians.

PLACE-NAMES IN APALACHEE PROVINCE

Overall the de Soto chronicles are useful for providing names and relative locations of native settlements and similar data. But in proportion to the five months that de Soto tarried in Apalachee, the chronicles' value for that province is surprisingly limited. Their principal contribution to our knowledge about Apalachee is their data on its productivity, the density of its population, and the persistent ferocity and valor of its people in their refusal to come to terms with the intruders, in contrast to many of the other native peoples that de Soto encountered. Among the Apalachee villages that the de Soto chroniclers mentioned, only two are identifiable in documentation from the mission era: Ivitachuco, easternmost of the Apalachee settlements, and Anhaica Apalache or Iviahica or Iniahico, the names that various chroniclers gave for the settlement de Soto appropriated for his winter quarters. De Soto's Ivitachuco is clearly recognizable in documentation a century or more later as the mission San Lorenzo de Ivitachuco, which was still located on Apalachee's eastern frontier, although it may not have occupied precisely the same site as de Soto's Ivitachuco.

De Soto's Anhaica is similarly linked to the other most important settlement of the mission era, San Luís de Talimali, center of Spanish authority in that period. When the native component of the name of the San Luis mission was first mentioned in the 1657 visitation as San Luis de Xinayca (Hann 1986:93), its native component was clearly a variant of the earlier Anhaica, perceived by Spanish ears not yet well attuned to the inflections of the natives' tongue. Even the alternate de Soto names for Anhaica, namely Iviahica and Iniahico, are recognizable in the 1657 visitation's second mention of San Luis as San Luis de Nixaxipa (Hann 1986:95). The important twin centers of Ivitachuco and Inihayca also appeared a half century earlier, in 1608, when Spaniards reestablished contact with the Apalachee for the first time after the de Soto intrusion (Oré 1936:114).

The more familiar name San Luis de Talimali did not appear in the documentation until 1675. The name from the de Soto era appeared as late as 1676 (Perete et al. 1676) in the form S[an]cti Ludouici de Inatafum, in which the Apalachee word for village, *tafum,* replaced the Timucua *hica* (also meaning "village") of Anhahica. The more common spelling for the Apalachee word is *tafun*. It appears repeatedly in the 1688 letter to the king written by the Apalachee chiefs, and it is the one used in the native component, Ychutafun or Deer Town, of the name of the Santa Cruz mission.

It is worthy of note that Timucua lexical forms appear in the names of Apalachee's two principal villages: Anhaica (Anhahica), or Iviahica, and Ivitachuco. *Hica* is Timucua for "settlement, town, village, or citizen" (Granberry 1989:167). In one mid-seventeenth-century document, the name Iniayca was rendered as Niayca, exactly the same as the name of a contemporaneous western Timucua village. On one occasion, that Timucua village's name was presented as Niahica, showing clearly that the *ica* was meant to be *hica*. It is of possible significance that *nia* means "woman" or "female" in the Timucua language. Another important Apalachee village in mission times, Cupaica, also included *hica* in its name.

The Timucua form *ibi* meant "water" or any body of water, such as a lake or pond or stream. Natives attached *ibi* in the forms *ibita* or *ivita* to a number of geographic features in Timucua territory, most of which were identified clearly as arroyos. Two Spaniards traveling in 1675 and 1716 recorded the names of a number of such arroyos. The examples include a large arroyo known as *ajano ybitta*, others called *apixa yvitta* and *ajano yvitta chirico*, and *pepa yvitta*. The traveler of 1675 gave the meaning of "Ajano hibitachirico" as river of little acorns (Hann 1996:248). West of the Suwannee River, still another arroyo bore the name Usiybitta. On crossing into Apalachee territory, the traveler of 1716 stopped for the night near the arroyo *ybitachuco* on the *ycapacha* of *ybitachuco*. *Hicapacha*, literally "village-old," was the Timucua word for "abandoned village site," the same as the Apalachee *chicasa* (Peña 1716). Late in the seventeenth century, a Timucua village between the St. Johns River and present-day Gainesville bore the name Ivitanayo, meaning White or Silver Lake.

Mission-era documents bear no trace of the other Apalachee place-names the de Soto chroniclers mentioned: Calahuchi, Uzela, Ochete, Aute, and the River of Guacuca, the first river de Soto encountered as he was leaving Apalachee. The name Guacuca, however, may have been a garbled version of the name of the mission village of Bacucua, located on or near a northwesterly trail leading out of Apalachee to a crossing point on the Flint River, the route de Soto is generally believed to have taken. De Soto's Rio de Guacuca would be the present Ochlockonee, known in the mission era by the native name Lagni, Yellow River, or variants of Lagni. If my theory is correct, Ranjel simply assigned the name of the nearest Apalachee settlement to the river.

Among the native place-names the de Soto chroniclers recorded for Timucua territory between Ocale and Ivitachuco, a much higher percentage reappeared in mission times or in other periods than was the case for the Apalachee names. The Timucua names are *Ocale*, Uqueten, *Acuera*, Itara, *Potano*, *Utina*, Aguacaleyquen, *Uriutina*, Cholupaha, *Apalu*, Napituca, Usachile, and *Agile*, with the italicized names being those that appear elsewhere. These names represent slightly more than half of the thirteen settlements for which native names were given. Ocale or Etocale reappeared as Eloquale on the Le Moyne map and in a 1630 document that mentioned the mission of San Luis de Eloquale. Acuera reappeared as a general name for people allied to the Freshwater leader Outina in the 1560s, the inhabitants of a distinct province that the Spaniards called Acuera. In the seventeenth century, Spaniards alluded to the province of Acuera also as the province of Diminiyuti or Ibiniyuti. One of Diminiyuti's villages bore the name Mocoso, a name associated with the Tampa Bay region in the de Soto narratives (Worth 1992:429, 456). The Acuera lived initially along the Oklawaha River but by the 1670s were ranging along the middle St. Johns River and westward into Potano territory in the vicinity of modern Gainesville (Hann 1992:451, 454, 461–64). Two missions bore the Acuera name, San Luis de Acuera and Santa Lucia de Acuera. Potano reappeared in French and Spanish documents from the 1560s and in Spanish documents into the early eighteenth century in the name of the mission San Francisco Potano.

The Utina or Utinamocharra of the de Soto chronicles did not reappear as the name of a Potano village after de Soto's time. In the rare later mentions of central Potano villages other than San Francisco de Potano, Spaniards gave only saints' names for the mission villages. But the name or title *utina* reappeared in the 1560s as part of the name of the Freshwater Timucua paramount, Olata Ouae Outina, mentioned by Frenchmen and Spaniards, and in 1602 as Nyaautina, the name of a village and its chief (Lussagnet 1958:101, 102; Valdés 1602). Jerald T. Milanich (1978:71) identified *utina* as "a Timucuan word meaning chief or king," noting that its "usage might have been widespread through the area in which Timucua was spoken." De Soto's Uriutina, of the province north of Potano, and the early seventeenth-century mission village of Santa Isabel de Utinahica, deep in south-central Georgia, are illustrations of Milanich's point. Uriutina reemerged in the 1630s as the mission of Urihica, last mentioned in 1655 as San Agustin de Urica. Apalu reappeared on the Le Moyne map from the 1560s and as the name of a mission station in 1616, but both of the later villages bearing that name appear to be different settlements than the one the de Soto chroniclers mentioned (Oré 1936:129).

De Soto's Agile is the familiar San Miguel de Asile of the mission era, westernmost of the villages of the province of Yustaga (Hann 1990:42–43, 44, 52, 53–54, 59–60).

The chroniclers' differing renditions of the names of two of the Spaniards may be a source of confusion. The first is Juan Ortiz. Elvas used the Portuguese form João for Juan, while Oviedo y Valdéz used Johan, derived from the Latin form of the name Johannes and ultimately from the Hebrew Yohanan. Ortiz was a Spaniard associated with the Narváez expedition who had fallen into the hands of the Indians. The Tampa Bay–area chief whom he served in 1539 released him to contact de Soto. Because of the Indian languages he had learned, Ortiz proved invaluable as an interpreter. The second Spaniard was Juan de Añasco. His name appears also as Joam danhusco and as Johan de Añasco.

Among the four de Soto accounts, the one by Garcilaso de la Vega is the most voluminous by far, particularly his chapters devoted ostensibly to Apalachee. Unfortunately, this account is also the least reliable, as many writers have observed. Much of what Garcilaso has to say about Apalachee is compromised considerably because of Garcilaso's placement of Vitachuco in Timucua territory. Careful reading of his account about events occurring in his Vitachuco, in conjunction with the other chroniclers' description of de Soto's experiences in Napituca, demonstrates clearly that Garcilaso's Vitachuco is Napituca. This knowledge raises a question about which, if any, of Garcilaso's statements about Vitachuco, whether they concern the man or the place, can be applied to Apalachee's Ivitachuco, as they often are. The Garcilaso statement that is used most often by others describes Vitachuco as having 200 houses. Henry Dobyns (1983:196) uses that figure in remarking that Yustaga's "Osachile Town consisted of a reported 200 houses, the same size as Vitachuco." Dobyns was speaking of the Timucua town to which Garcilaso gave the name Vitachuco and which he erroneously placed in Potano Province. Hann (1988:25), prior to his intensive study of the de Soto accounts, interpreted Garcilaso's description of Vitachuco's size as applying to the Apalachee town of Ivitachuco.

In telling of de Soto's entry into Apalachee, Garcilaso's account agrees with those of the other chroniclers only in his mention of the swamp and river, the extensive woods bordering them on either side, and the stiff resistance the Apalachee raised to the Spaniards' advance. Garcilaso made no mention of Asile, westernmost of the Timucua settlements. Neither did he mention any settlement in eastern Apalachee comparable to mission-era Ivitachuco or its near neighbor, Ayubale. Garcilaso's first-mentioned village in Apalachee is "a small village that marked the beginning of the fields, . . . great fields of corn, beans, squash and other vegetables which had been sown on both sides of the road as far as the eye could see across two leagues of the plain." The eastern Apalachee of Garcilaso had no towns, only "sprinklings of settlements" among the fields, "with houses set apart from each other and not arranged in the order of a town" (Varner and Varner 1951:181–82). The lack of organized settlements in eastern Apalachee portrayed by Garcilaso does not agree with the other chroniclers' portrayals of Ivitachuco as the gateway to Apalachee Province or with what is known about eastern Apalachee during the mission period. In the mission era, Ivitachuco and its near neighbor, Ayubale, had significant populations, and several other missions were clustered around them, not to mention the satellite villages that belonged to each mission center.

Cabeza de Vaca's accounts of Narváez's experience in Apalachee pose problems of credibility similar to those noted for Garcilaso's description of eastern Apalachee. Cabeza de Vaca's Apalachee does not seem to be the place that de Soto visited a decade later. Garcilaso himself noted the difference between what his sources told him and the image of Apalachee portrayed by Cabeza de Vaca. As Garcilaso began his description of Apalachee after de Soto's arrival in Apalachee's principal town, he interrupted the narrative:

> It seemed appropriate to me not to go on forward without touching on what Alvar Núñez Cabeça de Vaca writes in his *Commentaries* about this province of Apalachee, where he portrays it as harsh and full of brambles and briars (*fragosa*) obstructed (*ocupado*) by many woods and swamps, with rivers and bad passages (*malos pasos*), poorly populated and sterile, everything the opposite of what we are writing about it. From this, giving credence to what that gentleman writes as to one who is worthy of it, we believe that his trip did not take him so far inland as the one the governor Hernando de Soto made, but rather close to the shore of the sea, for which reason they found the land so harsh and full of woods and bad swamps, as he says, as the captain Juan de Añasco . . . encountered. (my translation)

Garcilaso went on to speculate that the village that Cabeza de Vaca called Apalache was not de Soto's Apalache but some other Apalachee village closer to the sea. Garcilaso wrote that "a great part of the account that Alvar Núñez writes about that land is what the Indians told him, as he himself says that those Castilians did not see it, because, as they were few, and almost or completely exhausted, they had no possibility of tramping (*rendido*) over it (*hollarla*) and seeing it by their own eyes" (my translation).

Although Garcilaso's argument has a certain plausibility, and although Cabeza de Vaca noted that Narváez did rely on information about Apalachee gathered from Indians that they had held, the argument does not square well with Cabeza de Vaca's remark that during the twenty-five days that Narváez remained in the village of Apalache, "we made three expeditions through the land," which was "very poor in people and very bad for moving about because of the bad trails and woods and ponds that it had" (my translation, p. 35). There seems to be no thoroughly plausible explanation for the discrepancies between the de Soto chroniclers' description of Apalachee and that left by Cabeza de Vaca. It could be that the Narváez expedition's hardships in Apalachee—failure to find the expected gold, the mauling that the men took, illness, and the beginning of long years of trauma in which most of the expedition perished—made Cabeza de Vaca remember Apalachee far more negatively than he otherwise would have, the opposite as it were to viewing the world through rose-colored glasses. The multitude of fallen trees that he mentioned suggests that Narváez reached Apalachee shortly after a hurricane had swept through the region. Diego Peña recorded similar difficulties when he encountered a hurricane as he journeyed from St. Augustine across north Florida to the Lower Creek country along the Chattahoochee River (Boyd 1949:15–17). Conceivably the village of Apalache had been destroyed by the storm, and the settlement Narváez appropriated was a makeshift temporary abode set up after the storm.

The various de Soto accounts and the Cabeza de Vaca narratives agree in attesting to the renown of Apalachee among other natives of Florida. Despite Cabeza de Vaca's poor-mouthing of what the Narváez expedition found there, Apalachee's principal town and its people are still the only place and natives in Florida whom Cabeza de Vaca identified by name, except for Aute, whose people were allied to the Apalachee. This in itself says something about Apalachee's importance for Cabeza de Vaca, even if the reasons for his retention of the name had faded into his subconscious. At the time of de Soto's arrival in Florida, so great was Apalachee's renown among the natives that one whom de Soto captured at Ocale described Apalachee as "a very large province" (Elvas 1932:32). Conceivably that estimate reflected the reality of an earlier day when the Lake Jackson center was flourishing and Apalachee played a leading role in a far-flung trade network that linked Mississippian mound centers. A similar image of grandeur is reflected in early seventeenth-century documents that describe "Great Apalachee" province as extending all the way to Panuco in New Spain and having 107 villages (Capilla 1609; Méndez de Canzo 1601; Peñaranda 1608). If the two chapters on Apalachee in Charles de Rochefort's *Histoire naturelle et morale des Isles Antilles de l'Amérique* have any basis in fact, Apalachee's former grandeur may be reflected there as well.

In de Soto's time seemingly, and in mission times definitely, Apalachee occupied a small area. Its borders extended from the Aucilla River on the east to a little beyond the Ochlockonee River on the west, from the area of the Georgia border to the Gulf of Mexico. But it was the most densely populated native province in Florida. Early in the mission era, 10 principal villages housed its people together with thirty-plus lesser settlements that were satellites. The settlements formed eastern and western clusters separated by the St. Marks River Valley. In de Soto's time, most of the villages probably were relatively close to the positions they occupied a century later when they became mission centers, strung out along the southern part of the Tallahassee area's red clay hills from western Leon County through eastern Jefferson County, not far from the Cody Scarp that marks the descent into the coastal lowlands. Their location was a most favorable one because of its combination of rich upland soils, access to lowland aquatic resources, an abundance of lakes and ponds, and relative proximity to estuarine resources as well. Apalachee's closeness to the coast also guaranteed it a bountiful supply of prime-quality yaupon holly (*Ilex vomitoria*), source of a native tea prized throughout the lower Southeast. Leaves from shrubs growing along the coasts were preferred over those from inland areas.

In de Soto's time the Apalachee chiefdom is considered to have been a complex one with an elaborated ruling hierarchy and a clear distinction between elite and commoners. The de Soto chroniclers provide little information about the head chief's power. They describe Anhaica Apalachee's chief as "lord of the province." But from the beginning of the seventeenth century through the destruction of the Apalachee missions at the beginning of the eighteenth century, Spaniards and natives repeatedly alluded to or acknowledged Ivitachuco's chief as paramount. If the Muskogean institution of peace chiefs and war chiefs existed in Apalachee, it would provide an explanation for the dichotomy. De Soto's invasion would have put the province on a war footing, which might have brought Anhaica Apalachee's chief to the fore. Anhaica's chief remained a powerful figure throughout the seventeenth century, second only to Ivitachuco's chief.

The Apalachee lived in somewhat permanent villages and were already a sedentary people in de Soto's time, depending primarily on agriculture for subsistence. They also relied on fish and game and wild fruit, nuts, and acorns to supplement the food they grew. The de Soto chroniclers remarked on the extensive fields of maize, beans, squash, and other vegetables that they encountered along the trail in Apalachee. Although it was still early in the fall, they also found caches of dried venison. That abundance in the fields and the adequacy of stored supplies of food were major factors motivating de Soto's decision to winter there. The Apalachee settlement's proximity to the coast doubtless was another consideration. It facilitated the transport to the winter camp of supplies that remained aboard ship when the major part of de Soto's forces headed inland from Tampa Bay. From the coast, canoes could take the St. Marks River, and tributaries that have disappeared since de Soto's time, to a point within a short distance of the upland Apalachee settlements. The camp's nearness to the coast also permitted de Soto's men to explore westward by ship during the winter for a good harbor suitable as a rendezvous point for resupply or return to Cuba the following summer or fall. De Soto planned to explore the interior of the Southeast by that time as far north as the mountains named for the Apalachee a generation later by French explorers.

THE DE SOTO CHRONICLERS

The account by the Gentleman of Elvas was the first of the four de Soto chronicles to appear. It was published in Portuguese in Evora, Portugal, in 1557. His account and the one based on Rodrigo Ranjel's diary are the most useful of the four accounts in that they are the most reliable and most detailed of the three accounts written by participants in de Soto's expedition. Ranjel's account is generally regarded as the most important single source of information, but the one by the Gentleman of Elvas is not far below it in importance. The identity of the Gentleman of Elvas has never been established, even though the names of most of the "Portuguese gentlemen" who accompanied de Soto to Florida are known (Swanton 1985:4, 86). Patricia Galloway (1995:104) prefaced her comment on this mystery with the remark "If there was a gentleman of Elvas."

Garcilaso de la Vega's account was the second to appear in print. The first edition appeared in Spanish in Lisbon only in 1605, although the manuscript had been completed by 1591. It is a secondhand account, although Garcilaso's major source, Gonzalo Silvestre, took part in de Soto's expedition, as did two others whom Garcilaso consulted to some degree. He also used a written account that has since disappeared. Garcilaso's account is the most detailed of the four, but today many of the details are believed to have been drawn from Garcilaso's imagination rather than from the participants he spoke to. He appears to have been as much interested in telling a good story as in writing a strictly historical account (Henige 1986; Swanton 1985:5–6).

Gonzalo Fernández de Oviedo y Valdés's account based on Rodrigo Ranjel's diary was not published until 1851, although it was written in the sixteenth century. Fernández de Oviedo y Valdés was a historian who had spent time in the New World himself. He published most of Ranjel's account as a minuscule part of his multivolume general history of the first years of the Spanish Indies. Ranjel's manuscript itself has been lost. Ranjel was de Soto's private secretary and kept a diary in which he made entries at frequent intervals, if not daily. The detail and the accuracy on the whole of the Gentleman of Elvas's account suggest that he also kept notes of some sort during the expedition.

Luys Hernández de Biedma's account, the briefest of the four, was first published in Spanish in London in 1857 by an American, Buckingham Smith. It appeared in a collection of various documents pertaining to the history of Florida and lands adjacent to it. Hernández de Biedma held an official position in the expedition as the king's factor or agent. Consequently his account was written as a sort of official report to the crown on the expedition.

MORE RECENT TRANSLATIONS

Since I prepared my translations in 1988 and this introduction in the early 1990s, the University of Alabama has published new translations of three of the de Soto accounts that are more attuned to the needs of archaeologists, anthropologists, and ethnohistorians than were the published translations that existed in 1988. John E. Worth, now anthropologist with the Fernbank Museum of Natural History of Atlanta, translated the accounts of Luyz Hernández de Biedma and of Rodrigo Ranjel. His translations were prepared specifically for the De Soto publication project of the University of Alabama Press. Charles Hudson, of the University of Georgia, collaborated with Worth in providing footnotes for Worth's translations. The third "new" translation is new only in the sense that it was published for the first time in 1993, in the University of Alabama Press's *De Soto Chronicles*. Charmion Shelby prepared her translation of the Inca Garcilaso de la Vega's account for the 1935 United States De Soto Expedition Commission. Lack of funds prevented the commission from including it in 1939, when it published John R. Swanton's *Final Report of the United States De Soto Expedition Commission*. Interestingly, Shelby's translation was being considered for publication by Oxford University Press at the time the Varners' translation was being readied. Oxford apparently abandoned the project on learning of the plans by the University of Texas Press to publish the Varners' translation. David Bost, of Furman University's Department of Classical and Modern Languages, edited the Shelby manuscript for Alabama's publication. The University of Alabama's archaeologist-anthropologist Vernon James Knight, Jr., one of three general editors for this project, annotated the Shelby translation concerning matters in his field of expertise.

For the Fidalgo de Elvas's account, the Alabama Press republished James Alexander Robertson's translation, published initially in the early 1930s in a limited edition by the Florida Historical Society. I updated Robertson's notes to his translation and added a few additional notes. (*Fidalgo* is the Portuguese equivalent of the Spanish *hidalgo*, reflecting more closely the Old Spanish form *fijo dalgo*, literally "son of something," from which the modern Spanish form developed.)

Like the Robertson translation, the new University of Alabama Press translations are careful literal ones. Worth noted in his introduction to Biedma's account, "Throughout, the goal has been to present as closely as possible in English the account as Biedma related it in Spanish. The following translation is therefore largely literal, with only occasional and minor restructuring of the original syntax in order to render specific passages into English more effectively." In comparing my translation of a brief portion of the Biedma account with Worth's translation, I found that his rendition of those passages lived up to his promises.

In Worth's introduction to his translation of the Rodrigo Ranjel account that was first published in Gonzalo Fernándes de Oviedo y Valdés *Historia general y natural de las Indias*, Worth noted that, while he had preserved all Indian names as originally printed in the Oviedo text, he had modernized the spelling of Spanish names. Worth said his interpolations to Oviedo's text had been set off by brackets. He noted also, "While minor restructuring of the original syntax was necessary at times, the present translation is largely literal, following Oviedo's paragraph and sentence structure as closely as possible." He has substantially fulfilled these promises. If anything, Worth's translation is too literal in places, in my opinion. The instances of excessive literalness may have flowed from his relative newness to the translator's art when he undertook this project.

In the matter of interpolations, Worth in a few instances added words to the text without enclosing the words in brackets, but none of those additions changes the meaning or involves matters of substance. Conversely, there are instances in Worth's translation in which he has deleted words that appear in Oviedo's text. Most such deletions do not change the meaning, such as shortening Oviedo's "year fifteen hundred and forty" to "fifteen forty." But a few of the deletions change the meaning somewhat. On page 271, line 18, Worth rendered Oviedo's "son unas mantas como de lienço basto y algunas delgadas" as "some blankets of coarse and fine linen," in effect deleting the word *como* ("like"). A more literal rendering would be "some cloaks [like those] of coarse linen and some fine." On page 263, line 24, he deleted the word "si" or "if" before "deceptions," changing the meaning somewhat. On page 269, line 25, he added a detail not found in Oviedo's text, identifying a wound as being "in the head." The translation's one outright error occurs just two lines below "in the head." There he misread Oviedo's "diez e siete" or "seventeenth" as "sixteenth."

On a few occasions Worth emulated the Varners' penchant for choosing English words that are more generic than the Spanish words they represent. A conspicuous example is his repeated use of "supplies" rather than "provisions" for Oviedo's "mantenimientos." His translation of "castañas pequeñas apiladas" as "small chestnuts piled up" on page 263, line 4, merited a footnote indicating that *apiladas* as applied to chestnuts also has the special meaning of "dried" or "peeled" because that would be of special interest to ethnohistorians and ethnobotanists. But such failings, if they deserve to be so categorized, do not detract from the overall value of Worth's translations of Oviedo and Biedma, which are far more faithful to the originals than earlier ones were.

My comparison of Charmion Shelby's translation with my own translation of a part of Garcilaso's account revealed her work to have been a literal rendering of the original as well. I found relatively few differences between her rendition and mine in matters of significance, even though she made her translation from the original 1605 edition and I used the 1723 edition.

For the portion that I have translated, there are differences involving numbers between the 1723 edition and Shelby's translation. Some of the discrepancies may simply reflect differences between the two editions that did not catch her eye or the attention of Bost. Some of the differences are significant, others are not. The first one that I noted is not. It appears on page 171, line 7 up, of the Shelby translation. The number "four" that qualifies "Indians" in the 1723 edition does not appear in Shelby's translation. Page 184, line 2 up, contains a more significant difference. There Shelby's translation gives six leagues as the distance between Vitachuco and Osachile, in contrast to the 10 leagues posited by the 1723 edition. It is conceivable that six leagues was the distance cited in the 1605 edition. But the fact that David Bost did not note this difference when editing the

Shelby translation suggests that it may be an error in the translation that the editor did not perceive.

Another possible error appears on page 209, line 2, where the Shelby translation states, "On the fourth day they marched eighteen more leagues." In the 1723 edition the Spanish text is "otros diez y siete leguas" (another seventeen leagues). The statement in the preceding sentence, that they had covered seventeen leagues on the third day as well, suggests that the "eighteen leagues" of Shelby's translation may be an error, particularly as Bost did not remark on the discrepancy between Shelby's rendition of the passage and the text of the 1723 edition.

On line 3 up of that same page, Shelby or her editors changed the spelling of Rio de Ochali to Rio de Ocali without indicating that such a change had been made. The Varners, who checked both early editions in preparing their translation, noted that the Ochali spelling appears in both.

On the discovery of evidence that the Martin site might contain at least part of de Soto's first winter camp, I translated portions of the four major chronicles from the de Soto expedition and two versions of Cabeza de Vaca's account of the Narváez expedition's experiences. The translations were designed for the guidance of the archaeologists working on the Martin site project and were part of the contributions of the staff at the San Luis site to the project's success. The length of the "Soldier of Fortune" manuscript has ruled out inclusion of the translations from the two Cabeza de Vaca accounts and a sizable piece of my translation of the Inca's account, which covers de Soto's progress from Ocale to the province of Yustaga. Copies of those portions of the translations will be on file at Florida's Bureau of Archaeological Research and available there on request.

8 · The Apalachee Section of the Fidalgo de Elvas's *True Relation of the Labors that the Governor Don Fernando de Souto and Certain Portuguese Gentlemen Experienced in the Exploration of the Province of Florida. Now Newly Made by a Gentleman of Elvas*

The translation here is based on the facsimile reproduction of the original Portuguese edition of 1557 that the Florida State Historical Society published in 1932–1933 along with a translation by James Alexander Robertson, who also edited that two-volume edition. Because of the difficulties of reading the Gothic lettering of the 1557 edition and the peculiarities of the mid-sixteenth-century Portuguese that the Fidalgo used, I prepared a typed transcription of the Fidalgo's text to facilitate the translation. In the transcription I maintained the peculiarities of the Fidalgo's text except in cases where that was not possible with the ordinary typescript.

One of the most prevalent peculiarities of the Fidalgo's text is the use of a letter that resembles a lowercase Greek delta. That symbol was used almost invariably to represent the letters *de* of the preposition "of" or "from" and occasionally to represent the initial *de* in other words, such as *deixar* (to leave or let) and *delles* (a combination of *de* and *elles,* the pronoun "them"). The Fidalgo's word for "and" somewhat resembles an undotted *i.* "And" is *e* in modern Portuguese. The Fidalgo seems to have had a marked aversion to using the letters *m* and *n,* which he represented frequently by a tilde. He also used a tilde occasionally to represent a suppressed *e* in words such as *trra* for *terra.* The old-style *s* of his text is virtually indistinguishable on occasion from an *f.* The similarity of the printing of *h* and *b* presents a similar problem when the context does not make clear which of those two letters the Fidalgo meant to use. The representations of the letters *y* and *x* present a similar problem. As in early Spanish, *i* and *y* are interchanged frequently in words such as *maiz.* Another peculiarity of the Fidalgo's Portuguese, by modern standards at least, is his frequent substitution of *r* for *l* and vice-versa, as in his spelling of *Florida* as *Frolida* and *frechar* for *flechar.* Infrequently used ornate capital letters presented problems at times, particularly when they appeared in names or in Roman numerals. In the portion of the text that I have translated, the Fidalgo wrote out all numbers and dates or presented them in Roman numerals rather than Arabic numerals. In my translation, I have transformed his Roman numerals into Arabic.

The Fidalgo made the first mention of Apalachee on the last folio of chapter 10 in describing de Soto's arrival at Cale, the first place in Florida where the Spaniards encountered an abundance of maize that was ripe. Up to that point, de Soto's men had been surviving largely on greens, cabbage palm, and the stalks of immature maize plants, after exhausting the food they brought with them on leaving the base camp near Tampa Bay in the territory of Chief Mocoso. The camp is believed to have been in the vicinity of Hillsborough Bay, on the Alafia and Hillsborough Rivers (Milanich and Hudson 1993:124). Because of that abundance of food, de Soto left a part of his force encamped at Cale, whose people had fled before his arrival. De Soto set out with the remainder of his force in search of Apalachee, which a captured Ocale Indian had described as a very large province that had an abundance of maize. Cale's exact location has not been established, but it was probably in southwest Marion County near the Withlacoochee River, most likely in the vicinity of Ross Prairie (Milanich and Hudson 1993:92–96). The translation begins with the context in which the first mention of Apalachee occurred.

True Relation of the Labors that the Governor Don Fernando de Souto and Certain Portuguese Gentlemen Experienced in the Exploration of the Province of Florida. Now Newly Made by a Gentleman of Elvas

Two horsemen came there [to Cale] whom the governor had sent out [ahead], who brought news that there was a lot of maize in Cale. They all rejoiced over this. As soon as they arrived in Cale, the governor ordered the gathering-in (*encerrar*)[1] throughout the countryside of all the maize that was ripe (*seco*),[2] which was sufficient for three months. The Indians killed three Christians while it was being harvested and one of those (*dos*)[3] who were captured told the governor that there was a very large province seven days away by trail that was called Apalache and [had] an abundance of maize. He set out from Cale at once with fifty horsemen and sixty foot-soldiers. He left the campmaster, Luis de Moscoso, with all the rest of the people and under orders that they should not stir from there until they received word from him. Because there was still no one to serve them, [the meal] for the bread that each one was going to eat was made in a mortar (*morterro*)[4] or bowl-shaped vessel (*gral*) made from a log with a pestle like a door bar (*tranca*). Some sifted the flour with their coats of mail. The bread was baked on some lid-like ceramic pieces (*testos*)[5] that they placed over the fire in the manner that I have already spoken of as being done in Cuba. It is so laborious to grind that there were many who formerly would not eat it without its being ground and [now] ate the maize parched and cooked (*cozido*).[6]

Chapter 11. How the governor arrived at Caliquen and how,
bringing the cacique with him, he went from there to Napetaca,
where the Indians tried to remove him from his control, and as
a result many were killed and captured

On the eleventh of August of the year 1540 (MQxl)[7] the governor set out from Cale. He went to a small village called Ytara to sleep; and the next day at another that was called Potano, and on the third one to Utinama. And [then] he reached another one on which they placed the name of Bad Peace (*mala paz*) because an Indian came in peace saying that he was the chief, that he with his people wished to serve the governor, that he order the release of the twenty-eight Indian men and women prisoners that they had taken from him on the preceding night, that he would order the bring-ing of provisions, would give a guide for the [journey] onward. The gover-nor ordered them released and to put him under guard. Many Indians came during the morning of the next day and situated themselves around the settlement close to the woods. The Indian, whom they were bringing along with them [as a prisoner], said that he wished to speak to them and to reassure them; that they would do what he ordered them to. And as soon as he saw that he was close to them, he lunged away abruptly and fled from the Christians. That there was no one who was able to catch up with him and they [the Indians] all took off fleeing through the woods. The governor ordered the release of a greyhound that he brought along already trained to their scent (*nelles . . . cevado*).[8] This [hound], after pass-ing many other Indians, proceeded to seize hold of the pretended cacique who had fled from the Christians and held him until they came to take him. From there the governor went to sleep at a settlement that was called Cholupaha. And because it had a great deal of maize, they gave it the name Fat City (*Villafarta*). On forward there was a river over which a wooden bridge was made and [then] he passed through uninhabited lands for two days. On the 17th (xvii) of August he reached Caliquen, [and] he was informed about the province of Apalache. He was told that Narváez had reached there and that he had set sail from there because of not find-ing a trail on forward; that there was no other settlement [there], but rather that it was all water in every direction. They were all saddened by this news and advised the governor that he should return to the port and depart from the land of Florida so that he should not become lost like Narváez. That, if he went on forward, when he should want to turn back, he would not be able to. That that little bit of maize that he had, the Indians would finish off on rebelling. The governor replied to this that he would not turn back without seeing what was spoken of with his own eyes; that he could not believe it and that we would be stranded there.[9] And he ordered Luys de Moscoso that he should leave at once from the Cale,[10] that he was waiting there [at Caliquen]. It seemed to Luys de Moscoso and to many others that they would have to turn back from Apalache and [consequently] they buried hardware (*ferragem*)[11] and other things in Cale. They reached Caliquen with great toil because the land through which the governor had passed had been laid waste and left without maize. After all his people came together there, he ordered a bridge to be built on a river that passed close to the settlement. He departed from Caliquen on the tenth of September [and] he brought the cacique with him. After his having traveled for three days, peaceful Indians came, who were coming to see their lord and they went out to the trail each day, playing [music] with flutes, which is the signal that they have so that it may be understood that they are coming in peace. They said that on forward there was a cacique who was called Uzachil, a relative of the [one] of Caliquen, their lord, awaiting him with great services and they begged the governor that he might free the cacique. He did not wish to release him, fearing that they would rise up and that they would not be willing to provide guides. And day after day he dismissed them with good words. He traveled for five days [and] passed by some small settlements [and] arrived at a settlement by the name of Napetuca on the fifteenth of September. There fourteen or fifteen Indians came and begged the governor that he might release their lord, the cacique of Caliquen. He replied to them that he was not holding him prisoner, but that he wanted him to go with him as far as Usachil. The governor learned from João Ortiz that an Indian had revealed to him that they had decided to assemble and to come upon him to give him battle and to remove the cacique from his control. On the day that had been agreed upon the governor ordered his [men] to ready themselves and to the horsemen that they should be armed and mounted, each one within his own lodging so that the Indians would not see them and so that, accordingly, they might approach the settlement without apprehension. Four hundred Indians came within sight of the camp with their bows and arrows and situated themselves in a wood. And they sent to tell the governor by means of two Indians that he should give them the cacique. Taking the cacique by the hand and talking with him to reassure the Indians, the governor with six men on foot went toward where they were and, on seeing the time to be favorable, he ordered the sounding of a trumpet and at once those who were in the settlement [scattered] through the houses, those on foot as well as those on horseback, came out after the Indians who became so surprised that the greatest concern that they had was by which way they should flee. They killed two horses. One was that of the governor and he was soon provided with another. Thirty or forty Indians were lanced. The others fled toward two very large ponds (*alagoas*)[12] that were distant (*desviados*)[13] from one another. There they went swimming about and the Christians around them. The harquebusiers and crossbowmen shot at them from the edge and because the distance was great and they shot from afar, they did them no harm at all. The governor ordered that they should keep one of the lakes surrounded during that night; that because they were large the people that he had did not suffice for surrounding both of them. Being encircled, as soon as night fell, the Indians came swimming toward the edge quietly with the determination of fleeing and so that they would not see them, they placed a water lily leaf on their head. As soon as those on horseback saw the water bubble, they dashed in until the water came up to the horses' chests and the Indians took off fleeing toward the center. This night passed in that fashion with neither they nor the Christians having any rest. João Ortiz said to them that inasmuch as they could not escape that they should surrender themselves to the governor. This they did, forced by necessity and by the coldness of the water, and one by one, first the one whom the hardship of the cold vanquished first, [who] would cry out to João Ortiz, saying that they should not kill him, that he was coming now to place himself in the hands of the governor. By the fourth of the moon they had finished surrendering except for twelve of the leading men, who as more honorable and valiant resolved to die rather than to come under his power. And the Indians from Paracoxi, who were already walking about loose, went in after them swimming and dragged them out by their hair. And they were all placed in chains and on the following day they were distributed among the Christians for their service. On being imprisoned thus, they determined to rebel and they charged one of the Indians who was an interpreter and whom they considered valiant, so that as soon as the governor should arrive to speak with him, he should throw his hands around his throat and strangle him. As soon as he saw an opportunity for that, he caught ahold of the governor and before putting his hands around his throat he gave him so strong a blow to his nostrils (*focinhos*), that he bathed them in blood and at once they all rebelled. He who could put his hands on weapons or the pestle with which one grinds the maize worked as best he could to kill his master or the first person who appeared in front of him. And the one who was able to put his hand on a lance or a sword swung about with it as if he had been using it all his life. One Indian in the plaza among fifteen or twenty men on foot fought with a sword like a bull in the arena until some of the governor's halberdiers arrived who killed him. Another one with a lance climbed up on a raised structure of canes (*sobrado de canas*) that they call *barbacoa*[14] that they build in order to store the maize and he raised an uproar there as if there were ten men inside. And while he was defending the door, they knocked him down with a crossbow shot (*passador*).[15] There were about two hundred Indians in all. They were all subdued (*sogigados*)[16] and the governor gave some of the youngest ones to those who had good chains and an admonition not to let them get away. And he ordered all the rest to be executed tied to a post in the middle of the plaza. And the Indians from Paracoxi shot them with arrows.

Chapter 12. How the governor reached Palache and was informed that there was much gold in the hinterland

The governor left Napetaca on the twenty-third of September [and] went to a river to sleep where two Indians brought him a deer on the part of the Cacique of Uzachil. The next day he passed by a large settlement called Hapaluya. And he went to Uzachil to sleep and found no people in it; for, because of the news that the Indians had of the slaughter at Napetaca, they did not dare to remain. In that village he found a great deal of maize, beans, and pumpkins (*abobaras*)[17] which is their sustenance and with which the Christians sustained themselves there. The Maize is like Sorghum (*Milho Zaburo*)[18] and the pumpkins are better and more delicious than those of Spain. From there the governor sent out two captains in search of Indians, each one in his own direction. They took one hundred head (*peças*) between men and women. From these, consequently, there, as in any other place where such expeditions were carried out, the captain set aside one or two head for the governor and divided the others between himself and those who participated [in it] with him. They brought these Indians along in chains with collars around the neck and they served to carry the baggage and to grind the maize and for other services that they were capable of doing restrained (*psos*)[19] in this fashion. It happened sometimes as they were going with them for firewood or maize that they would kill the Christian who led them and flee with the chain. Others would file it at night with a piece of stone with which they cut it and [that] they use in place of iron tools. Those who were detected paid for it for themselves and for the others so that they would not attempt the same on the next day. The women and young people of little age were no longer a concern once they were a hundred leagues from their land. They brought them along unshackled. They served thus and in a very short time they understood the language of the Christians. From Uzachill the governor set out for Apalache and after two days on the trail he reached a settlement that was called Axille. And because of not yet having had news of the Christians the Indians were caught unaware.[20] Because the settlement was surrounded by woods, the majority fled. On the morning of the next day, the first day of October, he set out from there and ordered the building of a bridge on a river over which he had to pass. There was a stone's throw to be swum to where the bridge was built and for a crossbow-shot on forward the water was waist-deep and there was a very tall thick woods through which the Indians came to see whether they would be able to defend the passage and [to harass] those who were building the bridge. The crossbowmen came to their aid and made them desist and some logs were thrown across, over which people passed who secured the passage. The governor crossed on Wednesday, the day of St. Francis. He went to a settlement that was called Uitachuco to sleep [that was] subject to Palache. He found it burning, as the Indians had set it on fire. The land was heavily settled from there on forward and [had] a great deal of maize. He passed by many groups of houses like hamlets (*muitos casaes como aldeas*). On Sunday the 25th of October he reached a settlement that was called Uzela and on Monday Anhayca Apalache where the lord of all that land and province resided. In this settlement, the field master, whose duty it is to assign and provide lodging, lodged everyone round about this settlement. At [a distance of] half a league and a league there were others where there was a great deal of maize, squash, and beans and dried plums of the land[21] that are better than those of Spain and that grow through the fields without their being planted. From these settlements on to Anhaica Apalache the provisions were gathered that appeared would be sufficient to last through the winter. The governor was informed that the sea was ten leagues from there. At once he sent out a captain with people on horseback and on foot and at six leagues along the trail he found a settlement that was called Ochete. And he reached the sea and found a large tree cut down and made into troughs (*couchos*) like mangers (*mãjadoiras*) with their piles (*estacas*) and he saw the skulls of horses. He came back with this report. [With that] he considered what was said about Narváez to be true, that there he had built the vessels with which he departed from the land [and] in which he was lost at sea. At once the governor sent Joam Danhusco[22] to the port of the Holy Spirit with thirty horsemen where Caldeiram was, so that they would abandon the port and all would come to Apalache. He left on Friday the seventeenth of November. In Uzachill and in other settlements that there were along the trail he found many people off guard already. He did not attempt to take Indians lest he be delayed, because it behooved him not to provide any opportunity for them to assemble. He passed by the settlements at night and once away from the settlement, he rested for three or four hours. He reached the port in ten days. He brought along twenty Indian women whom he took in Ytara and Potano near Cale. He sent them to Doña Isabel in two caravels that he sent to Cuba from the port. And he brought all the foot-soldiers in the brigantines and headed for Palachee from point to point along the coast. And Calderã went by land with the horsemen and some crossbowmen on foot. In some places the Indians attacked him and they wounded some of his men. As soon as he arrived at Palache the governor ordered prepared planks carried to the sea and nails (*crauçam*) with which a small vessel (*piragua*) was built into which 30 well-armed men entered. The latter set out to sea from the bay and sailed about waiting for the brigantines. On some occasions they fought with the Indians who sailed along the docking place (*caez*)[23] in canoes (*almadias*).[24] On Saturday the twenty-ninth of November an Indian came through the sentinels without being detected and set fire to the settlement and because of the strong wind that was blowing, two areas of it quickly burned. Joã Danhusco arrived with the brigantines on Sunday the twenty-eighth of December. The governor ordered Francisco Maldonado, captain of the foot-soldiers, to sail along the coast toward the west with fifty men and to search for some port because he had decided to go exploring by land in that region. That day by order of the governor eight horsemen set out through the countryside two leagues around the settlement in search for Indians because they had become so bold[25] now they came within two crossbow-shots of the village to kill the men. They found two Indian men and an Indian woman picking beans. The former could have fled, [but] in order not to leave the Indian woman behind, who was the wife of one them, they resolved to die fighting. Before they could kill them they wounded three horses. One of those died a few days later. While Caldeiram was going along on the seacoast trail (*caminho do mar*)[26] with his people some Indians came out against him from a woods that was near there and made him leave the trail and made many of those who went with him leave behind some necessary provisions that they were carrying. Three or four days after the time limit that the governor had set for Maldonado to go and come back, with the governor already resolved and determined to wait no longer if he had not come in another eight days, he came and brought an Indian from a province that was called Ochus, 60 leagues from Apalache, where he found a port with a good depth and sheltered. And because he hoped to find good land on forward, the governor was very content and sent Maldonado to

Havana for provisions and that he should wait for him at the port of Ochus that he had discovered. That he would go in search of it by land and that should he be delayed and not come during that summer, that he should return to Havana and return to the port to await him during the following [summer] because he would do nothing other than to go in search of Ochus. Francisco Maldonado went and Joam de Guzmã remained in his place as captain of the foot-soldiers of his company. Of the Indians that were taken in Napetuca the treasurer, Joã Gaytã, had a youth who said he was not of that land but that he belonged to another one very far away in the direction of where the sun comes up and that it was many days ago that he had come to see [new] lands. And that his [land] was called Yupaha and that a woman ruled over it and that the settlement where she lived was of remarkable grandeur (*grandeza*)[27] and that many of her neighboring lords paid tribute to that lady. And some gave her clothing and others gold in quantity. And he told how it was taken from the mines and smelted and refined as if he had seen it done or the devil had taught it to him. As a result, whoever learned anything about this said that it was impossible to give so good an account without having seen it. And all believed whatever he said to be true, when they saw it, because of the signs that he provided.

Chapter 13. How the governor set out from Apalache in search of Yupaha and what happened to him

On Wednesday, the third of March of 1540, the governor set out from Anhaica Apalache in search of Yupaha. He ordered that all his [men] should be provided with maize for sixty leagues of uninhabited territory. The horsemen carried their maize on their horses and those on foot on their backs, because, [of] the Indians that there were for work, most had died with the hard life that they had endured that winter, naked in chains. On the fourth day on the trail they reached a torrential (*caudaloso*)[28] river. And a pirogue was made and because of the strong current a hawser of chains was made. It was fastened on either side of the river and the pirogue crossed over alongside of it and the horses swimming with windlasses that they pulled by them. Having crossed the river in a day and a half, they arrived at a settlement called Capachiqui. On Friday, the eleventh of March, they found the Indians run off (*alçados*—literally, "risen in revolt"). On the following day, five Christians went to search for mortars that the Indians have for grinding the maize. And they went to some houses surrounded by woods, separated (*entresposta*)[29] from the camp (*real*).[30] And there were many Indians who came to spy on us walking about within the woods. Another five separated from these and attacked us. One of the Christians came running toward the camp (*real*) sounding a call to arms. Those who were most ready responded to the alarm. They found one Christian dead and three badly wounded. The Indians fled through a swamp (*alagoa*)[31] with a very thick woods into which the horses could not enter. The governor left Capachiqui [and] passed through an uninhabited territory (*hũ despovoado*). He reached a settlement that was called Toalli on Wednesday, the twenty-first of the month. And they noted a difference in the houses from there forward, because those on behind were covered with hay (*feno*) and those of Toalli were covered with reeds (*caniços*) after the fashion of a tile roof. These are very tidy (*muy limpas*). Some had the walls covered with clay (*enuarradas*) that they appeared to be of mud (*de taipa*).[32] Throughout the cold land the Indians each have their house for passing the winter plastered with mud (*euarrada*) within and without, and the door very small. They close it at night and they make a fire inside it so that it warms up like an oven (*forno*). And it remains so all night long so that no clothing is needed. And they have others for the summer in addition to these and kitchens close to them where they make a fire and cook their bread. And they have corncribs (*barbacoas*) in which they hold their maize, which is a house built up in the air above four posts (*esteyos*) with a wooden frame like a two-story building (*madeirado como sobrado*) and a cane floor (*ho solo de caniços*). In addition to being larger, the difference that the houses of the lords or leading men have from the others is that they have large balconies in the front (*grãdes balcoes diãte*) and down below cane seats (*assentos de caniços*) like chairs (*a maneira descanhos*).[33] And many and large corncribs roundabout in which they collect that which their Indians give them in tribute, which is maize and deerskins and blankets (*mãtas*)[34] of the land, which are like mantillas (*mãtilhas*). They make them from the bark of trees, from the inner skin (*de cascas darvores da tez de dentro*), and some from a plant (*erva*) like *abroteas*[35] that becomes like linen when pounded. The Indian women cover themselves with these blankets. They place one around themselves from the waist down and another over the shoulder with the right arm uncovered after the fashion and custom of the Gypsies. The Indian men wear nothing more than the one, over the shoulders in the same manner and with their private parts covered with a breechclout of deerskin (*bragueiro de veado*) like the little trousers (*panetes*)[36] that used to be customary in Spain. The hides are well cured and they give it the color that they wish, so perfect that if it be red it looks like very fine grenadine cloth (*pano de graã*)[37] and the black, perfect; and they make shoes from it. And they give the same colors to the blankets. The governor set out from Toalli on the 24th of March.

Notes

1. The usual meaning of *encerrar* today is to enclose, encompass, or adjourn, but it still has the meaning of "to get in" in Spanish.

2. *Seco* literally means "dry."

3. This could possibly be rendered as "two," as Robertson has done, on the presumption that the Spanish form for two was still being used rather than to-day's *dois*. I have assumed it was meant to be the Portuguese compound of *de* plus *os*.

4. The two letters in this word that appear to be an *i* without the dot are distinct from the usual *i* here, which does have a dot.

5. A *testo* is a lid or cover for an iron or clay vessel.

6. *Cozido* could be rendered as "cook," "bake," or "boil." Robertson rendered it as "sodden."

7. The year obviously should be 1539, but the Roman numerals clearly are those for 1540. Robertson (1933:55) rendered it as 1540, in contrast to Smith (1968:39), who rendered it as 1539 without indicating what the original was.

8. *Cevado* could also be rendered as "fatten on" or "baited on them."

9. The Portuguese here, y que estiuessemos ay sellados, has been rendered by other translators "and that we should be ready saddled" (as in Robertson 1933:57) and, in Buckingham Smith's (1968:40) very free translation as "Then he ordered us to be in readiness for the saddle." This passage can well be rendered literally "and that we should be there saddled," but in the context, "isolated" or "stranded" seems to be an equally likely interpretation of "ay sellados."

10. The Portuguese, "de ho Cale," has the article "the" before "Cale," as it does in the sentence that follows. The article was not used before Caliquen or Uzachil or the other settlements named in this section.

11. In addition to the general sense of "hardware made of iron," *ferragem* has the specific meaning of "horseshoes," which might be of significance archaeologically.

12. This word could be rendered also as "lake" or "lagoon" or "pool." There is no justification in the Portuguese text for Robertson's qualification of the lakes as "shallow lakes."

13. "Distant" in the sense of being "removed" some distance from one another or possibly on opposite sides of the settlement.

14. This word of Arawakian derivation was also used in Florida to designate the framework used for smoking meat and fish, for the benches that lined the walls of the council houses, and for the raised bench of the chief. The appearance of this word in Florida at so early a date could be evidence of contact between Florida's natives and those of the Bahamas or Cuba if Elvas's use of the term accurately reflects Florida usage. *Barbacoa* does not appear in Granberry's *Grammar and Dictionary.*

15. *Passador* in Spanish is among other things a very sharp arrow or dart fired from a crossbow. In Portuguese it can mean "marlin-spike" or "fid." Robertson (1933:63) rendered it as "javelin" and Smith (1968:44) as "battleaxe."

16. This is probably a variant of *subjugar*.

17. *Aboboras* could be rendered also as "squashes."

18. Both Robertson and Smith rendered *Milho Zaburo* as "coarse millet." In my Portuguese dictionaries, *milho zaburro* is defined as sorghum. Taylor (1958) gives *milho da Italia*, *milho-miudo*, and *milho-painco* as names for millet. *Milho* by itself is the Portuguese word for maize.

19. *Psos* presumably is an abbreviated form of *presos*. There are other instances in this text in which words beginning with *p*, such as *provincia* and *proposito*, omit the two following letters.

20. Uzachil's failure to warn Asile of the Spaniards' approach raises a question about Asile's status, as do the two leagues of apparently unpopulated land between Uzachil and Asile and Asile's proximity to Ivitachuco.

21. These would appear to be dried persimmons.

22. This name appears elsewhere as Juan de Añasco.

23. Robertson (1933:69) rendered this word as "keys," while Smith (1968:48) translated it as "estuary." It is probably the modern *cais*, meaning wharf or pier.

24. *Almadia* is a canoe used in India or a raft.

25. The Portuguese here is *andaua ja tam feitos foutos* (or *soutos*). The context calls for "bold" or "daring" even though *soutos* is not defined thus in dictionaries.

26. This could conceivably be rendered as "trail of the sea" in the sense of "to the sea," but it is unlikely that that is what was intended. In Brazilian Portuguese, *caminho do mar* definitely connotes a trail that runs along the beach.

27. *Grandeza* also signifies more explicitly "largeness, bigness, size."

28. *Caudaloso* connotes a river that carries much water.

29. This appears to be a variant of *interposto*, a cognate of the English "interposed." Thus it signifies that there was something between the houses and the camp, rather than the houses being "contiguous" to the camp. "Contiguous" is Robertson's rendering (1933:74).

30. From the repetition of *real* three lines below, it appears that *real* here refers to de Soto's camp and not the village of Capichiqui.

31. *Alagoa* can also mean "pond" or "lake," but the trees in it seem to indicate that it was a swamp.

32. *Taipa* could be rendered also as "wattle and daub," "tabby," or "lathes and plaster."

33. *Escano* in Spanish is a bench with a back. I have not found *escanho* in my Portuguese dictionaries, only *escano*, meaning footstool, and the diminutive *escaninho*, a small compartment in a box or drawer, a recess, retreat, or hiding place.

34. This might be rendered also as "cloak" or "shawl."

35. *Abrotea* is the name of a medicinal plant of the lily family and also of a fish, the squirrel ling (*Phycis chuss*). Robertson (1933:76) rendered it as "daffodils" and Smith (1968:52) as "nettle."

36. I did not find this word in my Portuguese dictionaries, but it is a diminutive of *pano*, the word for cloth. It appears in Spanish as *panetes*, "a kind of trousers worn by fishermen and tanners" (Velásquez de la Cadena 1960).

37. *Graa* or *grã* in modern Portuguese is a gall from a species of oak, or an insect used as a source of dye, or the color scarlet. In Spanish its meanings include "cochineal," "scarlet grain," "fine scarlet cloth," and "fresh red color of the lips and cheeks." As the Fidalgo may not have been familiar with cochineal at this early date, I have presumed that the "red" in question is that of grenadine.

9 · The Apalachee Section of the Narrative about the de Soto Expedition Based on the Diary of Rodrigo Ranjel, de Soto's Private Secretary

GONZALO FERNÁNDEZ DE OVIEDO Y VALDÉS

This translation is made from the Royal Academy of History's 1851–1855 four-volume edition of the work of Gonzalo Fernández de Oviedo y Valdés. The narrative based on Ranjel's diary appears in the first volume, *El Capitan Gonzalo Fernández de Oviedo y Valdés. Primer Cronista del Nuevo Mundo,* edited by D. José Amador de los Rios (Madrid: Imprenta de la Real Academia de la Historia, 1851–1855). The portion of the Ranjel account translated here appears in book 17, chapter 24 and part of chapter 25, pages 551–58.

Chapter 24. How the governor Hernando de Soto, proceeding on his conquest, passed on forward, and how the Indians tried to kill him or to take him by surprise, in order to free a cacique whom he was bringing along with him, and how a cacique gave the governor a blow that bathed his teeth in blood: and other things are treated of appropriate for the course of the story

On the eleventh of August of the same year the governor departed from Ocale with fifty horsemen and one hundred foot-soldiers in search of Apalache because it had great fame that it had many people. And Luís de Moscoso remained there with the rest of the camp until they should see what happened on forward. And that day they went to Itaraholata to sleep, a fine settlement with an abundance of maize. There an Indian pressed in on captain Maldonado and wounded his horse badly and he would have seized the lance from his hands, if the governor had not come up by chance, even though Maldonado was a good horseman and among the most valiant of that army. But the Indians of that land are very warlike and wild and robust. They went to Potano on the next day, and the following day, Wednesday, they reached Utinamocharra and from there they went to the settlement of Bad-Peace (*Mala-Paz*). That name was given to it because Johan de Añasco, having taken thirty persons from that cacique on the trail, he [the chief] sent to say that he wanted peace so that he would give them back. And to negotiate it, he sent an impostor in his place, who was believed to be the chief himself, and the people were given to him. On the next day it happened that this Indian, while fleeing from the Christians, sought to lose himself in the midst of the Indians in a rough bramble thicket (*arcabuco*). A fine Irish greyhound dog that ran up at his call and went into the midst of all those Indians, while he passed by many, he seized no one except that one who had fled, who was in the midst of the crowd. And he took him by the fleshy part of the arm in such a way that the Indian was thrown down and they seized him. The next day the Christians reached a pretty (*bonico*)[1] settlement where they found a great deal of food and many small, very flavorful dried chestnuts (*castaños . . . apilados*),[2] wild chestnuts; but the trees that bear them are not any taller than two spans of land (? *dos palmos de tierra*)[3] and they grow in prickly burrs (*capullos eriçados*). There are other chestnuts in the land that the Spaniards saw and ate, which are just like those of Spain. And they grow on such big chestnut trees and the trees [are] mighty and with the same leaf and prickly husk or burrs, just as plump (*gordo*)[4] and of very good flavor.

This army went from there to a river which they call of Discords. And the one who gave this account wished to remain silent [about the reason] because, as he was a just man, he did not believe in telling of the faults and weaknesses of his friends. On that day they built a bridge of pines as there were many there. And on the next day, Sunday, they crossed that river with as much or more difficulty than that of Ocale. The next day, Monday, they reached Aguacaleyquen and Rodrigo Ranjel and Villalobos, two hidalgos, horsemen, but gentlemen (I say horsemen as they were cavalrymen in this army), captured an Indian man and woman in a maize field. And she showed them where the maize was hidden and the Indian man led the captain, Baltasar de Gallegos, to where he captured seventeen people, and among them an Indian woman, a daughter of the cacique; that this would serve as a reason for her father to come in peace. But he would have liked to free her without [doing] this, if his hoaxes and cunning had not been less than those of these conquistadors. On the twenty-second of August a great multitude of Indians appeared. And the governor seeing that the land seemed to be more populous now and better provisioned, sent eight horsemen in full haste to summon the fieldmaster, Luis de Moscoso, so that he might join up with him with all his camp. And the fieldmaster made no little effort to comply with that order and arrived where the governor was on the fourth of September. And they all rejoiced to see themselves united again, because, as they were holding the cacique prisoner, it was feared the Indians would be likely to assemble. And they were not far wrong in view of what occurred on forward. On the ninth of September they all left Aguacaleyquen together, taking the cacique and his daughter with them and a leading Indian who was named Guatutima as a guide, because the latter said that he knew a great deal about the [land] on ahead and gave very great reports [about it]. And they built a bridge of pines to cross the river of Aguacaleyquen and they went to a little settlement to sleep. On the next day, Friday, they were at Uriutina, a settlement of pleasant appearance and of abundant food. And there was a very large council house (*buhio*) in it, in the middle of which there was a large open space (*patio*). Already there was a good population in that area. Ever since they left Aguacaleyquen, messengers were coming and going from Uçachile, a great cacique, playing on a flute by way of ceremony. And on Friday the twelfth of September these Christians reached a settlement that they called of the Many Waters, because it rained so much that they were not able to leave from there on either Saturday or Sunday. And they left on the following Monday, the fifteenth of that month, and they encountered a very bad marsh (*çienaga*)[5] and they found all the path very difficult. And they went to Napituca to sleep, which was a very fine (*alegre*) settlement in an exquisite spot and with much food. There the Indians used all their tricks and cunning to recover their cacique of Aguacaleyquen, and the matter reached a point where the governor found himself in great danger. But their hoaxes and tricks were seen through and he devised another better one in this fashion. Seven caciques from those districts (*comarcas*) assembled with their people and sent to the governor to say that they were subjects of Uçachile and that by his mandate and their own will they wished to be friends of the Christians and to help them against Apalache, a strong (*recia*) province hostile to Uçachile and to them and that they had come for this [purpose] at the persuasion and behest of Aguacaleyquen (who is the cacique whom the Christians brought along as a prisoner) and that they feared to enter into the camp lest they be detained. Therefore, let the governor bring Aguacaleyquen with him and come out onto a large savannah that was there to speak with them in order to discuss this business. Their proposal was understood and their message accepted, and the governor went out to speak to them, but he ordered the Christians to arm themselves and to mount upon their horses and that at the signal from the trumpet they should fall upon the Indians. Thus, having gone out to the savannah with only those of his guard and a chair (*silla*)[6] in order to seat himself [and] the cacique of Aguacaleyquen with him, when the governor had scarcely seated himself as the discussion was beginning, he saw himself surrounded in an instant by Indians with their bows and arrows and countless others were coming from many directions in such a fashion that the danger that the governor was in was seen at once to be obvious. And before the trumpet was sounded, the fieldmaster, Luis de Moscoso, struck the legs of his horse shouting, "Hey, horsemen, Sanctiago, Sanctiago,[7] and at them." And thus the people on horseback took off all at once, spearing many Indians, and the stratagem gained them [the Indians] nothing except momentarily, and our people got the jump on them in the fighting. Nonetheless those [Indians] defended themselves and fought like men of great spirit and they killed the governor's horse and they killed another belonging to a hidalgo named Sagredo, and they wounded others. And after the fighting had lasted for quite a while, the Indians took flight and sought refuge in two ponds (*lagunas*). And the Spaniards surrounded the one, and the other they were not able to. And they maintained that siege, keeping a vigil all night long and until the morning when they surrendered. And they took out three hundred Indians from there as prisoners and among them five or six caciques. At the last Uriutina remained [there] alone; that he refused to come out until some Indians from Uçachile went in for him swimming and pulled him out. And after having come out, he asked for a messenger [to send] to his land. And when he had been brought, he spoke to him thus: "Look, go to my people and tell them not to worry about me; that like a valiant man and lord, I have done what had to be done, and I struggled and fought like a man until they left me [there] alone; and if I sought refuge in that pond, it was not in order to flee from death or not to die as is appropriate for me, but rather in order to encourage these who were there within [it] so that they would not surrender. And that after they surrendered, I never surrendered until these Indians from Uçachile, who are of our nation, begged me to, saying that this was what was best for all. Therefore, that what I charge them [to do] and what I implore of them is that they have nothing to do with these Christians out of respect for me or anyone else; that they are devils and are mightier than they and that they can be very certain about me that, if I have to die, it will be as a valiant man." Johan Ortiz, that interpreter, who is that Christian whom they found in the land by lucky chance, as history has recounted, related all this immediately to the governor and made it known to him. The Indians who were taken in the manner already described were taken to be put into a lodge (*buhio*)[8] with their hands tied behind them. And the governor, walking among them in order to become acquainted with the caciques, encouraging them in order to bring them around to peace and harmony and making them untie them so that they would be better treated than the other common Indians, one of those chiefs, as soon as they untied him, as the governor was near him, raised his arm and gave the governor so strong a blow that he bathed his teeth in blood and made him spit up a lot. For the latter act, they tied this fellow and others to great posts (*á sendos palos*)[9] and they were shot with arrows. Other Indians did many other heroic feats that we could not begin to describe, as the historian said who was present there. On seeing that with so few Indians and without arms the Christians were put to such grief and he himself not being any less so, the governor, on account of this, spoke thus: "Oh God help me, and if those lords of the Council had been here so that they might see how His Majesty is served in these parts." And precisely because they do know, the chronicler [i.e., Oviedo himself] says, they have ordered a cessation of the tyrannies and cruelties and that better order be observed in the pacification of the Indies so that God our Lord and his Caesarean Majesty will be better served and so that the consciences of the conquistadors may rest more easily and the natives of the land not be mistreated.

On Tuesday the twenty-third of September the governor and his army left Napituca and arrived at the river of the Deer. This name was given to it because Indian messengers from Uçachile brought some deer [to them] there. That there are many and good ones in that land. And in order to cross this river, they made a bridge of three large pine trees [set] lengthwise (*en luengo*)[10] and four in width (the which pines are perfect and like the very large ones of Spain). And after all the army had completed the crossing of the river, which was on the twenty-fifth day of that month, they passed through two little settlements on that very day and one very large one that was called Apalu and they arrived at Uçachile to sleep. But in all these settlements they found the people [had] fled and some captains sallied out to forage through the huts of the countryside (*á ranchear*)[11] and they brought back many people. They left Uçachile on the following Monday, the twenty-ninth of the month and, [having] passed a large woods (*un gran monte*),[12] they went to a pine grove to sleep. And a young man named Cadena went back for a sword without permission and the governor wanted to have him hanged for both offenses. And he escaped because of the plea of good people. The next day, Tuesday, the thirtieth of the month of September, they arrived at Agile, subject to Apalache, and some women were taken. And they are of such [spirit] that one Indian woman grabbed a bachelor (*bachiller*)[13] named Herrera who remained alone with her and behind his other comrades and she grabbed him by the genitals and she had him very worn out and overcome, and if other Christians who came to his assistance had not come by by chance, the Indian woman would have killed him, because he had no wish to lay hands on her in a lustful way but rather she wished to free herself and flee. On Wednesday the first of October the governor, Hernando de Soto, left Agile with his people, and they reached the river or swamp (*çienaga*)[14] of Ivitachuco and they built a bridge. And there was an Indian ambush on the other side in a patch of reed grass and they hit three Christians with arrows. And they completed the crossing of that swamp on the Friday following at noon. And they lost a horse to drowning there. And they went to Ivitachuco to sleep and found the settlement burning because the Indians had set fire to it. On Sunday the fifth of October they went to Calahuchi and two Indian men and an Indian woman were captured and strips of dried venison (*tasajos de venados*)[15] in great quantity. And there the guide who led them fled from them.

They went on forward the next day, bringing along an old Indian as a guide, who led them astray. And an Indian woman brought them to Iviahica and they found that all the people had taken off. And the next day two captains went out from there and they found that all the people had fled. Johan de Añasco had set out from this settlement and eight leagues from it he encountered the port where Pamphilo de Narvaez had embarked in the vessels that he built. This was known because of the skulls (*calavernas*)[16] of the horses and the site of the forge and the slips (*pesebres*)[17] and the mortars that they had made for grinding maize and because of the crosses made on the trees. And they wintered there and remained until the fourth of March of the year one thousand and five hundred and forty, in the which time many notable things happened with the Indians, who are the bravest of men. And from what will be said now the discerning reader will be able to conjecture their great spirits and daring. Two Indians challenged eight horsemen and they burned the settlement on two occasions and they killed many Christians with ambushes on some occasions. And although the Spaniards pursued them and burned them, they never showed any desire to come to peace. If they cut off the hands and noses of some Indians, they took no more account of it than if each one of them were a Roman Mucius Scaevola. Not one of them for fear of death denied being from Apalache. And, on being taken, when they asked one where he was from, he replied with pride: "Where would I be from? I am an Indian of Apalache." Like one who was letting one know that whoever thought he was from some people other than the Apalache would be offending him.

The governor decided to go farther into the interior because an Indian boy was giving great reports about what there was in the interior. And he sent Johan de Añasco with thirty horsemen for Captain Calderon and the people who had remained behind in the port and they burned the provisions that they left behind and the settlement. And Captain Calderon came by land with all the people and Johan de Añasco came by sea with the brigantines and small vessels (*vergantines y bateles*) to the port of Apalache. Johan de Añasco reached the port on Saturday the nineteenth of November and at once Maldonado was dispatched along the coast in the brigantines to look for a harbor in the direction of the west-occident (*la via del hueste-occidente*). And during this time Captain Calderon arrived with all the people, except for two men and seven horses that the Indians killed on the trail. Maldonado discovered a very good port and brought an Indian from a province that is close to (*junto á*) that coast, that is called Achuse. And he brought a good mantle (*manta*)[18] of sables (*martas çebellinas*) (although they had seen others already in Apalache, but not such as [those]). Captain Maldonado was dispatched to Havana and left Apalache on the twenty-sixth of February of the year one thousand and five hundred and forty with instructions and orders from the governor that he should come with supplies to the port that he had discovered and along that coast to which the governor was thinking of coming. The province of Apalache is very fertile and most abundant in provisions, with much maize, kidney-beans (*fésoles*) and pumpkins and different fruits and many deer and many diversities of birds and close to the sea for fishes of which there are many and good ones. It is a pleasant land, although there are swamps (*çienagas*) but they are solid (*tiesas*) because of being over sand.

Chapter 25. How the governor Hernando de Soto and his people departed from Iviahica in search of Capachegui and how the guide whom they brought along, once he knew nothing more about what there was on ahead, became possessed by the devil (se hizo endemoniado);[19] and diverse matters are discussed and very notable ones

The departure from Iviahica in search of Capachequi was begun on Wednesday, the third day of March of the year one thousand and five hundred and forty. And the governor went with his army to sleep at the river of Guacuca, and [having] departed from there, they went to the river of Capachequi, which they reached early on the following Friday. And they built a canoe or pirogue (*canoa o piragua*)[20] in order to cross it. And the river was so wide that Chripstóbal [*sic*] Mosquera, who was the best arm, did not succeed in his purpose of throwing a stone across it. And they took the chains in which they brought the Indians and with some stout S's of iron [they were] joined together. And, [having] made a chain of all [of them], they tied one end of the chain to one bank and the other to the other so that the pirogue might cross. And the current was such that it broke the chain twice. And, on seeing this, they tied many ropes together and made two from them. And they fastened one to the stern and the other to the prow and pulling from the one side and from the other, the people and clothing passed over. In order that the horses might cross over, they made long ropes and tied them to their neck and, although the current carried them downriver (*los derribaba*),[21] by pulling on the ropes they pulled them over, but with difficulty (*trabaxo*)[22] and some half drowned. And on Wednesday the ninth of March[23] all of the army completed the crossing of the river of Capachequi and departed to sleep in a pine grove. They reached the first settlement of Capachequi on the next day, Thursday. This [settlement] had abundant provisions, but [was] in between craggy places full of brambles (*entre arcabucos*)[24] or land thickly covered with trees (*tierra muy cerrada de arboledas*) and for this [reason] they passed on to sleep at another settlement farther on and they encountered a bad swamp (*çienaga*) adjacent to (*junto al*) the village, with a strong current, and before reaching it [the current], they passed through a very long stretch of water up to the cinches and the bags of the horses' saddles (*bastos de las sillas de los caballos*), as a result of which all the army was not able to finish the crossing on that day because of the poor passage. One hundred soldiers[25] with swords and shields strayed away there (*Alli se desmandaron*) and an equal number of Indians attacked them and killed one of them and would have killed all of them if they had not been assisted.

They departed from Capachequi on the seventeenth of March and went to the White Spring to sleep. This is a very beautiful spring with a strong and good flow of water, and it has fish. On the following day they went to the river of Toa to sleep, where they made two bridges and the horse of Lourenço Suarez, son of Vasco Porcallo, was drowned. And on the Sunday following, the twenty-first day of the month, they reached the crossing place (*passo*) of the river of Toa and they made a bridge of pines twice and the strong current broke them and another bridge was made with braces [placed] in a certain manner (*otra puente de tijeras en cierta forma*)[26] that a hidalgo named Nuño de Tovar suggested, at which everyone laughed. But what he said proved to be true. And it [having been] made, they crossed over very well with that ingenious structure. And all the army completed the passage on Monday and they went to a pine grove to sleep, although scattered over many areas and in bad order. And early on Tuesday they reached Toa, a large settlement. And the governor wanted to go on farther and they did not let him. On Wednesday the twenty-fourth of the month the governor departed secretly from there at midnight with up to forty horsemen, gentlemen and hidalgos (*con hasta quarenta de caballo, caballeros e hijos dalgo*) and such [others] that for different reasons (*y tales que por diversos respectos*) he had not wished to place under another captain (*no los avia querido poner debaxo*). And they traveled all that day until night, when they encountered a bad water crossing and a deep one. And, although it was night, they crossed it and they covered twelve leagues that day. And the next day, which was Holy Thursday of the Supper (*Jueves Sancto de la Çena*) they reached the settlement of Chisi during the morning. And they crossed an arm of a large very wide river wading and swimming (*a vuela pie*)[27] and a good piece of it, swimming. And they came upon a settlement that was on an island of this river, where they captured some people and found [something] to eat. And as the place was dangerous, they turned back, leaving the way they had entered, before canoes should come, but first they lunched on some hens of the land that they call *guanaxas*[28] and on loins of venison that they found roasted on a grill (*barbacoa*) which is like on a gridiron (*ques como en parrillas*). And, although it was Holy Thursday, there was no one so Christian that he had scruples about eating meat. And the boy Perico led them there, whom they brought from Apalache as a guide. And they passed on to other settlements and to a bad crossing of a swamp (*çienaga*) [where] some horses were about to go under (*se ovieran de anegar algunos caballos*) because those began to swim with the saddles (*porque los que echaron á nado con las sillas*) while their owners were crossing by means of a log that bridged the current of water. And, while crossing thus, one Benito Fernandez, a Portuguese, fell from the log and was drowned. This day they reached a settlement to which leading Indians came as messengers from Ichisi. And one of them questioned the governor and spoke three words to him one after the other in this fashion: "Who are you? what do you want? where are you going?" And they brought presents of skins, blankets (*mantas*) of the land, which were the first gifts in sign of peace. All of this was [on] Holy Thursday and day of the Incarnation. The governor replied to the questions of the Indian that he was a captain of the great king of Spain; that he was coming in his name to make the sacred faith of Christ known to them and so that they might become acquainted with it and be saved and give obedience to the apostolic church of Rome and to the Supreme Pontiff and Vicar of God who resides there and that in the temporal sphere, so that they as his vassals might acknowledge the Emperor, king of Castile, our lord, as king and lord; and that they would treat them well in everything and that he would maintain them in peace and justice as [he does] for his other Christian vassals.

On Monday the twenty-ninth of March they departed from there for Ichisi. And it rained so much and a small river rose in such a manner that, if they had not made great haste in crossing it, all those of the army would have been in danger. Indian men and women came out to receive them on this day. They [the women] came clothed in white and made a fine appearance and gave maize cakes (*tortillas*) to the Christians and some bunches of tender little onions (*cebolletas*) just like those of Castile, as thick as the end of one's thumb and bigger. And that was a food that aided them greatly from there on forward and they ate them with the cakes, roasted and boiled and raw. And they were a great help because they were very good. The white clothing with which the Indian women came clothed are some cloaks like [those] of coarse linen and some delicate (*son unas mantas como de lienço basto y algunas delgadas*).[29] They make the thread for them from the bark of the mulberry tree (*morales*), not from the first [layer] but from the one in the middle. And they know how to process (*beneficiar*) it and to spin it into thread and to prepare (*aparejar*) it and weave it. That they make very beautiful cloaks and they wear one from the waist down and another tied by one side and with the end (*cabeça*) thrown over the shoulders like those Bohemians or Egyptians (*egipçianos*)[30] who are accustomed to wander about Spain at times like vagabonds. The thread is such that one who has seen it assured me that he saw the women spin it from the bark of the mulberry trees and make it as good as the best thread from Portugal, that the women in Spain obtain for [their] work, and thinner [*mas delgado*] and somewhat like it and stronger (*mas reçio*). The mulberry trees are just like those of Spain and as big and bigger; but the leaf is softer and better for silk and the mulberries are better to eat and even bigger than those of Spain, and the Spaniards also availed themselves of them greatly many times in order to sustain themselves.

On that day they reached a settlement of a cacique subject to Ichisi, a pretty good (*bonico*)[31] settlement and with abundant food. And he gave them of what he had with good will. And they rested there on Tuesday, and then early on Wednesday, the last [day] of March, the governor and his army departed and reached the Rio Grande, where there were many canoes in which they crossed very well and reached the settlement of the lord, who was blind in one eye (*tuerto*). And he fed them very well and he gave them fifteen Indians for burdens. And as he was the first who came in peace, they did not want to impose on him too much. They remained there on Thursday the first of April and they placed a cross for them on the mound (*cerro*)[32] of the settlement and through the interpreter they informed them of the sanctity of the cross. And they received it and they adored it with much devotion to all appearances. On Friday, the second day of the month of April, this army left there and slept in the open country. And they reached a good river on the following day and they encountered deserted huts (*buhios despoblados*) and messengers from Altamaha arrived there and brought them to a settlement where they found an abundance of food and a messenger from Altamaha came with a present. And on the next day they brought many canoes and the army crossed well. And from there the governor sent to call the cacique Çamumo. And they said that he always ate and slept and went about armed [and] that he never laid his arms aside because he was on the frontier of another cacique named Cofitachequi, his enemy, and that he would not come without them. And the governor replied and said that he might come as he wished. And he came and the governor gave him a large feather colored with silver embroidery. And the cacique accepted it, very happy, and said to the governor: "You are from the heaven and that feather of yours that you give me, I can eat with it; I shall go out to war with it; I shall sleep with my wife with it." And the governor said to him, yes, that he could do all that. This Çamumo and those others were subjects of a great chief who was called Ocute. And this [fellow] with the feather asked the governor to whom he was to give tribute from thereon forward, whether he was to give it to the governor or to Ocute. And the governor suspected that this question was spoken cunningly and he replied that he considered Ocute as a brother; that he should give his tribute to Ocute until the governor should order otherwise. From there he sent messengers to call Ocute and he came there and the governor gave him a yellow satin cap and a shirt and a feather. And he set up a cross there in Altamaha and it was well received. And the next day, Thursday, the eighth day of April, the governor set out from there with his army and he brought Ocute with him and they went to some huts (*buhios*) to sleep and on Friday they reached the village of Ocute. And the governor became angry with him and he was trembling from fear. And soon a great number of Indians came with provisions and gave as many Indians for cargo as the Christians wanted and he set up a cross and they received it with great devotion to all appearances and they adored it on their knees as they saw the Christians were doing. Monday, the twelfth of April, they departed from Ocute and arrived at Cofaqui and leading men came with gifts. This cacique Cofaqui was an old man with a full beard, and a nephew of his was governing for him. The cacique Tatofa came there and another leading man and they gave their present, both food and *tamemes,* all those that were needed. That in their language *tameme* means precisely the same as cargo-Indian. On Thursday, the fifteenth of that month, that Perico, who was the Indian boy, whom they were bringing along as a guide since Apalache, began to act in an incoherent manner[33] because he no longer knew anything about the land. And he made believe he was possessed by the devil. And he knew how to do it so well that the Christians thought it was true. And a religious whom they brought along, named fray Johan the Evangelist, said so. Consequently, as a result they had to take guides that Tatofa gave them in order to go to Cofitachequi through an uninhabited region for nine or ten days of trail.

Notes

1. *Bonico* could be rendered also as "neat," "good," or "passable." Bourne rendered it as "fair-sized."

2. *Apilados* could be rendered as "peeled" as well as "dried." These chestnuts were chinquapins and were known to natives living along the St. Johns River in the late seventeenth century as *pinoco*.

3. A *palmo* can be 8 1/4 inches as a measure of length or 3 inches in the sense of a handsbreadth. There is also an indefinite expression, "en un palmo de tierra," which means "in a short space of ground." The expression "dos palmas de tierra" may also have some such idiomatic meaning rather than representing a specific measurement.

4. Bourne rendered *gordo* as "rich."

5. Though this word could be interpreted as "swamp" as well, as Bourne has rendered it, *çienaga* has more the sense of "bog" or "muddy place" than the deeper water usually described as a "swamp" or *pantano*.

6. Bourne rendered this as "saddle," which is correct, but "chair" is a primary meaning of this word as well. A folding canvas camp chair would seem a more practical thing to carry.

7. Like the English battle cry "For St. George," "For St. James" or "Santiago" was the traditional Spanish battle cry from the early days of the wars against the Moors. The Reconquista began from the mountain fastnesses of northwest Spain, where the tomb of the Apostle St. James was believed to have been found. His great shrine at Santiago de Compostela was a popular place of pilgrimage.

8. Bourne rendered this as "wigwam." There is no evidence that Florida's Indians used wigwams. The structure may well have been a *buhio grande* or council house, as this *buhio* would have had to be of considerable size to house the three hundred Indians.

9. Bourne rendered *sendos palos* as "stakes." The correct modern meaning of *sendos* is "either," "each of two," "one for each," or "respective." Dictionaries also note that *sendos* is used nonacademically or incorrectly to mean "good," "great," "abundant," "strong," or "heavy." I chose the latter incorrect usage as it is the one that I have encountered most often in Spanish American literature and because the dictionaries' mention of the incorrect usage suggests that the usage is common.

10. This seems to be the sense of *en luengo* here, but it can mean also "finally" or "in the end."

11. Bourne rendered this simply as "to forage." However, as the word *ranchear* means "to build huts" or "to form a mess" and its derivatives, *rancheadero, rancheria,* etc., all have the connotation of huts or hamlets, such may also be implied in the choice of this term.

12. Bourne rendered this as "high mountain," not something that one finds in Florida. In this era and even today in Cuba, *monte* is used much more commonly for "woods."

13. Bourne rendered *bachiller* as "young fellow," but it is more likely that it was meant in the scholastic sense of "bachelor" as a college graduate. It also could have the meaning of a loquacious person or prattler.

14. *Çienaga* in this case is used clearly in the sense of "swamp" rather than marsh. This raises a stronger possibility that it was so used also in the earlier case that was noted.

15. *Tasajos* is the word for jerky or dried beef. Salt is used in making dried beef.

16. Bourne rendered this as "headpieces" for some reason.

17. Bourne translated this as "mangers." Although dictionaries define *pesebre* as "crib, rack, or manger in a stable," "slip" for building vessels seems more appropriate here.

18. *Manta* could be rendered also as "blanket."

19. Bourne has "made believe that he was possessed." The Spanish text does not seem to justify such a value judgment.

20. Bourne rendered *piragua* as "barge." The usual meaning of *piragua* is a dugout or canoe-like vessel and the phrase *canoa o piragua* points in that direction as well.

21. Literally, *derribar* means "to knock down."

22. *Trabajo* literally means "toil" or "labor."

23. Bourne noted that "Wednesday was the 10th."

24. *Arcabuco* is defined by Cassell as a "densely wooded mountain." Bourne rendered this as "They passed through much undergrowth or land closely covered with bushes."

25. Bourne noted that Oviedo obviously erred here in transcribing *cient* rather than *cinco* or five. Five is the number given by Elvas for this incident.

26. *Tijeras* has the sense of scissors or X-shaped. Bourne rendered this as "with timbers crisscrossed."

27. *Volapié* in modern Spanish, which among other things signifies a difficult crossing requiring a combination of wading and swimming.

28. *Guanajo* in Cuba is "turkey."

29. *Delgadas* might be rendered also as "thin."

30. By Egyptians, Oviedo probably meant Gypsies.

31. *Bonico*, a derivative of *bueno* or "good," has the sense of "pretty good," "passable," "neat," "sly," or "clever."

32. *Cerro* literally is a hill or high land, but in this context seems to mean "mound."

33. The Spanish here, *començó á desatinar aquel Perico*, might also be rendered as "began to act deranged."

10 · Report of the Outcome of the Journey That Hernando de Soto Made and of the Characteristics of the Land through Which He Traveled

Luys Hernández de Biedma

The Luys Hernández de Biedma account is the only one of the de Soto narratives for which the original manuscript exists. As John R. Swanton (1985:6) noted, "The manuscript was formerly conserved in the archives in Simancas, but was later transferred to the Archivo General de Indias in Seville. A copy of it was made (probably in the Simancas archives) by Juan Bautista Muñoz, which is now vol. 81 of the Papers of the Muñoz Collection in the Real Academia de la Historia in Madrid."

The translation here was made from a transcription of the Muñoz copy made by Buckingham Smith, which he published in London in 1857 through the House of Trubner and Company. Smith's transcription appears with other Spanish documents concerning the history of Florida and lands adjacent to it on pages 47–64 of *Colección de varios documentos para la historia de la Florida y tierras adjacentes,* vol. 1. I used a copy held by the University of Florida's P. K. Yonge Library of Florida History.

In view of the brevity of Hernández de Biedma's account, I have begun the translation of it from the beginning of his account rather than beginning it with de Soto's arrival at Ocale, as I have done with the other chronicles.

The following note precedes Smith's transcription of the document:

Florida
1539–1545
Report of the Outcome of the Journey That Hernando de Soto Made and of the Characteristics of the Land through Which He traveled.
Copy taken from the original existent in Simancas, Patronato Real, Indies, Bundle 7, by D. Juan Baptista Muños, which is found with notes of the same in tome 81 of his collection.

Report about the Island of Florida

We arrived at the port of Bayahonda. We disembarked six hundred and twenty men and two hundred and twenty-three horses. Soon after we landed, we learned from some Indians who were taken that there was a Christian there in that land, who was of those who had gone with Pánfilo de Narváez. We went in search of him. That a chief had him, who would be eight leagues from the port. We met him on the trail as he was already coming toward us. When the cacique learned that we had landed there, he asked the Christian whether he wished to come to where we were. And when he said, yes, he sent nine Indians with him. He came naked like them, with a bow and some arrows in his hand, with his body decorated like an Indian's. When the Christians encountered them, they thought that they were Indians who were coming to spy on their people. They took off after them and they fled toward a little woods that was nearby. When the horses reached them, they gave a lance thrust to an Indian and would even have killed the Christian because he remembered little of our language, which he had forgotten. But he remembered to call out to Our Lady, by which he was recognized to be the Christian. With great rejoicing, we brought him to where the governor was.

He had been among those Indians for twelve years. And he had also learned their language. And it had been so long that he had had to speak it [only], that he was among us for more than four days before he learned to put one idea together with another without speaking four or five words in the Indians' language for the one word in Spanish that he spoke until he reached the point of relearning to speak our language well.

He had so little knowledge of the land that he did not know anything [about it] only twenty leagues from there, either from [having] seen it or from [having] heard about it. But it is true that he told us as soon as he saw us that there was no sign of gold in the land.

We set out from the port of Baya Onda to explore the hinterland with all the people who disembarked [except for] twenty-six horsemen and sixty foot-soldiers who remained behind guarding the port until the governor should send word to them or send someone to call them. We set out on our way in the direction of the setting sun (*en la bia del poniente*) and taking that of northwest (*norueste*). We carried a report of a cacique whom the Indians told us they all paid tribute to and that he was called Hurripacuxi. He lived up to twenty leagues from the coast. From here we went crossing some swamps (*cienagas*) and rivers another fifteen or twenty leagues from there to a village that the Indians represented to us as very remarkable (*mui grande*)[1] to such an extent that they told us that its people made the birds that were flying past drop by giving shouts.

We reached this village, which is called Etocale. It was a small village. We found some food [consisting of] maize, beans (? *crisoles*)[2] and little dogs, which was no slight refreshment for the people who were dead from hunger. We remained here for seven or eight days during which we made some expeditions in order to capture Indians who might guide us to the province of Apalache, of which there was great report in all its land. Three or four Indian men were captured. That the one of them who knew the most was not acquainted with anything more than two leagues onward from that village. We departed from here still traveling toward New Spain. We were going diverted (*iriamos desviados*) ten or twelve leagues from the coast.

In the five or six[3] days that we traveled until (*hasta*) we reached a moderate-sized (*razonable*) settlement (*poblazon*) that was called Aguaca-lecuen, we passed some villages (*Pueblos*). We found that all the Indians [had] run off, [having] fled to the woods. We stopped here for another six or seven days in order to search for some Indians who might guide us. While going in search of some [male] Indians, ten or twelve women were captured, among whom we were told that one was a daughter of the cacique. For this [reason] the cacique came to us in peace and said that he would give us interpreters and Indians[4] for [the trail] on forward, but he never gave them to us [and] we had to bring him along with us. And continuing traveling along the trail, after we had marched for six or seven days, about three hundred and fifty Indians came out against us with bows and arrows with the intention of taking the cacique away from us, whom we were bringing along with us. We killed some of them and captured all the rest. Among them were some Indians who had reports (*noticia*) of the rest [of the country] inland. And they told us very great lies there.

We crossed another river that was in a province that was called Vea-chile. And we encountered some villages on the other bank, all [of the inhabitants of which had] fled, although in them we did not fail to find that which we needed, which was some food. From there we set out for another settlement that was called Aguile, which borders on that province of Apalache. That a river separates one province from the other.

We made a bridge on this river from many pine trees tied to one another. And we crossed it with a great deal of danger as there were Indians on the other side who opposed our crossing. As the Indians saw that we had crossed the river, they went to a village that was closest to there, which is called Ivitachuco. And they waited for us there until we arrived in sight of the village, and on seeing us begin to appear, they set fire to the entire village and fled.

There are many villages in this province of Apalache and it is land with an abundance of food. They call all this other land that we were traveling through the province of Yustaga. We went to another village that is called Iniahico. And here it seemed to us that it was time to learn about those who remained behind in the port and that they should know about us because we were thinking of pushing on into the interior to such a degree that we would not be able to receive any report from them. We had already marched one hundred and ten leagues to there from where we had left them. And the Governor sent to call them so that they might come to be where we were.

We went from here[5] to look for the sea, which would be nine leagues from this village. And at the edge (*orilla*) of it we found where Pánfilo de Narváez built the boats, because we found the site of the forge and many bones from the horses. And through the interpreter the Indians told us how the other Christians had built those boats there.[6] Juan de Añasco made certain signals on some trees there that were at the edge of the sea, because the Governor ordered that he should go to call the people who had remained in the port and that he should send them by land by the route by which we had come and that he should come by sea in two brigantines and a small vessel (*vatel*) that were there and that he should bring them to that province of Apalache. And in the meantime we would remain there waiting for him.

Juan de Añasco sent the people by land and he himself came by sea as the Governor had ordered. He suffered plenty of labor and danger in this because he did not find that coast which he had seen from the land before [leaving]. When he went there by the sea he did not find any trace of them (*memoria dellos*) [the markings] because they were [in] shallow bays (*oncones vaxos*)[7] that held water with the rising of the tide and that became dry with the ebbing tide. We made a pirogue, which went two leagues out to sea every day to see if the brigantines were coming in order to show them where they were to stop. God willed that both should come, both those by the sea and the other people by land.[8]

When the brigantines had come, the governor ordered them that they should go toward the west in order to see if they should be able to find some port that there might be near there in order to know the coast if they should find (*fallase*)[9] something in the hinterland. Francisco Maldonado, a gentleman from Salamanca, went in the brigantines.[10] He went along sailing along the coast and entering all the coves (*caletas*), bays (*ancones*) and rivers that he saw until he reached a river on which he found a good entrance and a good harbor and an Indian village on the seacoast; that some came to trade with him and he took one of those Indians and came to where we were. He spent two months on this voyage which had begun to seem to us like a thousand years because it detained us there so long on account of the reports we had about what [there was] in the interior.

Maldonado [having] come, the Governor told him that, as we were going in search of that land that that Indian was telling us was on another sea, that he should go in those brigantines to the Island of Cuba, where Doña Isabel de Bobadilla, the wife of the governor was. And that if he did not hear anything from us within six months, that he should come in those brigantines and that he should sail along the coast as far as the River of the Holy Spirit [the Mississippi] because we would have to return there again. And the brigantines went to Cuba and we set out on the trail toward the north in order to go to see what the Indians were telling us about.

We traveled for five days through uninhabited land [and] we reached a large river [with] a strong current. We were not able to build a bridge because of the strength of its current, [so] we made a pirogue in which we crossed to the other side. [There] we found a province that is called Acapachiqui, very abundant in the food that the Indians were accustomed to eat. We saw some of its villages and we could not see others because of its being a land of very large swamps. And that we encountered differences in the houses (*casas*) of the Indians because we found them like cellars (*cuebas*)[11] under the ground (*debajo de terra*). And heretofore they were covered with palm-thatch and with straw (*de palmas i de paja*). We went on forward and came across two other rivers over which we had to build bridges of pines tied together as we were accustomed to make them. We reached another province that was called Otoa. We encountered a fair-sized village (*pueblo razonable*) larger than any we had encountered up to there (*que fasta alli abiamos fallado*). We went on from there to other villages of another province that would be two days from there, where we captured some people who were not vigilant, as they had not learned about us. They agreed to come to serve us peacefully so that we would return the people whom we had taken from them. The governor returned them as they did not take any except some who were guides [and] interpreters for [the lands] on forward. We spent (*tardamos*) five or six days in crossing this province that is called of Chisi. We were well served there by the Indians from the little (*de la pobreza*) that they had.

We passed on from here for another three days without a settlement (*sin poblazon*) until another province that is called Altapaha. Here we encountered a river that did not flow toward the south like the others that we had crossed as it went running toward the east to the sea to where the Licentiate Lucas de Ayllón came. On account of this we gave much more credit to what that Indian was telling us and we believed all the lies (*mentiras*)[12] that he had told us to be true. This province was well populated by Indians and they all served us in turn (*todos nos bolbian de serbir*).[13] When the Governor asked them about that province that we were going in search of, that was called Cofitachyque, they told us that it was not possible to go there; neither was there a road by which [to do so]; nor anything on the trail to eat and that we would all die of hunger. We went on forward to other caciques who were called Ocute and Cofaque and they gave us of the foods that they had. And they told us that if we wished to go to make war on the Señora of Cofitachique, that they would give us everything that we might wish for the trail. But they made us understand that there was no trail by which to go because they did not have dealings with one another because of the war that they had except for the occasional times when they went to make war on one another and this was by way of hidden and secret areas where they would not be detected. And that they spent twenty to twenty-two days on the trail in [which] they did not eat anything except plants (*ierbas*) and some toasted maize that they carried. In view of our determination they gave us eight hundred Indians that they might carry our loads of foodstuffs and clothing and other Indians who would guide us. The latter took the trail directly to the east and thus we went traveling for three days. . . .

NOTES

1. Literally, *mui grande* means "very large" or "very great," and this passage could well be rendered as "that the Indians represented to us as very large." But the context suggests that the rendering I have given may be preferable.

2. Presumably this was meant to be *frijoles,* as *crisoles* means "crucible."

3. Bourne (1904:51), who presents Buckingham Smith's translation, has "four or five days' march" here.

4. The Spanish here, Smith noted in a footnote, is *lenguas i dias.* Smith believed that *dias* was meant to be either "Indias" or "guias," i.e., "Indian women" or "guides."

5. Smith transcribed this as *as qui,* but observed in a footnote that he believed what was meant was *aqui* or "here."

6. Smith rendered the Spanish text here, *como alli habian hecho los otros Christianos aquellas barcas,* as "what others like us there had done," deleting the direct references to "Christians" and to "those boats."

7. In a footnote Smith observed that what he had transcribed as *oncones* he believed should be *ancones* or "bays." Smith rendered *ancones* here as "inlets."

8. Smith rendered this very freely as "I was thankful when the people arrived not less those that came by land than those by water."

9. In modern Spanish this would be *hallase*.

10. Smith rendered this as "had the command," making no mention of the brigs.

11. *Cuevas* in modern Spanish can also be "cave, grotto, a subterraneous cavity, or den" (either "of thieves" or "of wild beasts").

12. Smith rendered this blandly as "stories," which could be misleading. Although a lie can be referred to euphemistically as a "story," *mentira* has no other meaning than "lie, falsehood" or "error, mistake in writing."

13. Smith rendered this as "all desired to serve us," which is a rather free translation. The expression *volver de* followed by another verb usually indicates repeated action.

11 · The Florida of the Inca: *History of the Adelantado,*
Hernando de Soto, Governor and Captain General of
the Kingdom of Florida, and of Other Heroic Spanish
and Indian Cavaliers written by the Inca Garcilaso de la
Vega, Captain of His Majesty, Native of the Great City
of Cozco, Head of the Kingdoms and Provinces of Peru.
Dedicated to Our Lady the Queen

Many errors of the First [Printing] Are Corrected in This Printing:
and a Copious Table of the Notable Events added.
And the Chronological Essay That Contains the Happenings up to the
Year of 1722.

With Privilege: in Madrid

In the Royal Workshop, and at the Expense of Nicolás Rodríguez Franco,
Printer of Books. Year 1723
They will be found in his House.

I began my translation of the Inca's narrative with Chapter 19 of the first
part of its second book. Chapter 19 is titled "The Spaniards Make a
Bridge and Cross the River of Ocali and Reach Ochile." The length of the
manuscript required excision of a substantial part of my translation of
the Inca's account and all of my translation of two accounts about the
Narváez expedition written by Alvar Núñez Cabeza de Vaca. I concurred
with those deletions except for insisting that the starting point be pushed
back one chapter so that the translation would include what the Inca had
to say about Osachile, to which I had given considerable attention in my
introductory essay. That chapter on Osachile is important as well because
the Inca's ostensible description of the Spaniards' crossing of the Suwannee River to enter Osachile Province appears to be, instead, a misplaced
description of the Spaniards' crossing of the Aucilla River to enter Apalachee Province. The deleted translations are available at the Bureau of
Archaeological Research.

Chapter 30. The Governor Passes on to Osachile. The Way in Which the Indians of Florida Establish (fundan)[1] Their Villages Is Told

After the battle that we have told about [that was] worthy of laughter, although bloody and cruel for the poor Indians, the governor remained in the village of Vitachuco for four days, repairing the damage that he and his [men] had received. On the fifth day they set out in search of another province called Osachile that was near that one.[2] They traveled four leagues on the first day. They lodged (*alojaronse*)[3] on the bank of a large river that separates the limits of these two provinces. In order to cross it, it was necessary to build another bridge like the one that was made on the River of Ochile because it could not be forded.

When the Castilians had the platform (*tablaçon*) ready for throwing it into the water, the Indians on the other side rushed up to oppose the work and the passage.[4] The Christians, abandoning the manufacture of the bridge, built six large rafts on which one hundred men crossed between crossbowmen and harquebusiers and fifty armed horsemen, who carried the saddles for horses on the rafts.

When these had touched land, the governor (who remained present for everything even though his face [was] covered with plasters) ordered fifty horses to be driven into the river, that crossed swimming.

The Spaniards who were on the other side, having received them and saddled them, set out for the plain with the utmost diligence. The Indians, seeing horses on land that was clear of woods, abandoned the post and left the Christians free to build their bridge. And with the customary diligence they completed it in a day and a half and threw it onto the river.

The army crossed the river, traveled through two leagues of land without woods and at the end of them encountered large plantings of maize, beans, and pumpkins of the type that in Spain is called Roman. With the planted fields began the settlement, with houses scattered and distant from one another without the order of a village, and these proceeded for the space of four leagues up to the principal village, called Osachile. This had two hundred large and good houses and was the seat and court of the curaca and lord of that land. And it had the same name, Osachile.

The Indians, who for two leagues of clear and level land had not dared to wait for the Spaniards, as soon as they saw them among the planted fields, turning back on them and concealing themselves in the maize fields, shot many arrows at them, attacking them from all sides, without the loss of any time or place or occasion that was offered to them that would enable them to do harm to them. They wounded many Castilians with this [attack], but neither did the Indians succeed in covering themselves with glory, because the Christians, on recognizing the insolence and rabid courage that the heathen showed in order to kill or wound them, when they caught them out in the open, lanced them without sparing any, as they took very few as captives.[5] Thus the rigorous game proceeded over the four leagues of planted fields with losses on the one side and the other as is always wont to happen in war. There are ten leagues of pleasant (*apacible*) and level land from the village of Vitachuco to that of Osachile.[6]

The Spaniards found the village of Osachile abandoned as the curaca and the Indians had gone to the woods. The governor then sent messengers to him from the few Indians whom they had captured in his land, inviting him with [the offer of] peace and friendship. But the curaca Osachile neither came out nor replied to the messages; nor did any Indian of those who had carried them return. This might be due to the short time that the Christians remained in his village as they were [there] no more than two days. During those [two days], the Spaniards, placing themselves in ambushes (*emboscadas*)[7] captured many Indians to use them as servants. After [having] surrendered, they were tame (*domesticos*) and good servants[8] even though they had shown themselves fierce with their arms in their hands.

During the short time that the Spaniards remained in this province, and because of its being small, although well populated with people and abundantly supplied with food, few things happened [there] to tell about beyond those that have been spoken of. For this [reason] it will make sense, so that we do not depart from it so quickly, that we should describe the site, plan, and manner of style (*el Sitio, traça, y manera*) of this village, Osachile, so that by it one may see the state of things (*asiento*) and the usual arrangement (*forma*) of the rest of the villages of this great kingdom called Florida. Because, as all of its land is almost of one same type and character (*casi de vna misma suerte, y calidad*), flat and with many rivers that run through it, so all its natives make villages (*pueblan*), dress, eat, and drink almost (*casi*) in one same manner. And even in their heathenism (*Gentilidad*), in their idols, rites, and ceremonies (of which they have a few), and in their weapons, social status (*condicion*)[9] and ferocity they differ little or nothing from one another. From which, [having] seen one village, you will have seen almost all, and it will not be necessary to portray them individually unless someone appears [that is] so different that it may be necessary to make a report about it by itself.[10]

For this [purpose] it is to be noted that the Indians of Florida always tried to settle on a height (*procuraron poblar en alto*), at least the houses (*casas*) of the caciques and lords, when all the village cannot be. And because all the land is very level and few times do they find an elevated site (*sitio alto*) that has the rest of the useful and necessary conveniences for settling (*para poblar*), they make it with the strength of their arms, as, after piling up a very great quantity of earth, they go about stomping strongly on it, lifting it up in the form of a hill (*en forma de cerro*) of two or three pikes in height (*de dos, y tres picas en alto*)[11] and on top they make a level area capable of ten or twelve, fifteen or twenty houses for the dwelling (*morada*) of the lord and his family and serving people in accord with his capability (*posibilidad*)[12] and the grandeur of the state. On the level area at the foot of the hill (*en lo llano, al pie del cerro*), either natural or artificial, they make a squared plaza (*una Plaça quadrada*)[13] in accord with the size of the village that is to be settled (*segun el tamanho del pueblo, que se ha de poblar*)[14] and around it the most noble and leading people build their houses and then the rest of the common people theirs. They try not to be distant from the hill where the house of the lord is, instead they work to crowd about it (*cercale*)[15] with theirs.

In order to climb up to the house of the curaca they make passages straight up the hill (*calles derechas por el cerro arriba*)[16] two or three or more as are needed of fifteen or twenty feet in width. For the walls (*paredes*) of these paved ways they drive thick logs (*hincan gruesas maderas*) that go together one with the others (*que van juntos vnos de otros*) and enter more than an estate (*estado*)[17] into the earth. For stairs they cross other logs no less thick than those that serve as walls and they fasten one to the other (*los travan vnos con otros*). These logs that serve as steps are worked on all four sides so that the climb will be smoother (*mas llana*). The steps are four or six or eight feet apart from one another in accord with the proportions (*disposición*) and steepness of the hill, more or less elevated. The horses went up and came down by it easily because they are wide. All the rest of the hill, except for the stairs, they cut in the form of a wall with the result that they cannot climb up by it, because the house of the lord becomes more fortified in this fashion. From this model and plan Osachile made his village and house, [but] he abandoned it because the woods appeared stronger. He remained there, unwilling to accept the friendship of the Spaniards or to reply to their messages.

Second Part of the Second Book of the History of the Florida of the Inca wherein Will Be Seen the Many and Fierce Battles That the Indians and Spaniards Had in Difficult Passages in the Great Province of Apalache. The Labors They Endured in Discovering the Sea. The Events and the Unbelievable Toil That the Thirty Horsemen Endured, Who, in the Going and the Coming, Returned for Pedro Calderón. The Ferocity of the Apalache. The Capture of

Their Cacique, His Strange Flight, and the Fertility of That Great Province. It Contains Twenty-Five Chapters.

Chapter One: The Spaniards Reach the Famous Province of Apalache, and About the Resistance of the Indians

The governor and his captains, having learned in the village of Osachile that the province of Apalache was now close, of which they had heard so many praises and wonders (*tantos loores y grandeças*), both about its abundance and the fertility of the soil and the military deeds and ferocity of the people, about whose ferocity and valor the Indians along the trail had made so many threats to them, telling them that the Apalache would riddle them with arrows, butcher them, burn, and destroy them, desiring to see them now and to spend the winter in it if it should be as fertile as they were saying, did not want to stop more than two days in Osachile. At the end of them he departed from the village and in another three they traveled without opposition through some twelve leagues of uninhabited area that exists between the two provinces.[18] And at noon of the fourth day they reached a swamp, very large and hard to cross, because the water alone, not to mention the woods that there were on either side of it, had a width of half a league and in length was like a river. At the edges of the swamp, beside the water, there was a woods of many tall and thick trees, with many briar thickets (*con mucha maleça de çarças*)[19] and another low woods (*y otro Monte bajo*)[20] that, intertwining themselves with the thick trees, thickened and closed the woods in such a fashion that it looked like a strong wall.[21] Through this there was not any passage by which to cross through the woods and the swamp except for a footpath (*senda*)[22] that the Indians had made, so narrow that two men could scarcely walk abreast on it.

Before coming to the woods the camp was set up on a good plain, and, because it was early, the governor ordered that one hundred foot-soldiers, between crossbowmen and harquebusiers, and shield bearers, and thirty on horseback, with twelve swimmers, assigned to assess the depth of the water, so that they might go to reconnoiter the passage through the swamp and to take note of the difficulties that there might be on it so that they would be prepared for them on the following day.

The Spaniards set out and a few steps after they had penetrated the narrow lane (*callejon*) through the woods, they encountered Indians prepared to defend the passageway; but as the lane was so narrow that neither the faithful nor the infidels were able to fight except for the two foremost of each band. For this reason, placing the two best-armed Spaniards out front with their swords and shields and another two crossbowmen and gunmen just behind them, they confronted the Indians all through what there was of the woods until coming to the water. There as both the one side and the other could scatter and spread out, there was a great battle and many and very good shots by one side against the other with people killed and wounded on both sides.

Because of the great resistance that the Indians in the water offered, the Christians could not then reconnoiter how great was its depth, concerning which they advised the general, who went to their assistance in person [and] brought the best foot-soldiers of the army with him. The enemy, likewise, for their part rushed many more than they had earlier into the fray as reinforcements and the battle became more cruel and bloody. The one and the other continued fighting with the water halfway up the thigh and to the waist with great difficulty and the roughness that there was in walking through it, because of the briar thickets, the bushes (*matas*)[23] and fallen trees that they encountered under the water. But despite all these problems, as the Spaniards saw that it would not be appropriate to turn back without having reconnoitered the passage, they made a great charge against the enemy and threw them back to the other side of the water and they found that it could all be forded [with water] up to the waist and to the thighs except in the middle of the channel, as for the space of forty paces (*pasos*) because of its great depth, it was crossed by a bridge, made of two fallen trees and other timbers (*maderos*) tied to one another (*atados vnos con otros*).[24] They saw also that in the same fashion that there was a narrow lane under the water through the woods, cleared of the bushes (*matas*) and briars (*maleças*) that there were beyond the path on either side. [Having] crossed the swamp beyond the water on the other side, there was another woods (*monte*) as closed and thick as the one we have spoken of. It was also impossible to walk through the latter except by another narrow lane (*callejon*) and narrow path (*camino angosto*) made by hand. These two woods and the swamp, each one by itself measured half a league across, so that in all it was a league and a half.

After having reconnoitered the passage well and having considered the difficulties that there were in it, the governor returned to his encampment with his [people] to make plans, in accord with what he had seen and noted, for what had to be done on the following day. And, after having consulted with the captains over the problems and dangers that existed in the case, he ordered a hundred men to be readied from the cavalry, who because they were better-armed people than the foot-soldiers, always received less injury from the arrows,[25] the latter, taking shields because the horses were not needed[26] were to go ahead on foot, forming a shield for

the other one hundred foot-soldiers between crossbowmen and harquebusiers, who were to follow behind them.

He ordered likewise that all of them were to be equipped with axes and
billhooks, and other instruments (*hachas, y hocinos, y otros instrumen-
tos*)[27] for felling a piece of the woods that was on the other side of the
swamp as a campground for the army,[28] because, with the Spaniards having to cross one by one, with the path being narrow, and with the enemies
who had shown themselves so ferocious on that day being bound to contest the passage, it seemed impossible to the governor that his people
would completely cross the two woods of the swamp in one day. For this
[reason], he wanted the campground prepared, achieved by dint of labor
(*a fuerça de braços*)[29] in the second woods, because he would not be able
to have it in any other fashion.[30]

Chapter II. The Spaniards Gain the Passage of the Swamp and the
Intense and Fierce Struggle That Occurred in It

With the preparations and arrangement that have been spoken of, with
each one of the soldiers carrying the food for that day in his stomach
(*seno*) which was a little bit of toasted or cooked maize without anything
else, two hundred of the most select Spaniards that there were in it left the
campground. And two hours before the dawn came, they entered the narrow lane of the woods and with the utmost silence possible traveled by it
until they reached the water, where, on recognizing the pathway cleared of
briars that went under the water they followed it to the bridge made from
the fallen trees and timbers tied [to them] that crossed the deepest part of
the channel of the swamp. They crossed that bridge without any Indian
coming out to its defense, because it had seemed to them that the Spaniards would not dare enter the thickness of the wood and the depth of the
water and the briars that there were in it, at night. As a result of this they
had neglected to rise early to defend the passage. But on seeing the day and
realizing that the Christians had crossed the bridge, they rushed out with
the greatest fury, shouts, and outcry for the defense of what remained to
be crossed of the water and swamp, which was a fourth of a league. And
with anger, that they had with themselves for having been negligent and
for having slept so much, they charged upon the Castilians with great
ferocity and impetus. However, they went well prepared and were desirous that that struggle should not last for much time [and so] they pressed
the Indians strongly. One and the other walked in water to the waist. They
pushed them out of it [the water] and confined them in the narrow path
through the second woods, which [the woods] was so closed and thick

that the Indians could not flee by way of it in a spread-out fashion, but only single file confined by the narrow path. The Indians [having been] confined in the narrow path through the woods, as few Spaniards were needed to defend it because of the narrowness of the passage, they agreed that one hundred and fifty of them should undertake the clearing of a site for the establishment of the camp and that the other fifty should protect and defend the passage, if the Indians attempted to come to interfere with the work, because, as there was no other path for them to enter [the place] where those were who were clearing the woods except by the path or narrow way, the few Christians who were at the passage sufficed to defend it.

In this manner they remained all that day, the Indians giving shouts and howls in order to disturb their enemies with the noise now that they could no longer do so with weapons, and the Castilians, with some working at defending the passage, others cutting the woods, others burning what [had been] cut, so that they would not obstruct the site (*porque no ocupase el sitio*). When night came, each one of ours remained where it found him without sleeping during any part of it because of the many sudden assaults and the noise that the Indians made.

Daylight [having] arrived, the army began to cross and, although it met no opposition from the enemies, it had it from the pathway itself, which was very narrow, and from the briars that there were in the water that did not let them pass as they wished to. For this [reason] it was necessary to travel one by one. Because of this delay, which was great, they had enough to do that day in arriving at the campground to install themselves in the cleared area. There the following night, because of the noise and the unexpected attacks which the enemy made, they slept as little as during the preceding one. They provided the food for those who were defending the passage, passing it from hand to hand, from one to another until it reached those on the front line.

As soon as dawn came, the Spaniards traveled by the narrow path of the woods, pushing the Indians before them. The latter went along continually firing arrows and retreating little by little, not wishing to cede them any more room than what they could gain at the blow of a sword.

Thus they covered the half league that there was from that closed and thick woods. Coming out of the heavy one, they entered into another lighter and open woods through which the Indians, being able to spread out and come and go among the trees, gave many a headache to the Castilians, attacking them from both sides of the path, shooting many arrows at them; but with order and system as when those on one side attacked, those on the other [side] did not attack until the former had pulled back in order not to wound one another with the arrows that went astray.[31] The latter were so numerous that it seemed like rain that was falling from heaven (*Cielo*).[32]

The woods where the Indians and the Spaniards were now continuing to fight, which we said to be lighter, was not so much so that the horses could run through it. As a consequence the heathen went about it most boldly darting in among the Christians and pulling back so that they paid no heed to them. And, even though the crossbowmen and the harquebusiers went out to resist them, they affected them not at all, because while a Spaniard was firing one shot and preparing for another, the Indian was shooting six and seven arrows. They are so skillful and fire them so quickly that they have scarcely released one when they have another placed in the bow.

The Indians had closed off the pieces of open land that existed in the middle of the woods through which the horses would have been able to run and obstructed them with large logs that were tied between various trees to provide themselves with safety from the horses. And where there was a closed woods, through which the Indians were not able to move, they had cut entryways and exits in places so that they might attack the Christians without being attacked by them.

They made these preparations beforehand because they knew that, because the woods of the swamp was as dense as it was, they would not be able to attack the Castilians as they would have liked and would have been able to if the woods were more open and clear as [was] the one that they were now encountering. For when they saw themselves with the advantage by reason of the location that the Spaniards held, they did not neglect to attempt and to employ whatever effort, stratagem, or trick that they could in attacking the Christians in their eagerness to wound or kill them.

Through the woods the Castilians gave more attention to defending themselves from the enemies than to attacking them because they could not take advantage of the horses because of the impediment of the woods. For this [reason] they were beset more by their own anger than by the weapons of their opposites. The Indians, on seeing their enemies encumbered, pressed them more and more from all directions with an eagerness and a desire to break them and rout them. They gathered new spirit for other [assaults] and new strength from the memory and the recollection of having ten or eleven years earlier in this same swamp, although not on this passage, broken and routed Pámphilo de Narváez. They recalled the latter feat for the Spaniards and for their general, saying to them among other effronteries and insults, that they were going to do the same to them and to him.

With the difficulties of the trail and with the headaches that the enemies were giving them, the Spaniards passed through the two leagues that were left of the woods until they came out into open and level land. Once they had reached there, giving thanks to God, who had released them from that prison, they loosed the reins of the horses and clearly demonstrated the anger that they bore against the Indians because in the more than two leagues for which the open land extended until it reached the fields of maize they did not come across any Indian whom they did not either capture or kill, especially those who showed any sign of resistance. Among the latter not one escaped. Thus they killed many Indians, as the slaughter was great that day, and they took few as prisoners. With this, these Castilians avenged the attack and the damage that the Apalache inflicted on Pámphilo de Narváez and disabused them of the idea and arrogant opinion that they had of themselves, that they were going to kill and destroy these Castilians as they had the earlier ones.

Chapter III. Of the Continuous Fighting that There Was until Reaching the Principal Village of Apalache

As it seemed to the governor Hernando de Soto that he had done enough for that day in having come out of the woods where he had met so much opposition and in having punished the Indians in part, he decided not to move on forward but rather to lodge his army on that plain because it was land clear of woods. The camp was set up near a small village that initiated the settlement and fields of the province of Apalache so renowned and famous in all that land.[33]

The Indians did not want to rest during the ensuing night nor to let the Christians recover from the bad days and nights that they had given them after they had reached the swamp, as during all that night they did [not][34] cease to give shouts and hollerings, and alarms and attacks at all hours, firing many arrows into the camp. Both sides passed the night with this disturbance without coming to blows.

The day [having] come, the Spaniards marched through some large fields of maize, beans, and pumpkins and other vegetables (*legumbres*) the fields of which stretched out over those plains on both sides of the trail as far as the eye could see and it took two leagues to cross it. A great settlement of scattered houses was spread out among the fields and separated from one another without the order of a village.[35] The Indians came out of their houses and fields with the utmost diligence to shoot arrows at the Castilians, obstinate in their desire and eagerness that they had to kill or wound them. The latter, fed up with such persistence and rankled by the anger and animosity they felt toward them, [having] lost their patience, lanced them without any compassion through the maize fields in order to see whether they could tame them or teach them a lesson with the rigor of their tactics. But it was all in vain, because the more the Christians desired to avenge themselves all the more did the anger and the rage that they held against them seem to increase among the Indians.

[Having] crossed the two leagues of the fields, they reached a deep arroyo with much water and a thick woods that existed on either side of it. It was a very difficult (*dificultoso*)³⁶ passage and one the enemies had reconnoitered well and prepared beforehand for attacking the Castilians in it. The latter seeing the difficulties and the defenses that the passage had, the best armed of the horsemen dismounted and by dint of sword and shield and others with axes gained the passage and tore down the palisades (*paliçadas*) and barricades (*barreras*) that he had made so that the horses could not pass or their masters attack them. Here the Indians attacked with the greatest force and fury, placing their last hope of conquering the Christians on this bad passage because it was so difficult, where the struggle was savage and where many Spaniards were wounded and some killed because the enemy fought overboldly, making a last attempt as desperate men [will do]. But they were not able to achieve their wicked desire because the Castilians gained the victory by means of the spirit and the strength that they demonstrated and the great diligence that they exercised so that the damage would not come to be as great as they had feared it might be in so difficult a passage.

[Having] crossed the arroyo, the Castilians traveled another two leagues of land devoid (*limpia*) of planted fields and settlement (*poblaçon*). In them the Indians did not attack because in the open fields (*campo*) they could not cope with the horses. The Christians camped in that open country that was free (*limpio*) of woods because the Indians, with their fear of the horses, on seeing them outside of the woods, allowed them to sleep, as they had need of rest, as for four days and three nights they had worked and been on guard. But they slept as little during that night as on the earlier ones, because the enemy, trusting in the darkness of the night, even though in open land, during all of it never ceased to raise alarms and make attacks on every side of the camp, not letting the Castilians sleep in order not to lose the renown and reputation that those of this province of Apalache had won among all their neighbors and nearby peoples of being the most valiant and warlike.

The following day, which was the fifth since they had crossed the swamp, as soon as the army began to move, the governor went out ahead of it with two hundred horsemen and one hundred foot-soldiers, because he had learned from the Indian prisoners that two leagues from there was the village of Apalache and its cacique within [it] with a large number of the most valiant Indians, waiting for the Castilians in order to kill and to quarter all of them. The words are the very ones that the prisoners spoke to the governor, as, even as captives and in the power of their enemies, they did not lose their fierceness (*bravosidad*) and pride (*presuncion*) of being natives of Apalache. The general and his [troops] ran the two leagues, lancing as many Indians as they encountered on either side of the trail. They reached the village [and] found that the curaca and his Indians had abandoned it. The Spaniards, knowing that they had not gone far, followed them and ran another two leagues on the other side of the village, but, although they killed and captured many Indians, they could not overtake Capafi, as thus the cacique was called. This is the first one that we have encountered with a name different from his province. The adelantado returned to the village, which consisted of two hundred and fifty large and good houses. In these he found all his army lodged, and he took quarters in those of the cacique, that were to one side of the village and, as houses of the lord, surpassed all the rest.

In addition to this principal village, throughout all its district (*comarca*) there were many other villages at half a league and one and at a league and a half, and at two and three [leagues]. These had fifty and sixty houses and others of a hundred and more and [some] of less (*y de à mas, y de à menos*) not to mention another multitude of houses that there were scattered about without the order of a village. The site of the entire province is pleasant (*apacible*), the land fertile with a great abundance of food and a great quantity of fish that the natives catch all during the year for their sustenance and keep prepared.

The governor and his captains and the ministers of the royal treasury all became very content over having seen the good parts (*buenas partes*) of that land and its fertility. And, although all the provinces that we had left behind were good, this one had the advantage over them because the natives were indomitable (*indomitos*) and boldly warlike as has been seen and as we shall see further on in some notable cases that occurred in this province, between the Spaniards and the Indians individually and in general, although to avoid prolixity, we shall not tell about all of them. By those that are spoken of, one will see clearly the ferocity of these Indians of Apalache.

Chapter IV. Three Captains go to Explore the District (*Comarca*) of Apalache and The Report That They Bring

The army having rested for some days and recovered to some degree from the recent heavy labor, although the continual attacks and alarms that the enemy gave us both night and day were never lacking during this time, the governor sent bands of people on foot and on horseback with designated captains so that they might penetrate fifteen or twenty leagues into the hinterland to see and to discover what there was in the district (*comarca*) and neighborhood of that province.

Two captains penetrated toward the north side by different areas, the one named Arias Tinoco and the other Andrés de Vasconcelos. These returned without anything happening to them worthy of talking about, the one after eight days, the other nine days after they had left the camp, and they reported almost identically (*casi igualmente*) that they had encountered many villages with many people and that the land was abundant in food and clear of swamps and impenetrable woods (*Montes bravos*).[37] On the other hand the captain Juan de Añasco, who went toward the south, said that he had found a very harsh (*asperisima*) and most difficult land and almost impossible to walk about in because of the undergrowth (*maleças*) of the woods and swamps that he had encountered and steadily worse the farther south he went. On seeing this difference between very good lands and very bad lands, it seemed [appropriate] to me not to go on forward without touching on what Alvar Nuñez Cabeça de Vaca writes in his *Commentaries* about this province of Apalache, where he portrays it as harsh and full of brambles and briars (*fragosa*)[38] obstructed (*ocupada*) by many[39] woods and swamps, with rivers and bad passages (*malos pasos*), poorly populated and sterile, everything the opposite of what we are writing about it. From this, giving credence to what that gentleman writes as to one who is worthy of it, we believe that his trip did not take him so far inland as the one the governor Hernando de Soto made, but rather close to the shore of the sea, for which reason they found the land so harsh and full of woods and bad swamps, as he says, as the captain Juan de Añasco, who went from the principal village of Apalache to look for the sea, encountered and discovered the same thing as we shall see shortly. Many times the latter was very fortunate in not becoming lost because of the bad terrain (*la mala tierra*). The village that Cabeça de Vaca calls Apalache, at which he says Pámphilo de Narváez arrived, I believe that it was not this principal one that Hernando de Soto discovered but rather some other one among the many that this province has, that was closer to the sea and because of being under its jurisdiction was called Apalache like the province itself, because in the village that we have spoken of as being head of it (*Cabeça della*) was to be found what we have seen.[40] It is to be noted, moreover, that a great part of the account that Alvar Nuñez writes about that land is what the Indians told him, as he himself says that those Castilians did not see it, because, as they were few, and almost or completely exhausted (*rendido*), they had no possibility of tramping over it (*hollarla*)[41] and seeing it by their own eyes, nor for searching for food. And accordingly, the majority allowed themselves to die of hunger. And in the account that they gave to him, it is believable that the Indians would speak poorly rather than well of their country (*patria*) in order to discredit it so that the Spaniards would lose the desire to go to it. And with this [explanation], our history does not contradict that of that gentleman.

Chapter V. About the Hardships that Juan de Añasco Experienced in Order to Find the Coast of the Sea

We have said (*Digimos*)[42] that one of the captains who went to explore the district (*comarca*) of Apalache was Juan Añasco. Therefore, so that the toil that he endured may be known in more detail, it should be known that he brought along forty horsemen and fifty foot-soldiers. With him was a cavalier, a relative of the governor's wife, whose name was Gómez Arias, a great soldier, and, wherever he happened to be, he was a great asset, because, with his fine soldierly qualities, his great industry, and good advice and along with being a most excellent swimmer (a useful and necessary thing for the conquests), he eliminated the difficulties that arose both on the land and the water. He had been a slave in Barbary, where he learned the Moorish tongue and he spoke it so correctly that from many leagues into the hinterland he made his way to a frontier with the Christians without the Moors who happened to meet him taking any notice that he was a slave. This gentleman and the people that we have spoken of went toward the south with Juan de Añasco to discover the sea, of which there was a report that it was less than thirty leagues from Apalache. They brought along an Indian so that he would guide them, who had offered himself to serve as their guide, making much of his loyalty and of being a friend of the Christians.

In two days' travel of six leagues each (*en dos jornadas de á seis leguas*) that they marched on a very fine trail (*camino*), wide and level, they reached a village called Aute [and] they found it without people, but full of food. On this trail they crossed two small rivers and easy to cross (*y de buen paso*).

From the Village of Aute they set out in pursuit of their search, carrying food for four days with them. On the second day that they traveled by the same wide and good trail, the Indian who was guiding them began to mislead them, it seeming to him that it was a bad deed to serve as a good guide for his enemies. With this he pulled them off the level and good trail that they had taken up to there and took them through some thick and closed woods of great harshness with many fallen trees without trail or path; and some pieces of land that they encountered, like level pieces of ground where the rains make a pool without woods (*como navaços sin Monte*)[43] that were so spontaneously marshy (*era de suyo tan cenegosa*) that the horses and the foot-soldiers sank into it and on top it was covered with plants (*yerva*) and seemed like solid ground over which one could walk securely. On this trail, or to put it better, in this woods they encountered a variety of bramble (*çarças*)[44] with long and thick branches that spread out over the ground and covered much land. They had some long straight thorns (*puas*) that tore the feet of the horses and the people cruelly, and, although they sought to protect themselves from these bad brambles, it was not possible because there were many and they were stretched out between two [layers of] soil (*entre dos tierras tendidas*) and covered with mud or with sand or with water. With these difficulties and others such as can be imagined, these Castilians tramped about misled for five days, making a turn in one direction and then in others to wherever the Indian wished to lead them according to his whim in order to deceive them or to place them [somewhere] from whence they would never come out.

When the food that they had taken from the village of Aute ran out, they agreed to return to it to obtain more provisions and to continue their search. In returning to Aute they suffered even more hardships on the trail than on coming because it was necessary for them to backtrack over the same passages they had covered in order not to become lost. And as they found the ground already trampled down from the earlier passage, the horses and even the soldiers became mired in it more than they had when it was fresh.

In these difficulties and hardships the Castilians well knew that the Indian was leading them astray knowingly, because on three occasions in those woods, they found themselves so close to the sea that they heard the surf (*resaca*) from it. But the Indian, as soon as he noticed it, led them back inland again with the aim of entrapping them someplace from which they could not get out and so that they would perish from hunger. And, although he would die along with them, he was content with this in exchange for killing them. The Christians were aware of all of this, but they did not dare to let him know, lest he harm them more than what he was doing already on his own; and also because they had not brought any other guide.

Returned to Aute, which they reached dead from hunger, as any people would be who had been four days without having eaten [anything] except plants (*yervas*) and roots, they took provisions for another five or six days as there was [food] in the village in great abundance, and they returned to their exploration, not by better trails than the earlier ones, but rather by other worse ones, if there could be worse ones or if the diligence and malice of the guide were able to find those such as he desired.

One night among those that they slept in the woods, the Indian, for whom the time that he had set for killing the Christians was dragging on too long, not being able to endure it [any longer], picked up a burning brand (*tiçon*) from the fire and hit one of them in the face with it and injured him. The rest of the soldiers wanted to kill him for the effrontery and audacity that he had shown, but the Captain came to his defense, saying that they should put up with him for a time, as he was [their] guide and they had no other. [Having] returned to sleep, an hour later he did the same to another Castilian. Then by way of punishment they gave him many cudgelings, kicks, and punches, but the Indian had not been chastened, as before the day dawned, he hit another soldier with another firebrand.

The Spaniards now no longer knew what to do with him. For the present they contented themselves with giving him many cudgelings and putting him in chains by which he was tied to one of them themselves so that special care would be taken of him.

Soon after the day dawned, they returned to the trail very much afflicted by the great harshness of the earlier trail and the current one and exasperated with the wickedness of the guide. The latter, after they had traveled only a short distance, on seeing himself in the power of his enemies without being able to kill them or to flee from them, having despaired of life, he attacked the soldier who was bringing him along bound by the chain, and grabbing him from behind, he lifted him up in the air and threw him to the ground lengthwise (*tendido*)[45] and before he got up he jumped on top of him with his feet and gave him many kicks. The Castilians and their Captain, no longer being able to endure such effrontery, gave him so many gashes and lance-blows that they left him for dead (*cuchilladas y lançadas*).[46] However, a strange thing was noted; and it was that the swords (*espadas*) and tips of the lances penetrated into him and cut him so little that he appeared [to be] charmed, as he had many sword slashes (*cuchilladas*) that made no more of a wound than the welt (*verdugon*) that a quince tree rod (*vara de Membrillo*) or one from the wild olive tree (*Acebuche*) is wont to make when they hit with it.[47] Juan de Añasco was so enraged by this that he stood up in his stirrups and taking his lance with both hands, he gave him a blow with the lance with all his strength and, despite being a robust and strong man, he did not thrust the head of the lance in halfway. The Spaniards, having noted this, were all amazed and they loosed a greyhound so that it might finish killing him and feast on his flesh and fatten itself on him. Thus this treacherous and insolent Indian received what he deserved.

Chapter VI. The Captain Juan de Añasco Arrived (*llegò*) at the Bay of Aute, and What He Found on It

The Castilians had not gone on fifty paces from the Indian, whom they believed was dead and eaten by the dog, when they heard the greyhound let out some great howls, sounding as though they were killing it. Ours rushed back to see what it was, and they found that the Indian with the little life (*espiritu*) that he had left had thrust his thumbs into either side of the mouth and was tearing it without the dog's being able to defend itself. On seeing this, one of the Spaniards stabbed him many times, with which he finished killing him and another with a woods knife that he was carrying cut off his hands and after [having been] cut, they could not disengage them from the mouth of the dog so strongly had he grasped it.

After this incident the Spaniards returned to the trail amazed that one single Indian could have been enough to have given them so much trouble. But as they did not know which way to turn, they were confused, not knowing what to do. During this confusion fortune assisted them with an Indian whom they had captured on the earlier trip, when they returned to the village Aute, and whom they had brought along with them always. And, although it is true that before the death of the Indian guide, the Spaniards had questioned him many times whether he knew the path to go to the sea, he had never responded a word, remaining mute, because the other one had threatened him with death if he spoke. Therefore, on seeing this obstacle now removed and that he was free of his comrade, and fearing lest they should give him the same death [as they gave] to the other one, he spoke and replied to what they asked him then, and by signs and by some words that it was possible to understand he said that he would bring them to the sea to the very place where Pámphilo de Narváez had built his boats and where he had embarked; but that it was necessary to return to the village Aute, because from there one took the trail directly to the sea. And, even though the Spaniards said to him that he should look because it was close, because from where they were they heard its crashing and surf, he replied that never in their entire life would they reach the sea by the way they were thinking of and that the other Indian had brought them [there] because of the many swamps and the briars of the woods that lay in between. For this [reason] it was necessary to return to the village Aute. With this report the Castilians returned to the village, having wasted five days on this second trip and ten on the first one along with much personal hardship. And it was the loss of the fifteen days which was what they felt the most, for the concern that the governor would have over their delay.

While they were returning to the village, therefore, Gómez Arias and Gonçalo Silvestre, who went on ahead exploring the land, captured two Indians whom they encountered near the village. The latter, on being questioned whether they knew how to guide them to the sea, said they did, and in everything [that they said] agreed with the Indian that they brought along captive had said. With these hopes the Spaniards rested that night with somewhat more content than the past fifteen.

On the following day the three Indians guided the Christians along a level, clear, and pleasant trail through some large and good stubbles (*rastrojos*), [and] on coming out of them, the trail went on wider and more open and they did not encounter a bad passage in all of it except for one narrow and easy to cross swamp as the horses did not sink [even] to the pastern (*quartillas*). After having traveled a little more than two leagues, they reached a very wide and spacious bay (*Baía*) and on walking along its shore, they reached the site where Pámphilo de Narváez had lodged [and] they saw where he had the forge in which he made the nails for his boats [and] they found a great deal of charcoal round about it. And they likewise saw some thick beams hollowed out like troughs (*artesas*)[48] that had served as mangers (*pesebres*) for the horses.

The three Indians showed the Spaniards the site where the enemies killed ten Christians of those of Narváez, as Alvar Núñez Cabeça de Vaca tells of it also in his history.[49] They brought them step by step through all those [places] where Pámphilo de Narváez had tramped, indicating the places where such and such an event had occurred. Finally, they did not omit anything of the notable things that Pámphilo de Narváez did on that bay, about which they gave us an account (? *de que no diesen cuenta*)[50] by signs and words, [some] well and [some] poorly understood, and some spoken in Castilian, as the Indians of all that coast pride themselves greatly in knowing the Castilian tongue and with the utmost diligence try to learn isolated words at least, which they repeat many times.

The captain Juan de Añasco and his soldiers tramped about with great diligence, looking [to see] whether any letters (*cartas*) had been stuck in the holes of trees or whether any letters (*letras*)[51] written on their bark would tell of things that the earlier ones had seen and noted, because it has been customary and very common for the first discoverers of new lands to leave such messages for those who would come after them. The latter notes have many times been of great importance. But they were unable to find anything similar to what they wanted.

After having made this effort, they continued along the coast of the bay to the sea, which was three leagues from there, and with its outgoing [tide], ten or twelve swimmers entered into some old canoes that they found thrown across it and they tested the depth that the bay had in the middle of its channel.

They found it capable of heavy ships. Then they placed signals on the tallest trees that there were around there so that those who might come coasting along through the sea could recognize that site, that it was the same one where Pámphilo de Narváez had embarked in his five boats, so ill fated that none of them [ever] came to light.

After having taken those precautions that we have spoken of and recorded them in writing so that anyone who might go [looking] for it [later] would not miss the spot, they returned to the camp and gave the governor an account of everything that happened and what they had done. The general was very pleased to see them because he had been worried by their tardiness and he rejoiced on learning that there was a port for the ships.

Chapter VII. Thirty Lancers Prepared Themselves for a Return to the Bay of the Holy Spirit

While the three explorer captains went out and returned with the report of what each one of them had seen and discovered, the governor, Hernando de Soto, had not remained resting or idle. But rather with the utmost caution and vigilance, he took counsel with himself, studying and preparing what was best for his army. Seeing, therefore, that the winter was approaching (since it was October already), it seemed best to him not to go forward with his exploration during [the rest of] that year, but to pass the winter in the province of Apalache where there was plenty of food. He decided to send for Captain Pedro Calderón and the rest of the Spaniards who had remained behind with him in the province of Hirrihigua so that they might come to join forces with him, because, where they were, they were not doing anything of importance.

With these intentions he ordered the collecting of all the provisions that should be possible. He ordered the building of many houses in addition to those that the village had so that it would have suitable lodging for all his soldiers. He had the site fortified, which seemed to him to be appropriate for the security of his people. During this time he never ceased to send messengers to Capafi, lord of that province, with gifts and fine words, begging him to come out in peace and to be his friend. The latter refused to accept any terms (*partido*), but rather fortified himself in a very rugged woods, full of swamps and bad passages that he chose for defense and as a secure place for himself (*guarida de su persona*).

Having arranged and provided for the matters mentioned, the governor ordered the auditor Juan de Añasco to prepare for a return to the province of Hirrihigua because it seemed to him that this gentleman was the luckiest captain, who from the beginning of this expedition had achieved better fortune than any other of his [men], and that such a man, with the rest of the good qualities that he had as a soldier, was needed in order to pass through the dangers and difficulties that he would face. With this consideration [in mind] he gave him an order to return to the village of Hirrihigua by the same trail by which the army had come, with another twenty-nine lancers that had been readied and with him [as the] thirtieth so that the captain Pedro Calderón and the rest of the soldiers that were with him might learn what the general was ordering them [to do].

The assignment was a most difficult one as they would have to go back through almost one hundred and fifty leagues of territory inhabited by valiant and cruel enemies, obstructed by swollen rivers, woods, swamps, and bad passages where while [even] the entire army was passing, it had been in great dangers. How much more so now when no more than thirty lancers were going and when they were to find the Indians more prepared than when the governor passed through; and because of the injuries received, more irritated and desirous of avenging themselves.

But all this did not suffice to make the thirty horsemen summoned [for it] decline the journey, but rather they offered themselves in obedience with the utmost promptitude.

[The rest of this chapter is omitted as it contains nothing about Apalachee or Florida's Indians.]

Chapter VIII. What the Thirty Horsemen Did Until They Reached Vitachuco, and What They Found in It

These twenty horsemen and the other ten whose names are lacking [for filling out] the number thirty set out from the village of Apalache on the twentieth of October of the year one thousand five hundred and thirty-nine to go to the province of Hirrihigua where Pedro Calderón remained.[52] They carried the order, which will be spoken of further on, about what they were to do on both sea and land.

They were all traveling very lightly with nothing more than the helmets (*celadas*) and coats of mail (*cotas*) over their clothing and their lances in their hands and huge saddlebags (*sendas alforjas*)[53] on the saddles with some horseshoes and nails and with the provisions for horses and horse-men that could fit in them.

They set out from the camp a good while before the day dawned and so that the word of their coming would not precede them and with it the Indians be prepared to go out to take control of the passages, [and] they traveled with the utmost good speed, running where it was appropriate to run. On this day they lanced two Indians whom they encountered on the trail; they killed them lest, with some outcry, they should alert the others who were scattered through the countryside. They traveled always with this precaution so that the report [of their coming] would not precede them. Thus on that day they covered the eleven leagues that there are from Apalache to the swamp, which they crossed without any opposition from the enemy and this was no small piece of luck, because had a few Indians come, they would have been sufficient to shoot the horses with arrows on so narrow a trail as the one that there was in the woods and in the water.

The Spaniards slept on the plain beyond all of the woods, having run and traveled more than thirteen leagues on that day. While they were rest-ing they kept watch by thirds of ten on ten, as we have mentioned earlier.

Before daylight arrived, they set out in continuation of their trip and traveled the twelve leagues of uninhabited country that there are from the swamp of Apalache to the village of Osachile. They proceeded with fear, lest the Indians learn of their coming and come out to block the passage. For this [reason] they went along slowing down here so that night would overtake them and thus they passed by (por)[54] the village close to mid-night, running at half speed. A league beyond the village they rested at a spot off the trail for what remained of the night, keeping watch by thirds as we have mentioned. On this day they traveled more than another thir-teen leagues (mas de otras trece leguas).[55]

They resumed their journey at the crack of dawn, running at half rein because there were people through the fields, as they always did this while going through inhabited territory so that the news of their coming might not precede them, which was what they feared the most. Thus they ran the five leagues that there are from where they slept to the river of Osachile at the expense of the horses, but they were so good that they endured it all. On arriving close to the river, Gonçalo Silvestre, who was running out ahead because of having pressed his horse more than the others, gave it a glance with plenty of fear that he might find it more swollen than when the army crossed over it. But God was pleased that it should, rather, carry less water now than then. With the joy of seeing it so, he threw himself into it and crossed it swimming and got out onto the level ground (llano) on the other side. When his comrades saw him on the other shore, they were greatly pleased, because they all bore the same fear of finding the river swollen and they crossed it without trouble. To celebrate and rejoice over having crossed the river, they set themselves down to lunch. Then at a moderate pace they traveled the four leagues that there are from the river of Osachile to the village of Vitachuco, where the rashness of the Cacique Vitachuco occurred.

The Castilians went along with the fear of finding the village of Vitachuco as they had left it and they feared that if[56] they had to fight with the inhabitants and to gain the passage by force of arms (braços), in which it might happen that they would kill or wound some man or horse, such a misfortune would double their work and the difficulties of the trail for them. For this [reason] they agreed with each other that no one would stop to fight, but rather that they would all try to pass on forward without stopping. With this determination they arrived at the village, where the anxiety of mind that they had endured evaporated, because they found it all burned and leveled, the walls thrown down to the ground and the bodies of the Indians who died on the day of the battle and those whom they killed on the day that the Cacique Vitachuco struck the blow to the governor were all piled up through those fields, as they had not wished to bury them. They abandoned and destroyed the village, as the Indians told us later, because it was established on a luckless and calamitous site, and the dead Indians, as ill-fated men who had not accomplished their aim, they left without burial as food for the birds and wild beasts, as among them this punishment was one of great infamy. And it was inflicted on those [who were] unlucky and unfortunate in war, as to people accursed and excommunicated (descomulgado) in the eyes of their heathenism. And they did this to this village and to those who died in it because it seemed to them that the unlucky nature of the site and the bad fortune of the deceased had done more to cause the calamity that took place in it than the effort and the valor of the Spaniards as they were so few in number against so many and such valiant Indians.

[The text of Chapter IX is omitted because it is largely irrelevant to the events in Apalachee Province.]

Chapter X. The Governor Captures The Curaca of Apalache

The adelantado Hernando de Soto was not idle while the auditor and Captain Juan de Añasco and the thirty horsemen who went with him made the journey that we have spoken of but rather, perceiving the Indians of the province of Apalache, where he was, with the eagerness and concern that we have seen to kill or to wound the Castilians and that neither by day or by night did they pass up any occasion that arose for them to be able to do so, as it seemed to him that if he were able to have the cacique in his hands, the ambushes (*asechanças*) and treacherous attacks of the Indians would cease at once, put a great effort secretly into learning where the curaca was. And in a few days they[57] brought him a correct report that he was ensconced in some large mountains (*vnas grandes montañas*)[58] of great ruggedness. There, even though he was no more than eight leagues from the camp, it appeared to the cacique that he was secure both because of the quantity of briars (*la mucha maleça*) and difficulty of the trail, woods (*Monte*), and swamps that there were on it,[59] and because of the strength of the site and because of the many and good people that he had with him for its defense.

With this certain news the general decided to make the journey in person. And taking the horses and the necessary foot-soldiers, guided by the same spies, he went to where the cacique was. And after having traveled the eight leagues in three days and after [having] suffered a great deal of hardship on account of the difficulties of the trail, he reached the post. The Indians had fortified it in this manner. In the midst of a very large and thick woods they had cleared a piece where the curaca and his Indians had their lodgings. In order to enter this plaza they had opened a narrow trail more than a half league long through the same woods. Along the entire length of this trail they had built strong palisades (*fuertes paliçadas*) with heavy lumber (*maderos gruesos*) at one-hundred-foot intervals that blocked the passage. In each palisade (*palenque*) there were people on garrison duty assigned to it so that they might defend it. They had not made any exit in order to escape by way of the other side of this fort, as it seemed to them that the site was so strong by itself and the people for its defense so many and so valiant that, even if the Spaniards reached it, it was not possible that they should take it. The cacique Capafi was inside in it well accompanied by his own men, and all of them with the intention of dying rather than see their lord in the power of his enemies.

The governor, [having] reached the mouth of the trail, found the people well prepared for its defense and the Castilians struggled bravely, because, as the trail was narrow, none except the two in front were able to fight. With this difficulty, after receiving many arrow wounds they gained the first and the second palisades by the brute force of the sword. But as it was necessary to cut the bindings of willow rods (*maromas de mimbres*) and other cords (*sogas*) with which the Indians had tied the crosspieces together they received great damage from the enemy. But despite all these difficulties they gained the third palisade and the rest up to the last one, even though the Indians fought so stubbornly that, because of the great resistance that they put up, the Spaniards gained the trail only bit by bit until they reached the point where the curaca was in the cleared area.

There the battle was great because the Indians, on seeing their lord in danger of being killed or captured, fought like desperate men and thrust themselves in the midst of the swords and lances of the Spaniards in order to wound or to kill them, when they could not do so in any other way. For their part, the Christians, on seeing the prize that they desired so close, did everything possible in their struggle in order not to lose what they had worked for by the cacique's slipping away from them. The Indians and the Spaniards were engaged for a long time in this stubborn contest and combat with both sides showing the strength of their spirits even though the Indians received the worst of it because of their lack of defensive arms. The governor, who was desirous of seeing the cacique in his power, seeing him so close, fought to capture him like the very valiant soldier that he was and like a good captain he encouraged his own men by shouting to them by their names. With the latter the Spaniards made so great a charge and wounded the enemy with such ferocity and cruelty that they killed almost all of them.

The Indians, having done more than naked people could have been capable of, those few who remained, so that the Spaniards around them would not kill the cacique, on seeing that they could defend him no longer and also because the curaca himself ordered this to be done at the top of his voice, dropped their weapons and surrendered, and ranged before the governor on their knees, they all as one begged him to pardon their lord Capafi and to order them killed. The general received the Indians compassionately and said to them that he was pardoning both their lord and all of them for their past disobedience on the condition that they should remain good friends despite their past disobedience.

The cacique came on the arms of his Indians because he was not able to walk with his feet [and] managed to kiss the governor's hands. The latter received him with great affability, very happy to see him in his power. Capafi was a man very thick of body, so much so that on account of the excessive corpulence and on account of the chronic indisposition (*los achaques*) and hindrances that it is wont to cause, he was not able to take a single step or even to stay on his feet. His Indians carried him on litters. Whenever he walked about his house it was on all fours (*a gatas*). And this was the reason for Capafi's not having put greater distance between himself and the lodgings of the Spaniards, believing that the distance of the site and its strength would suffice along with the difficulties of the trail, so that it would protect him from them, but he found himself deceived in his confidence.

Chapter XI. The Cacique of Apalache Goes with an Order from the Governor to Bring His Indians under Obedience

With the capture of the cacique the general returned to the village of Apalache very happy because it seemed to him that with the imprisonment of the lord the impudence and audaciousness of his vassals would cease. The latter, since the Castilians entered into that village, had not ceased making sudden attacks by day and by night, raising alarms and making attacks with great frequency, proceeding so astutely and diligently in their ambushes that whenever the Spaniard strayed from the camp, no matter how slightly, they surprised him or wounded him at once. All of this, it appeared to the general, would come to an end with his having the curaca in his power. But all that hope failed to be realized because, with the loss of their cacique, the Indians became more free (*mas libres*)[60] and impudent and they were more persistent in their harassments of the Christians, because, as they no longer had a lord in whose protection and service to occupy themselves, all of them directed their energies into harassing and injuring the Castilians more obstinately than before. Irritated by this, the adelantado spoke to Capafi one day and told him of the disgust that he harbored over the great insolence and the lack of gratitude that his vassals displayed for the good treatment that he had given to their curaca and to them in not having imposed justice on their persons and property for the evil and harm they had done that they could have inflicted in punishment for their rebellion, but rather that he had treated them as friends [and] that, although he was angered with them, he had not killed or wounded any Indian, nor exerted himself to inflict damage on their villages and their planted fields, as he could have laid waste to and burned the entire province because they were the lands and houses of enemies as perverse as they; that he should order them to cease their treacherous conduct and insolent acts if he did not want him to make war on them with fire and blood (*a fuego y sangre*) and that he should keep in mind that he was in the power of the Spaniards, who were honoring him and treating him with great respect and feasting but that it could come to pass that the insults and the great pride of his vassals would cause his death and the total destruction of his land.

The curaca replied with great obsequiousness and signs of deep feeling, saying that it grieved him in the extreme that his vassals did not respond to their obligation from the mercy that his lordship was showing them and that they were not serving him as he desired and as he had sought [to bring about] since he had been in his power, with messengers that he had sent to them commanding them that they should cease to harass and create problems for the Castilians. However, that his notes had had no effect at all because the Indians had refused to believe that they were from the cacique, but rather from someone else (*sino agenos*).[61] Nor could they be persuaded to believe in the mercy and largesse with which his lordship treated him or that he was free. Rather they suspected that he had treated him very badly, held him in irons and in fetters and that this suspicion was the cause for their now proceeding more persistently and obstinately than before in their ambushes (*y que esta sospecha era la causa de que anduciesen aora mas solicitos, y porfiados en sus asenchancas, que antes*).[62] For this [reason] he was begging his lordship that he order his captains and people that, while carrying him with good caution, they should go five or six leagues from the camp with him to where he would guide them [and] that the most noble and important of his vassals had withdrawn there in a large woods, to whom he would call out with great shouts by day or by night, calling to them by their names, and they, on hearing the voice of their lord, would hearken to his call (*su llamado*)[63] and that after having been disabused of their unfounded suspicions, they would become pacified and they would do what they ordered them to, as he would see from doing so; and that this was the most correct and the quickest path for reducing the Indians to his service through the respect and veneration that they have naturally for their curacas. And that he would achieve nothing at all by means of messengers, nor would he negotiate anything with them because they would be bound to reply that they were false and dissembling reports that their enemies themselves were sending to them and not their cacique.

With these words and with a very pained expression Capafi persuaded Hernando de Soto that he should send him to where he spoke of and thus it was ordered and put into effect. Two companies went with him, one of horse, and the other of foot-soldiers. They went strongly charged about the guarding of the curaca and about [observing] the utmost caution lest he flee from them. With this caution they departed from the camp before dawn and traveled six leagues toward the south (*àcia el Mediodia*) [and] around nightfall they reached the post that the cacique spoke of, where his [people] were in some woods that there were in the vicinity (*donde el cacique decia, que estavan los suyos, en vnos Montes, que por alli avia*).

As soon as Capafi reached the spot indicated, three or four Indians of those who had gone with him entered into the woods and in a brief space another ten or twelve among those who were in the woods returned. The curaca gave orders to them that that night they should prepare all the leading Indians who were in the woods so that they might assemble and appear before him on the following day [and] that he wished through his own person to give them news of things that were of great importance for the honor, health, and benefit of all of them. The Indians returned to the woods with this message and the Castilians, after having placed their sentinels and a good guard on the person of the cacique, rested that night with great contentment over what had been arranged, it seeming to them that their mission (*pretension*) was well launched, from which they would return with honor and glory from their expedition, not keeping in mind that the greatest hopes that men of themselves promise themselves are accustomed to result more vain as happened to these Spaniards.

Chapter XII. The Cacique of Apalache, Being Crippled, Fled from the Spaniards on Hands and Knees

Our Castilians, both captains and soldiers, had set themselves to rest and to sleep with great contentment and general rejoicing, believing that they would return to their captain general on the following day with victory and the triumph of bringing along all the leading Indians of that province reduced to his friendship and service, as a result of which they all thought they would remain in peace and rest (*descanso*). Instead they found themselves mocked by their dreams because, as soon as the day dawned, they found themselves without the cacique and without any Indian among the few who had come with him. Surprised, they asked one another what could he have done? And they all replied that it was not possible unless the Indian had conjured up demons and that they had carried him away through the air, because, according to [what] the sentinels affirmed, there had been no carelessness at all by which the cacique could have fled.

But the truth of the matter is that the Castilians, both because of the fatigue from the long journey of the preceding day as well as because of the confidence they had gained from the friendship and from the fine words of Capafi and from his impediment and lameness, they had become careless and both the sentinels and nonsentinels had slept. The curaca, realizing his dream and the good opportunity, dared to slip away from them and put it into action, slipping out through the sentinels on all fours. And his Indians, who were not sleeping, went out before him to waylay the Spaniards [and] running into him, they had carried him on their shoulders. And it was a favor that God did for the Christians that the heathen did not return to behead them, because between their ferocity and the slumber of ours, they could have done so very much at their leisure. But they contented themselves with seeing their lord free from the power of the Castilians and so that they would not return for him, they sought to place him with greater security than there was before. And thus they carried him to where he never made an appearance either then or later.

The two captains, whose names we do not mention out of concern for their honor, and their good soldiers made great efforts, searching for Capafi through those woods, like a wild beast, but as hard as they labored all that day they did not find a trace of him, because it is difficult to catch the bird once he escapes from the net.

The Indians, having placed the curaca undercover, came out against the Christians and uttered a thousand insults and taunts to them, making fun of them and ridiculing them but without doing them any other offense, they let them return to their camp as they did not wish to fight with them. They arrived there crestfallen and ashamed that an Indian whom they brought along under such protection should now have fled from them and escaped on all fours. To the general and the rest of the captains they told a thousand fables in excuse for their carelessness and in support of their honor, all swearing that they had experienced most strange things[64] during that night and that it was not possible unless he had gone through the air with the devils, because, they swore, it was not possible in any other manner on account of the good guard that they had placed.

The governor, when he saw the poor security maintained and that there was no longer any remedy for it, in order not to affront those captains and soldiers, pretended to believe what they said and lent support to it by saying that the Indians were such great sorcerers that they could do much more than that. Nevertheless, he could not but regret the carelessness that had occurred.

[The rest of chapter 12 and all of chapters 13–16 are omitted in this translation as they cover the thirty horsemen's progress from Ocali back to Tampa Bay. The first paragraph of chapter 17 is translated here as it discusses some of the supplies that de Soto had brought with him to Florida and their disposition.]

Chapter XVII. About the Things That the Captains Juan de Añasco and Pedro Calderón Ordained in Fulfillment of That Which the General Had Ordered Them [to Do]

The curaca Mucuço remained for four days with Juan de Añasco and the rest of the Spaniards in which and in the rest [of the days] that our [people] remained in the village of Hirrihigua, his Indians never ceased to carry to their land, coming and going like ants, everything that the Spaniards were going to leave in that village, because of not being able to carry it with them, which amounted to a great quantity, because of manioc (Caçavi) alone, which is the bread of that island of Santo Domingo and Cuba and their neighbors, there remained more than five hundred quintals[65] not to mention a great quantity of cloaks (*Capas*), loose coats (*Sayos*), doublets (*Jubones*), trousers (*Calçones*), hose (*Calças*)[66], and footwear of all kinds (*calçado de todas suertes*), shoes (*Zapatos*), buskins (*Borceguies*), and *Alpargates*.[67] And of weapons (*armas*) there were many cuirasses (*Coraças*), shields (*Rodelas*), pikes, and lances and steel helmets (*Morriones*); that the governor brought a great abundance of all these things as he was rich, not to mention the other things that were necessary for the ships such as sails, tackle (*Jarcias*), pitch, oakum, and tallow, ropes (*Sogas*), panniers (*Espuertas*), hampers (*Serones*), anchors and cables (*Gumenas*); a great deal of iron and steel; that, although the governor carried what he could of these things with him, a great quantity remained; and as Mucoço was a friend, the Spaniards were pleased that he should carry them off, and so his Indians did so and they became rich and happy.

Chapter XVIII. Pedro Calderón Sets Out with His People and the Events of His Trip until He Reaches the Great Swamp

[My translation omits the first two paragraphs of this chapter and begins with the third paragraph, which provides an introduction to an incident recounted in the fourth paragraph that took place in Apalachee].

The Captain Pedro Calderón and his one hundred and twenty comrades covered their daily marches until they reached the great swamp without anything happening to them worthy of being remembered, except that one night before they reached the swamp when the Castilians having camped on a plain near a woods, many Indians emerged from it at all hours to launch surprise attacks and sudden assaults even to the point of entering into the camp and engaging them near at hand. And when the Spaniards pressed them, they returned to the woods fleeing, [but] then emerged again to disturb them. During one of these strikes a horseman rushed to close with an Indian who appeared more daring than the others, who fled from the horseman, but when he realized that he was going to overtake him, he turned around to receive him with an arrow set in his bow and he fired it from so close that at the same time that the Indian released the arrow the Spaniard hit him with a blow of the lance from which he fell dead, but his death was not in vain because, with the arrow that he fired, he hit the horse in the chest, and even though from so close, the shot was so fierce that, with both front and hind legs outstretched, without taking another step or moving at all, the horse fell dead at his feet. As a result the Indian and the horse and his master, all three fell together one on top of the other. And this horse was the famed one belonging to Gonçalo Silvestre, all the excellence of which availed it nothing so that the Indian[68] might respect it.

The Spaniards, astonished that an animal so spirited, ferocious, and courageous, such as is a horse, should have died so suddenly from the wound of solely one arrow fired from close by, as soon as the day dawned, wished to see what had been the nature of the shot. And they opened the horse and found that the arrow had entered by the chest and passed through the middle of the heart, and stomach, and gut, and stopped in the last of the intestines. The natives of this great kingdom of Florida are generally most fierce, strong, and skillful in the shooting of the arrows. But this is nothing to be surprised about if note is taken of the perpetual[69] practice that they have in it at all ages, because the children of three years [of age] and under, once they are able to move about on their feet, moved by their natural inclination and by what they see their fathers doing continually, ask them for bows and arrows and, when they do not give them, they themselves make them from the little sticks (*palillos*) that they are able to find and with them they went about unendingly (*desfenecidos*) after the lizards (or insects—*savandijas*) that they encountered in the house. And if they happen to see some mouse or little lizard (*lagartija*) as it enters into its hole they stay three and four and six hours with their arrow set in the bow waiting with the greatest attention that one could imagine for it to come out in order to kill it. And they do not rest until they have achieved their objective. And when they do not find anything else at which to shoot, they go about shooting at the flies that land on the walls or on the ground. With this practice so continuous and because of the habit that they acquire during it, they become very skillful and ferocious in shooting the arrows. They make the most unbelievable shots with the latter as we shall see and as we shall take note of in the course of the history. And because it is apropos, even though the incident occurred in Apalache, where the governor remained, it will be good to tell about it here as, when we reach that province, things will not be lacking for us to tell about the courageous deeds of its natives. Thus it was that in one of the first skirmishes that the Spaniards had with the Indians of Apalache, the fieldmaster Luis de Moscoso pulled out (*sacò*)[70] an arrow from a wound (*vn flechaço*) on the right side that passed through a leather jacket (*vna cuera de ante*) and another of mail (*otra de malla*) that he wore under it, which, because it was so burnished, had cost one hundred and fifty ducats in Spain, and the rich men had brought many of these as highly esteemed (*y destas avian-llevado muchas los hombres ricos, por muy estimadas*).[71] The arrow also passed through a quilted doublet (*vn jubon estofado*) and wounded him in such a way that in being at a slant it did not kill him. The Spaniards, astonished at so surprising an arrow-shot, wanted to see how good the highly polished coats were in which they had such great confidence. On reaching the village, they placed a basket (*cesto*) in the plaza, which the Indians make out of reedgrasses (*Carriços*), after the fashion of baskets for gathering grapes (*à manera de cestos de vendimiar*)[72] and, having chosen the most valued coat of mail among those which they brought, they placed it over the basket, which was very strong because of [the way] it was woven. And, releasing an Indian from those of Apalache from the chain in which he was, they gave him a bow and an arrow and ordered him to shoot at the coat of mail, which was fifty paces from them.

The Indian, after having shaken his arms (*braços*) with his fists clenched to awaken his strength, fired the arrow. The latter passed through the coat of mail and the basket so cleanly and with such force that, had it encountered a man on the other side, it would also have passed through him. The Spaniards, on seeing the little or no defense that one coat of mail provided against an arrow, wished to see what two coats of mail would do. And so they ordered the placing of another very prized one on top of the one that was on the basket, and, giving an arrow to the Indian, told him that he should shoot as [he had] the first one to see if he were man enough for [it] to pass through both.

The Indian, after shaking his arms once again, as if he were seeking new strength, for the opposing defense had been doubled for him, he released the arrow and hit the coats of mail in the middle of the basket and passed through the four layers of mail and the arrow remained protruding equally on either side. And, when he saw that it had not emerged cleanly from the other side, he said to the Spaniards with great irritation over it that he showed, Let them allow me to shoot another and, if it does not pass through both [sides] cleanly, as it did the one [coat of mail], let them hang me immediately, as this second arrow did not emerge from the bow as well as I wished and, for that [reason] it did not emerge from the [two] coats of mail like the first one.

The Spaniards refused to grant the Indian's petition so as not to see greater insult done to their coats of mail (*cotas*)[73] but from that time forward they remained very disenchanted with the slight [degree] that the very highly valued [coats of mail] could protect them from the arrows. And thus, with their very own owners making fun of them, they called them Dutch Linens, and in their place they made quilted coats (*sayos estofados*) of a thickness of three or four fingers with long flaps that covered the chest and the haunches of the horse. And these coats, made of blankets (*mantas*), resisted the arrows better than any other defensive arms. And the thick and padded coats of mail, that had not been held in esteem, with any whatsoever protection that was placed under them deflected the arrows better than the very stylish and polished ones. For the latter [reason] the ones that had been scorned came to be esteemed and the highly valued ones, disesteemed.

Farther on, in the places where they happened we shall make mention of other shots worthy of renown that took place during this exploration, for certainly they are to be admired. But in the end, taking into consideration that these Indians are conceived and born in the midst of bows and arrows [and] reared and nourished with what they kill with them and so practiced with them, there is no [reason] for us to marvel so.

[Chapters 19–21 are omitted since they are largely irrelevant to the events in Apalachee Province.]

Chapter XXII. Juan de Añasco Arrives at Apalache and That Which the Governor Provided for Finding a Port on the Coast

It should be known that when Captain Pedro Calderón arrived at the village of Apalache, the comptroller, Juan de Añasco, who left the bay of the Holy Spirit with the two brigs headed for Aute, had arrived [there just] six days before without having experienced while at sea anything worthy of remembrance. He landed in Aute without opposition from the enemy because the governor, after reckoning more or less the time that it could take for his voyage, sent a company of cavalry and another of foot-soldiers twelve days before his arrival at the port in order to secure the port and the trail up to the camp. The latter were replaced every four days as, after one group reached the bay, the others returned. And while they were in the port, they had flags placed in the tallest trees so that they might see them from the sea. Juan de Añasco saw them and came to the camp with the two companies, leaving a good crew on the brigs which remained in the bay. Consequently, as these two captains, Juan de Añasco and Pedro Calderón, now found themselves together in the company of the governor and the rest of the captains and soldiers, there was great pleasure and rejoicing because it seemed to them that as they [now] found themselves together in the tasks, no matter how great they might be, they would find them easy because the company of one's friends provides relief and tranquility in the tasks (*afanes*) [that face them]. With this general contentment the Spaniards passed the winter in the village and province of Apalache, where some things occurred that it will be good to give an account of, without paying attention to the order or the time [that they occurred] other than that they took place in this encampment.

A few days after that which has just been spoken of, as the governor was never idle but rather always imagining and outlining within himself what appeared to be appropriate for the exploration and the conquest and later for the settlement of the land, he ordered that a gentleman, a native of Salamanca called Diego Maldonado in whom he had the utmost confidence (who was a captain of infantry and who had served to the great satisfaction of all the army in everything that had been assigned to him up to then),[74] that after handing over his company to another gentleman named Juan de Guzman, native to Talabera of the Queen (*Talabera de la Reyna*) his great friend and comrade, he should go to the bay of Aute and with the two brigs that the comptroller Juan de Añasco had left there, he should go sailing along the coast toward the setting sun for the distance of one hundred leagues and with the utmost care and diligence he was to observe and reconnoiter the ports, inlets (*caletas*), gulfs (*Senos*), bays (*Baias*), estuaries (*Esteros*),[75] and rivers that he should encounter and the shoals (*bagios*) that there might be along the coast and that he should bring back a satisfactory report about all of this. That it was appropriate to have all of this known for what might occur in the future. And he set a limit of two months for him to go and to return.

The captain, Diego Maldonado, went to the bay of Aute and he set sail from there in pursuit of his commission and, after having proceeded sailing along the coast for two months, he returned at the end of them with a lengthy report of what he had seen and explored. He said among other things that at sixty leagues from the bay of Aute he had left behind explored, a most beautiful port named Achusi, sheltered from all winds, capable [of handling] many ships and with such a good depth [even] up to the shores that he could bring his ships close to the land and land on it without opening the hatch (*sin echar compuerta*).[76] From this voyage he brought back with him two Indians from the same port and province of Achusi and one of them was a lord of vassals, whom he captured with trickery and craftiness unworthy of gentlemen, because, when he had reached the port of Achusi, the Indians received him in peace, and with many signs of friendship they invited him to come on shore and take what he might need as if he were in his own [home]. Diego Maldonado did not venture to accept the invitation because he did not trust the unknown friends. Therefore when the Indians perceived this, they set about dealing freely with the Castilians in order to dissolve their fear and the suspicion of them that they might have. And so they went to the brigantines in [groups of] three in three and four in four to visit Diego Maldonado and his comrades, bringing them what they asked for. With this friendliness on the part of the Indians the Spaniards ventured to take soundings and in their small boats (*batelejos*) to reconnoiter everything that there was in the port and when they had seen and bought what was necessary for them to sail, they raised the sails and cast themselves free, carrying the two Indians with them whom they brought imprisoned, as they determined them to be the curaca and a relative of his. The latter, trusting in the good friendship that as heathen and faithful they had made with one another (although for them they were not [good friends]) and influenced by the report that the other Indians had given to them about the brigs, with the desire of seeing what they had never before seen, they ventured to enter onto them and to visit the captain and his soldiers. The latter, as soon as they learned that one of them was the cacique, were pleased to carry him away.

Chapter XXIII. The Governor Sends a Report of His Discovery to Havana. The Boldness of an Indian is Reported

With the report that the Captain Diego Maldonado brought concerning the entire coast and about the good port that he had discovered in Achusi, they were greatly pleased. . . .

[A little more than half a page of the Spanish text is omitted here that tells of this contentment and of the dispatch of Maldonado to Cuba and the instructions given him about his return to meet up with de Soto once more.]

. . . And we shall return to telling of some particular incidents that happened in the province of Apalache. Through these they shall be able to see the fierce qualities of the Indians of that province and along with them their audacity because their deeds show certainly that they knew how to dare and that they did not know how to fear, as will be seen in the following case and in others that will be recounted, although not all of those that occurred, as we shall dispense with the most [of them] in order to avoid becoming tedious.

It is thus: that one day among those of the month of January of the year one thousand five hundred and forty, it happened that the comptroller Juan de Añasco and six other horsemen rode in good conversation, proceeding on horseback along the streets (*Calles*) of Apalache; and, after having traversed them all, it pleased them to go out into the countryside surrounding the village without straying far because of the ambushes of the Indians who were to be found hiding behind each clump of trees [and] because the countryside was not secure. And as they were not going to stray from the village, it seemed to them that they could go out without weapons, at least defensive ones; and thus they went out wearing only their swords, except for one of them named Estévan Pegado, native to Yelves, who had the good sense to go armed and wore a helmet on his head and carried a lance in his hand. While proceeding thus in their conversation they saw an Indian man and an Indian woman who, in a clearing in a woods that was close to the village, were going along harvesting kidney beans that had remained planted from the preceding year. They must have been gathering them more to entertain themselves [or] even to see whether some Castilian would emerge from the village than for the need that they had for the kidney beans, because, as we have said, the province was full of every sort of provision. As the Spaniards saw the Indians they went toward them in order to capture them. The Indian woman on seeing the horses was confounded (*se cortò*) as she did not manage to flee. The husband took her in his arms and running, he carried her to the woods that was nearby and having placed her within the first cluster of trees (*primeras matas*), he gave her two or three shoves (*empellones*) telling her to lose herself within the woods. This done, and being able to have gone with the woman and to have escaped, he did not wish to. Instead he returned running to where he had left his bow and arrows and recovering them he emerged to challenge the Castilians with such determination and such boldness as if they were one other Indian alone like he. And he made this assault in such a manner that he obliged the Spaniards to say to one another that they would not kill him but instead take him alive because it seemed to them a mean thing [to do] that seven Spaniards on horseback should kill a lone Indian on foot, and also because they considered that a spirit as gallant as [the one] the heathen showed did not merit that they should kill him, but rather that they should show him every compassion and favor. With all of them going forward with this determination, they reached the Indian who, because of the distance being short, had not yet been able to fire an arrow and they ran him down and sought to subdue him without letting him get up from the ground, now one and then the other running into him always as he was about to get up and all shouting at him that he should surrender.

The Indian, the more pressure that they put on him, became all the more ferocious and fallen thus as he was, several times placing the arrow in the bow and shooting it to the extent that it was possible and other times, taking stabs at the bellies and hind legs of the horses, he wounded all seven of them, although with slight wounds because they did not give him room to be able to give greater ones. And [then], on escaping from within their feet, he stood up and taking the bow in both hands, gave such a fierce blow with it to the forehead of Estévan Pegado, who was the one who with blows from the lance had harassed him the most, that he caused the blood to spurt over his eyebrows and it ran down his face and half stunned him. The Portuguese Spaniard, on seeing himself attacked and treated so badly, inflamed with anger, said, I regret such [a decision], will it be well for us to wait until this lone Indian kills all seven of us? On saying this, he gave him a lance thrust through the chest that passed through to the other side and knocked him down dead. [Having] performed this feat (*Hecha esta haçana*), they inspected their horses and found them all wounded, although with slight wounds, and returned to the camp, marveling at the audacity and the strength of the barbarian and blushing and ashamed to recount that one lone Indian had stymied seven on horseback in such a fashion.

Chapter XXIV. Two Indians Offer to Guide the Spaniards to Where They May Find Much Gold[77]

All the time that Governor Hernando de Soto was wintering in the encampment and village of Apalache, he always took care to inquire and to learn what lands [and] what provinces there were on ahead toward the setting sun through the region that he planned and designed to enter during the following summer in order to see and explore that kingdom. With this desire he went about constantly gathering information from the Indians, who had been servants in his army from days past and from those whom they captured recently, importuning them for them to tell him what they knew of that land and its parts. Therefore, as the general and all his captains and soldiers went about [among them] with this concern and to this purpose, it happened that among the Indians whom those who were running through the countryside captured, was a young Indian of sixteen or seventeen years of age. Some Indians recognized him, who were servants of the Spaniards and had love for their masters. These gave them news, so that it might be given to the governor, of how that young man had been the servant of some trading Indians, who were accustomed to enter many leagues into the hinterland with their merchandise, buying and selling, and that he had seen and knew what the governor sought so much to learn. Let it be understood that these merchants did not go to seek gold or silver, but rather to exchange some things for others, which is the trading of the Indians (*que era el mercadear de los Indios*) because they do not have any use for money. With this report they inquired of the youth what he knew. He replied that it was true that he had news of some provinces that the merchants, his masters, had traveled through and that he would venture to guide the Spaniards twelve or thirteen days' journey along the trail that there was in that [portion] which he had seen. The governor handed the Indian over to a Spaniard, charging him with the responsibility of taking special care of him lest he flee from them. But the youth himself freed them of this worry, because in a short time he became so friendly and familiar with the Spaniards that he seemed to have been born and reared among them.

A few days after the capture of this Indian they captured another of almost the same age or a little older. And, as the first one knew him (*lo conociese*),[78] he said to the governor: lord, this young man has seen the same lands and provinces as I, and others farther on that he has traveled through with other richer and wealthier merchants than my masters.

The newly captured Indian confirmed what the first one had said and he very willingly offered to lead and guide them through the provinces that he had traveled through, which he said were many and large. Questioned about the things that he had seen in them, whether they held gold or silver, or precious stones, which was what they most desired to know, and after showing him jewels of gold and pieces of silver and fine stones from rings that were to be found among some captains and leading soldiers so that he might understand better the things that they were asking him about, he replied that in a province that was the farthest away (*postrera*) that he had traveled through, called Cofachiqui, there was a great deal of metal like the yellow one and like the white one and that the major business of the merchants, his masters, was the buying of those metals and the selling of them in other provinces. In addition to the metals he said that there was a very great quantity of pearls. And in order to tell of this he pointed to a mounted pearl (*Perla engastada*) that he saw among (*entre*) the rings that they showed him. Our Spaniards became very happy and joyful with these reports, desiring to see themselves in Cofachiqui already in order to be masters of the great amount of gold and silver and precious pearls. Returning to the particular happenings that occurred in Apalache between the Indians and the Spaniards. Thus it was that the month of March having already begun, it happened that twenty horsemen and fifty foot-soldiers went out from the camp and went one league from the principal village to another of that jurisdiction (*y fueron vna legua del Pueblo principal a otro de la jurisdicion*)[79] to bring back maize which there was in abundance throughout the little villages (*Pobleçuelos*) of all that district (*Comarca*) in such great quantity that the Spaniards during all the time that they remained in Apalache never went as far as a league and a half from the principal village in order to provide themselves with maize (*çara*)[80] and other seeds (*otras semillas*)[81] and legumes (*legumbres*)[82] that they ate. Therefore as they had collected the maize (*Maiz*)[83] that they were to take, they concealed themselves in the village itself with the desire of capturing some Indians if they should come to it. They placed a guard as a lookout (*Pusieron Vna Atalaya*)[84] in the highest part of a house (*casa*) that was very much different from the others[85] and appeared [to be a] temple (*Templo*). A good interval [having] passed, the lookout (*Atalaya*)[86] signaled that in the plaza, which was very large (*en la Plaça que era muy grande*)[87] there was an Indian looking about [to see] if there was anything in it.

A gentleman named Diego de Soto, nephew of the governor, who was one of the best soldiers of the army and a very good rider, galloped out to capture the Indian more in order to show his skill and courage than for [any] need that he had. The Indian, as he saw the horseman, ran a race with the horse with very great speed, to see whether he could escape from him by flight. That the natives of this great kingdom of Florida are fast and great runners and pride themselves on it. But, on seeing that the horse was gaining ground on him, he dashed in under a tree that was nearby, which is the shelter that the foot-soldiers (*Peones*)[88] always have recourse to in order to defend themselves from the horses in the absence of pikes. And, putting an arrow in the bow that, [for] as we have said on other occasions, they always go about armed with these weapons, he waited for the Spaniard to come within range. The latter, not being able to enter under the tree, passed by, galloping to the side [of it] and aimed a lance thrust at the enemy by running the lance over his left arm to see if it would be possible to reach him. The Indian, after protecting himself from the blow of the lance, fired the arrow at the horse at the moment that he came even with him and managed to hit him between the girth (*la cincha*) and the knee with such great force and skill that the horse went on forward stumbling for fifteen or twenty paces and fell dead without moving a hind foot or a forefoot. At this point another horseman named Diego Velázquez, an equerry of the governor, no less courageous and skilled in horsemanship than the earlier one, came galloping at half speed. The latter had followed Diego de Soto in order to assist him if it should be necessary. Therefore, on seeing the hit that the Indian had made on his comrade, he speeded up his horse and, not being able to enter under the tree, he passed to the side of it, aiming another lance blow [at him], like that of Diego de Soto. The Indian had the same luck as on the first shot because, as the horse drew abreast, he fired another arrow to the back of the knee, and like the earlier one, it made him go tumbling until it fell dead at the feet of its companion. The two Spanish comrades got up on their feet at full speed with their lances in their hands and, in order to avenge the death of their horses, rushed to attack the Indian. The latter, content with the two good shots that he had made in so brief a time and with such good fortune, took off running toward the woods, jeering at them and ridiculing them, turning his face toward them to make grimaces and gestures at them, and saying to them, while keeping the same pace as them, without trying to run as fast as he could, Let us all fight on foot and we shall see who are the best ones. With these words and others that he spoke in scorn for the Castilians, he escaped, leaving them behind sorely grieved over so great a loss as that of the two horses. Because these Indians realized the advantage that the Spaniards on horseback enjoyed over them, they sought and took more pleasure in killing a horse than four Christians. And thus with the utmost care and effort, they shot at the horse rather than at the horseman.

Chapter XXV. About Some Dangerous Moments of Fighting that Happened in Apalache and about the Fertility of that Province

A few days after the bad experience of Diego de Soto and Diego Veláz-quez, another occurred not much better, and it was that two Portuguese, the one called Simón Rodríguez, native to Villa de Maruan, and the other, Roque de Yelves, native to Yelves, went out beyond the village on their horses to gather green fruit (*fruta verde*)[89] that there was in the woods. And, although they would have been able to pick it from the lower branches from the backs of their horses, nothing would satisfy them but to dismount and to climb up into the trees to gather it from the high branches because it seemed to them that it was better [there]. The Indians, who never lost an opportunity that was presented to them to be able to kill or to wound the Castilians, on seeing the two Portuguese Spaniards [who had] climbed into the trees, went out after them. Roque de Yelves, who saw them first before his comrade did, giving the alarm, jumped down from the tree and went running to mount his horse. One Indian among those who came after him, shot at him with an arrow with a flint point (*vn harpon de pedernal*) and hit him in the back. And one-fourth of the arrow came out through his chest, from which he fell on the ground without being able to get up. They did not permit Simón Rodríguez to descend from the tree, [but] instead shot at him with arrows up above as if he were some wild beast [that had] climbed up there and they brought him down dead, pierced from side to side with three arrows; and he had scarcely fallen when they removed his head, I mean all the skin round about it (*todo el Casca en redondo*) (that it is not known with what artifice they remove it with such very great ease) and they carry it off as evidence of their feat. They left Roque de Yelves where he fell, without removing his scalp, because the help from the Spaniards on horseback was coming very close because the distance was short [and] gave no time for the Indians to remove it. The latter told of the incident in a few words, and, after asking for confession, soon expired. With the noise and the sudden assault of the Indians, the two horses belonging to the Portuguese fled toward the camp, and the Spaniards who went to help them, recovered them and found that one of them had a drop of blood on his hind leg and they brought it to a veterinary surgeon (*Albeytar*) so that he might heal it. The latter, after seeing that the wound was no greater than that of a lancet said that there was nothing there to be cured [but] on the following day when it dawned, the horse [was] dead.

The Castilians, suspecting that there must have been some arrow wound, opened him at the wound and following its mark through the length of the body, they found an arrow that after having passed through the thigh (*muslo*) and the gut (*tripas*) and the liver (*asadura*)[90] was lodged in the chest cavity, as it lacked only four fingers-width of flesh to have emerged through the breastbone. The Spaniards remained amazed, it seeming to them that a missile from an harquebus would not have passed through so much. Although of little importance these specific incidents are recounted [here], because they occurred in this encampment and because of their ferocity, which is notable. And because it is now the occasion for us to conclude telling of the things that occurred in the principal village of Apalache, we say in summary (because to tell of all of them would be a very lengthy matter) that the natives of this province during the entire time that the Spaniards were wintering in their land showed themselves [to be] very warlike and eager and that they showed concern and persistence in attacking the Castilians without losing an opportunity or occasion, no matter how slight it might be in which they might be able to wound or to kill those who strayed from the camp, even though it was a very short distance.

Alonso de Carmona in his Pilgrimage (*Peregrenacion*) notes particularly the ferocity of the Indians of the province of Apalache, about whom he speaks these words that are taken [from him] word for word: These Indians of Apalache are of great stature (*grande estatura*)[91] and very courageous and spirited. Because, as they had come to grips and fought with the earlier [men] of Pámphilo de Narváez and made them leave the land, as heavily as it weighed on them [to do so], they found us in their hair every day and each day we had skirmishes with them and as they were not able to gain anything with us because of our governor being very valiant, energetic, and experienced in war with Indians, they resolved to roam through the woods in gangs of four, and as the Spaniards went out for firewood and as they were cutting it in the woods, at the sound of the ax the Indians rushed up and killed the Spaniards and loosed the chains of the Indians whom they brought with them to carry it on their backs and they stripped the Spaniard of his scalp (*Corona*), which was what they prized most so that they might carry it on the arm (*braço*) of the bow with which they fought. And at the shouting that they did and at the alarm (*arma*) that they gave, we rushed out at once and found the bad business already done, and in this fashion they killed more than twenty soldiers and this happened on many occasions. And I recall that on one day seven on horseback left the camp to *ranchear,* which is to forage for some food and to kill some little dog in order to eat it, that all of us availed ourselves of in that land and we considered ourselves fortunate on the day that we obtained part of one, and not even pheasants tasted better to us. And, while roaming about in search of these things, they met up with five Indians who were awaiting them with their bows and arrows and they drew a line on the ground and they told us that we should not cross it because we would all die. And the Spaniards, as they would not put up with mockery rushed to do battle with them. And the Indians released their bows and killed two horses and wounded another two and they badly wounded one Spaniard. And the Spaniards killed one of the Indians and the others escaped through [the use] of their feet, because they are truly very swift and the adornments of clothing do not hinder them, but rather, their going about naked helps them a great deal.

Up to here is from Alonso de Carmona.

In addition to the vigilance against those who strayed, they maintained it also against the entire army, keeping it on edge with alarums and sudden attacks which they launched both day and night without choosing to engage in a battle of people assembled in an organized squadron, but rather with ambushes, concealing themselves in the clumps of bushes and little bunches of trees no matter how small they were and where one least thought they might be able to be, from there they would emerge like highwaymen to inflict the damage that they could. But this is enough in reference to the valor and ferocity of the natives of the province of Apalache. About its fertility, which is great, we have [already] spoken as well, because it has an abundance of Indian corn (*Zara*), Maize (*Maiz*),[92] and many other seeds (*semillas*) of beans (*Frijoles*) and squash (*Calabaça*) (that in the language of Peru they call *çapallu*) and other legumes (*legumbres*) of diverse species (*especies*), not to mention the fruits that they encountered like those of Spain, such as cherries (*Ciruelas*) of every type, three sorts of nuts (*nueces*), one of which is all oil (*aceyte*), acorn (*Bellota*) from the live oak (*Encina*) and the [deciduous] oak (*Roble*) in so great a quantity that it remains on the ground at the feet of the trees from one year to another because, as these Indians do not have any tame cattle that might eat it, nor do they have need of it, they allow it (*la*)[93] to spoil.

In conclusion, so that one may see the abundance and fertility of the province of Apalache, we say that the entire army of the Spaniards and the Indians whom they brought as servants, who amounted to more than fifteen hundred persons in all, and more than three hundred horses, during the five months and more that they spent wintering in that encampment, sustained themselves with the food that they gathered at the beginning and, when they needed [more] of it, they found it in the small villages of the district (*comarca*) in such great quantity that they never went as far as a league and a half away from the principal village to bring it back. In addition to this fruitfulness of the harvest, the land has very good suitability for the raising of every sort of cattle because (*porque*)[94] it has good woods, pasture-lands (*Dehesas*) with good waters, and swamps and ponds (*Lagunas*) with a great deal of sedge (*Juncia*) and reed (*Enea*)[95] for black cattle (*ganado prieto*)[96] which do very well on it (*que se cria muy bien con ella*) and when eating it (*comiendola*) they do not need grain. And this suffices for an account of what there is in this province and about its good qualities, one of which is the potential for producing a great deal of silk in it because of the abundance of mulberry trees that it has. Also it has a great deal of excellent fish.

End of Second Book.

NOTES

1. The Varners rendered this as "build."

2. Neither Ranjel nor Elvas provided a specific name for the province that de Soto entered after leaving Napetuca. They gave the name Uzachil or Ucachile to its head chief, which closely resembles the name Osachile, which the Inca gave to the province. But Hernández de Biedma identified it as Yustaga, a name confirmed by other sources from the 1560s on.

3. The Varners rendered this as "pitched camp." The verb *alojarse* has more the sense of taking lodging or billeting troops in some sort of existing structure, though there is no indication of any such structure beyond the choice of the verb *alojarse*.

4. Relative to the Indians' opposition to the Spaniards' attempt to bridge the river, it is likely that the Inca confused this crossing with the next one, between Osachile and Apalachee. Neither Ranjel nor Elvas indicates any such problem in crossing the Suwannee, which they named River of the Deer because Uzachil sent de Soto a deer carcass as a present when he reached the river. That gesture does not seem compatible with armed opposition.

5. In this paragraph the Inca seems to be talking about the reception the Spaniards received in their progress through the first half of Apalachee. No such conflict is reflected in the other chroniclers' account of the Spaniards' progress through Osachile Province, which was known later as Yustaga.

6. The Shelby translation gives six leagues rather than 10 as the distance between Vitachuco and Osachile.

7. The Varners rendered this as "ambush" in the singular, as though they had all been captured in one big operation. There were many forays according to Ranjel.

8. As they have done so often, the Varners telescoped this admittedly wordy phrasing into "made good domestics." The Spanish is *eran domesticos, y de buen servicio.*

9. *Condicion* might be rendered also as "natural temper or constitution" or as "quality," "rank," or "class in society."

10. Unfortunately, the Inca chose the wrong province for including a description of a mound complex. None is found in the province of Osachile. Again he may have been thinking of its western neighbor, Apalachee, which has a significant mound complex, although its Lake Jackson complex had been abandoned before de Soto's arrival in Apalachee territory. This misplacement of the mound complex was not remarked upon in the note for this passage in the Shelby translation.

11. A *pica* is among other things a pike or long lance or a bullfighter's goad and as a unit of measure 12 3/4 feet.

12. This might be rendered as "wealth."

13. Here the Varners deleted the word "squared" in their rather free rendition of this passage.

14. The Varners also deleted this important phrase, apparently because it detracts from the smooth flow of the sentence.

15. The words of this phrase, beginning with "instead," were deleted by the Varners.

16. "Streets," the usual meaning of *calles*, seems inappropriate here, though it is what the Varners used. *Calle* might also be rendered as "lane," "narrow way between hedges," or "paved way."

17. As a unit of measure, an *estado* is 2.17 yards. The Varners rendered this imprecisely as "more than the height of a man."

18. Close to the river was a last Timucua village named Asile, which the Inca omitted.

19. This is *maleza de zarzos* in modern Spanish.

20. The Varners rendered this as "and other low bushes."

21. In their rendition, the Varners have shortened this passage and moved the participle *entretegiendose* or "intertwining itself" so that it modifies only "the briars," whereas in the Spanish text it modifies both the briars and the understory or low woods. The Spanish here is *con mucha maleça de çarças, y otro Monte bajo, que entretegiendose con los arboles gruesos, espessavan y cerravan de tal manera el Monte, que parecia un fuerte muro.*

22. The Spanish here, *por lo qual no avia paso alguno por donde pasar el Monte y la cienaga, sino por vna senda,* was rendered thus by the Varners: "Through this entanglement and mud there was no passage except that of a small footpath."

23. *Matas* might also be rendered as "copse," or "grove of trees."

24. The Varners rendered this as "pieces of wood fastened together." *Atar* can be rendered as "fasten," but its primary meaning is "to tie or bind."

25. The term "better armed" here would seem to refer to the use of armor and indicate that the foot-soldiers had little or no armor.

26. In their somewhat free translation, the Varners dropped the parentheses here and broke this run-on Spanish sentence into two separate sentences. They ended the first sentence just prior to the material that is in parentheses in the Spanish text and in my translation (*porque no eran menester los cavallos*). In rendering *menester* as "useless" rather than "not necessary," they have changed the meaning slightly.

27. The Varners' rendering of *hocinos* as "hatchets" is somewhat misleading, as its usual meaning is "billhook," a sort of hatchet with a hooked point.

28. The Varners deleted the last six words of this sentence, *para alojamiento del Exercito.*

29. The Varners' rendition of this phrase as "by dint of arms" is correct technically, but possibly misleading because it might be understood as "by means of military power."

30. The Varners rendered this last clause as "this being the only way he could have *them*" (my italics). The Spanish, *pues no lo podia aver,* is singular. The Varners required the plural here because they had translated the preceding (singular) *alojamiento,* which I translated as "campground," as the plural "quarters."

31. This latter phrase was deleted by the Varners.

32. The Varners rendered this as "heavens" as though it were plural.

33. The Inca alone of the four de Soto chroniclers failed to mention Apalachee's important eastern gateway village of Ivitachuco by name, probably because he had confused it with Utina's Napetuca.

34. The verb *cesaron* here does not have the negative, but the context seems to require one if this passage is to make sense. The Varners rendered *cesaron* as "they continued." But Shelby rendered it as "they never ceased."

35. The Spanish here is *Entre las sementeras se derramava gran poblaçon de casas sueltas, y apartadas vnas, y otras, sin orden de Pueblo.*

36. The Varners rendered this as "tedious."

37. The Varners rendered this as "extensive forests."

38. *Fragosa* might be rendered also as "craggy," "rough," "uneven," or "noisy." The Varners chose "craggy," not a very appropriate choice for describing the sandy flat coastal plain.

39. The Varners deleted "many."

40. In their rendition the Varners rewrote this long sentence extensively, beginning it with the phrases with which it terminates in the Spanish text.

41. *Hollar* might be rendered also as "to humble, pull down, depress, or trample underfoot." The Varners rendered it as "to subject it."

42. The Varners changed this to the singular "I have said." They also edited the chapter's title to some degree.

43. The primary meaning of the term *navaço* or *navazo* in modern Spanish is "Kitchen-garden in Sanlucar upon a sandy shore." This is the only meaning given by Cassell. Velázquez adds "2. Level piece of ground where the rains make a pool."

44. *Çarças* or *Zarzas* in modern Spanish is specifically "blackberry brambles." These probably were dewberries, which are common in the area even today.

45. In their rendition the Varners deleted this detail, leaving simply "cast him to the ground."

46. A *cuchillada* is a cut or slash with a knife or other cutting instrument. From the subsequent lines it is evident that these were administered with a sword rather than a knife or *cuchillo*.

47. The Varners have rephrased this sentence and the one that precedes it and those that follow on the rest of this page and have given a somewhat free rendition, deleting details in places and embellishing the original text in others.

48. *Artesa*, a special trough in which dough is worked, can be rendered also as "canoe."

49. The Varners put this parenthetical remark in parentheses that are not found in the original.

50. I am presuming that *no* should be *nos* or "us," as a negative here does not make sense.

51. Here "letter" is used in the sense of "letter of the alphabet." In the preceding line, the Spanish *cartas* is "letters" in the sense of "missives."

52. In the omitted portion of the preceding chapter the Inca gave the names of twenty of the soldiers. The Inca, Elvas, and Ranjel all differed on the time of the departure of this expedition. According to Elvas they set out on Friday, November 17. According to Ranjel, Añasco reached Tampa Bay on November 19.

53. The correct meaning of *sendas* is "on either side," and that may well be what the Inca intended. But it was and is often used incorrectly or colloquially to mean "huge," "abundant," "heavy," "good," and "strong."

54. *Por* could also be rendered as "through," as Shelby has done.

55. The Varners rendered this as "another thirteen leagues," deleting *mas de* or "more than."

56. The "if" of the 1723 edition does not appear in Shelby's translation of this passage.

57. The Varners have edited Garcilaso's account here to identify the "they" of the Spanish text as "his spies."

58. Though this could be rendered conceivably as "large hills" or "heavily wooded wastelands," the Inca's use of *grande* before it suggests that he meant "mountains" or "hills." There are no mountains, of course, in the vicinity of Tallahassee.

59. Shelby's translation omits the words "both because of the quantity of briars and difficulty of the trail, woods, and swamps that there were on it."

60. The Varners rendered this as "more bold" and have rephrased this entire passage to some degree in their translation.

61. The Varners deleted this passage. They also placed the curaca's reply in quotation marks (not found in the 1723 text) and changed the person of the verbs to accord with that editorial liberty with the Spanish text.

62. The Varners have drastically altered the meaning of this passage in their translation: "And now because of this suspicion you [de Soto] should be even more solicitous and persistent in your artifices than previously, and I therefore beg your Lordship. . . . " Although the Spanish text has a period after *antes* or

"previously," the Varners have changed it to a comma, detaching this closing clause from the long sentence and joining it instead with the sentence that follows.

63. This is still within the long quotation created by the Varners that has required them consistently to change the "his" in such phrases to "my" as if the Spanish text were *mi llamado.*

64. The Varners rendered the Spanish here, *que avian sentido aquella noche cosas estrañissimas,* as "All affirmed that they had heard very strange noises that night."

65. A quintal is a hundredweight, a metric quintal one hundred kilograms.

66. The primary meaning of *Calzas* is "long loose breeches or trousers."

67. A cheap sandal or shoes made of hemp. In modern Brazil the footwear bearing this trade name usually has a canvas top and a hemp sole.

68. Here the Varners changed "the Indian" to "an infidel."

69. The Varners deleted the word *perpetuo,* but after "surprised" they added "at their prowess," which is absent in the Spanish text.

70. The Varners rendered *saco* as "was struck."

71. The Varners rendered this as "and it was the type which many rich men wore and highly esteemed." In the Spanish text "many" or *muchas* is feminine and thus cannot be a modifier of *ricos hombres* or "rich men." The words "the type" were added by the Varners.

72. The Varners rendered this simply as "use for harvesting," editing out the words "after the fashion of" and "baskets for gathering grapes." And the earlier reference to *cesto* or "basket" the Varners rendered by the more generic term "receptacle."

73. The Varners transformed "coats of mail" here into the generic "arms."

74. The Varners included the phrases "a native of Salamanca" and "in whom he had the utmost confidence" within the parentheses, even though they are not so included in the Spanish text.

75. *Caletas* might be rendered also as "coves," "creeks," or "small bays." *Esteros* could be rendered also as "a large lake near the sea" or "tidal creek," or "tidal marshes." The Varners rendered it as "creeks."

76. Shelby rendered this as "without building up breakwaters."

77. Here the Varners added "and silver," which does not appear in the 1723 edition.

78. This might be rendered also as "became acquainted with him." The Varners put this in the present tense, rendering it as "being acquainted." The form *conociese* does not appear in the declension of this verb in modern Spanish, but it is probably the equivalent of *conociera,* the third person singular past subjunctive of *conocer.*

79. The Varners telescoped this passage thus, changing the meaning in several respects: "went out from the camp to bring corn from the principal village of another district one league distant." In deleting "principal Village" as the point of departure, they transferred "principal" to make it a modifier of the village that was their destination. And *otro* or "other," which refers clearly to the village that was their destination, the Varners transformed into a modifier of *jurisdición* de-

spite the fact that *otro* is masculine and *jurisdición* feminine. The Varners have changed the meaning additionally by rendering *jurisdición* as the bland generic "district."

80. *Çara* is *Zara* in modern Spanish. It is from the Quechua *sara*, meaning maize.

81. The Varners rendered this as "other grains." As grains are seeds, such a rendering is legitimate, though possibly misleading in view of the more literal primary meaning of *semillas* as seeds.

82. The Varners rendered this as "vegetables," which again is a legitimate meaning. But the English cognate "legumes" seems preferable in view of the prominence of beans as an Indian crop. *Legumbres* also could be rendered as "pulse."

83. With their penchant for the generic term, the Varners here rendered *Maiz* as "food."

84. The term *Atalaya* means primarily a "watchtower or height from which a considerable tract of country can be viewed" and secondarily "a guard placed on such a height." The Varners rendered it simply as "guard."

85. Here the Varners have "from all the others," adding the word "all."

86. In the Varners' rendition he remained a generic "guard" here also.

87. In their interpretive rendition here, the Varners telescoped "the Plaza that was very large" into "the main plaza."

88. The Varners rendered *Peones* here as "pedestrian." This makes as much sense as referring to an infantryman as a "pedestrian."

89. The Varners rendered this as "fresh fruit" rather than "immature." They also rewrote the sentence by dropping the phrase "beyond the Village," and adding "lying near the village" after "woods."

90. This could also be rendered as "lungs" or "entrails."

91. The Varners rendered this as "gigantic in stature," which may be stretching the point a bit, though "huge" is one of the meanings given for *grande* in the dictionary. But it is more generally used simply in the sense of "large" or "big," without the connotation of gigantism.

92. The use of two separate words for maize suggests that Garcilaso is referring to separate varieties, as he subsequently does with oaks. *Sarah* may be derived from *Zea mays*. The Varners masked this by rendering this as "maize or corn."

93. The Varners rendered this as plural, "them." In the mid-seventeenth century, they are recorded as using acorns for food.

94. The Varners broke this link by deleting "because" and rendering what follows "because" as a separate sentence, with no link to what precedes it.

95. *Enea* is the common cattail reed or *Typha*. In rewriting this passage, the Varners eliminated Garcilaso's positing of two types of swamp foliage, translating it to read "lagoons with quantities of rushes."

96. Here the Varners stripped the cattle of their color, leaving "for cattle." Shelby's translation here has "hogs" rather than "black cattle."

Epilogue: What Is Next in de Soto Research?

Charles R. Ewen

Oftentimes the true events of history are more fantastic than the most lurid works of fiction. Such is the case of the four-year odyssey of Hernando de Soto in the southeastern United States. Coming fewer than 50 years after Columbus's first voyage, it was the longest overland reconnaissance of the United States during the sixteenth century, rivaling the Lewis and Clark expedition centuries later.

Given this amazing story, why do we know so little about the Spanish Colonial past of the southeastern United States?

Research Trends

Spanish Colonial archaeology during the twentieth century has loosely followed the general developmental trend in historical archaeology. The earliest work tended to focus on standing structures (Palm 1945, 1952; Goodwin 1946) and artifact studies (Mendoza 1957; Goggin 1960). In an interesting aside, one of the earliest Spanish Colonial studies in the Caribbean (Morales Patino and Acevado 1946) addressed the Contact period, preceding the Columbian Quincentennial emphasis by nearly half a century.

A recent assessment of the literature (Ewen 1990) employed a topical approach in a historiography of Spanish Colonial archaeology. This method permits the identification of certain "core interests" in Spanish Colonial archaeology: (1) Contact period, (2) missions, (3) settlements and architecture, (4) material culture studies, and (5) shipwrecks. However, by the eve of the Quincentennial, investigation had advanced to the point where the synthesis of archaeological and historical works on the Spanish Colonial archaeology of the southeastern United States was possible. Plans were also made to embark on major new field projects such as those at Isabela in the Dominican Republic and the mission of San Martín in north-central Florida.

Although Columbus kept sailing until 1504, most of the Quincentennial activities were over by the end of October 1992. Despite the anticipation, the popular boom was a bust. The North American public never really got behind the Quincentennial as it had the Bicentennial. A couple of disappointing movies, a mildly successful PBS series, an unsuccessful Jubilee, America's pathetic exhibit at Expo '92 in Seville (see Skowronek 1995), and a spate of "Columbus: The Man" books left little visible impression. The celebrations that did succeed focused not so much on Spain's efforts in America as on the consequences of contact (*Seeds of Change*, Viola and Margolis, 1991).

In an effort to explain the failed Jubilee, some scholars tried to blame the public's flagging interest in the Spanish chapter in American colonial history on the fact that the Quincentennial was touted as politically incorrect. Many of the Columbian texts vilified the role of Spain in America. Kirkpatrick Sale's *Conquest of Paradise* (1990) was not content merely to bash Columbus but indicted all European males as well. The University of California at Berkeley ignored the Spanish discovery and declared 1992 the year of the Native American, followed by the United Nations' declaring 1993 the year of indigenous peoples. The Episcopal church went along with this idea and produced literature comparing Columbus to a pirate and worse. In retrospect, though, one wonders how much these efforts really hurt interest in Spanish Colonial archaeology.

The Columbus bashing, if properly done, should only have served to heighten the public's interest in the Spanish Colonial period. The Florida Museum of Natural History's touring *First Encounters* exhibit couldn't buy the kind of advertising the exhibit got from picketing Native Americans. As for Berkeley's declaration, a colleague noted that, given the radical tendencies of that institution, the pronouncement would have been remarkable only if Berkeley had not condemned the Quincentennial. The Episcopal church (never a big fan of Catholicism or its practitioners for historical reasons) had some clever literature, but who saw it? (Now if the Baptists had taken up Columbus bashing. . . .)

The Quincentennial might have been expected to receive little attention. The United States is still largely an Anglo nation, which explains why the American Bicentennial got all the good press. However, Spanish Colonial archaeology *did* benefit from the Quincentennial, which raised scholarly interest. The effects have been chronicled in the Organization of American States' newsletter *Quincentennial of the Discovery of America: Encounter of Two Worlds*. Several synthetic works were published detailing recent Spanish Colonial archaeological research. Most notable were the three-volume *Columbian Consequences* (Thomas 1989–1991) and the popular *First Encounters* (Milanich and Milbrath 1989).

Fieldwork started during the eighties and nineties has been generally successful. A multiyear project initiated at Isabela, Columbus's first planned colony, focused on the excavation of the public and private sectors of that settlement. It will tell us much about Spanish Colonial adaptations. The community-oriented archaeological work has continued at St. Augustine, Santa Elena, San Luis, and other Spanish missions and settlements. The underwater archaeologists were far from idle during this period, with contract and academic-based research groups scouring the Caribbean and the Gulf of Mexico (R. C. Smith et al. 1985; Keith 1989). The recent excavations at the Pensacola wreck (possibly one of Tristan de Luna's ships) combined investigations on both land and sea (R. C. Smith 1991).

POST-QUINCENTENNIAL DEPRESSION?

What impact *did* the Quincentennial have on Spanish Colonial research as it heads into the twenty-first century? Even with the availability of recent synthetic articles (such as Deagan 1988), it is difficult to assess the state of recent research. However, it appears that the direction of scholarly pursuits has not been greatly altered. A decline in activity might have been anticipated following the end of the anniversary, but this does not seem to be the case: the same or slightly more work is being pursued today as when the Quincentennial began.

If the Quincentennial did nothing else, it provided a focus for Spanish Colonial research. Grant-hungry scholars eager to tap into the Quincentennial El Dorado, symposium organizers, book editors, professors on the lecture circuit, and others all tried to relate their research to the Columbian Voyage of Discovery or its consequences (*Columbus and the Land of Ayllon,* Cook 1991, which describes an early Spanish colony in Georgia). Leaving this theme, researchers are returning to previous research questions that are often site-specific or at most regional in nature.

This fragmentation of effort is perhaps the most unfortunate aspect of post-Quincentennial research. Admittedly, many of the research connections during the Quincentennial were tenuous and often concocted for mercenary reasons, yet they provided a focus for our research. Other general research topics, such as community studies or a reexamination of assumed demographic changes, have been proposed. It remains to be seen what integrating themes, if any, emerge.

FUTURE TRENDS

Continuity would seem to characterize the future of Spanish Colonial research in the Southeast. The Quincentennial, oddly enough, may have been more of a distraction than an impetus to pursue broad archaeological topics. Although some of the special funding is no longer available, it often had many strings attached, and researchers are returning to topics that they and not the media feel are important. Public education remains an important factor, but the tail is no longer wagging the dog.

That the themes of the Quincentennial are current and valid can be seen in the program of the 12th Annual CAI Visiting Scholar's Conference at Southern Illinois University in 1995. The conference focused on building a new framework for the study of culture contact in archaeology. Claiming that the Quincentennial both aided and hindered culture contact studies, this conference presented the merits and limitations of approaching culture contact through world systems theory, models of evolution, and theories of acculturation and ethnicity. Certainly these discussions will provide guidance for future research.

What are some of the research questions we could be looking into? We could begin by questioning the basis for the Spanish black legend. How bad was the effect of Spanish-introduced epidemics? Do we even know what a Contact-period plague site would look like? The hypothesis that disease was rampant in the sixteenth-century Southeast needs to be tested before it is accepted as fact.

A broad anthropological research topic that would complement the current research of Spanish Colonial archaeologists would be to define and test a Spanish Colonial pattern. Deagan (1983) derived such a pattern from her work in St. Augustine, which was tested at Puerto Real (Ewen 1991). Basically, the pattern is defined by conservatism in those socially visible areas associated with male activities, coupled with Spanish-Indian acculturation in the less visible female-dominated areas. Williams (1993: 118–19) had trouble accepting this pattern, citing the works of Foster and Fuentes pertaining to Spanish Colonial adaptations in Mexico and Peru. Does this questioning invalidate the hypothesis or merely require modification? Perhaps the Spanish Colonial pattern changes through time (see Skowronek 1989) or varies somewhat from place to place (Southeast v. Caribbean v. Southwest). Perhaps a pattern can be established by comparing Spanish Colonial sites with contemporary sites of other colonial powers. How are they different, how are they alike, and how do we account for this? Is there a universal colonial pattern? Why or why not? It is fertile ground for inquiry.

Spanish Colonial scholars in the post-Quincentennial era have more data at their command than did their predecessors. The advent and development of computerized databases will continue to increase the accessibility of references and the data themselves. New documents are being discovered in old archives, and with the end of the Cold War and an anticipated greater access to archival sources in Cuba, this trend is likely to continue. The expanding syntheses of the material culture permit better interpretation of new excavations and reinterpretation of old data. The task of Spanish Colonial archaeology in the Caribbean is to focus on the questions that count, whether reconstructing past lifeways or discovering patterns in the colonial process. Such work transcends the immediate "Did Columbus sleep here?" questions and keeps Spanish Colonial archaeology integrated into the larger frameworks of history and anthropology.

The expedition of Hernando de Soto was one of the most important events in the New World during the sixteenth century. *La Florida* had proven to be a hostile wilderness devoid of easily exploitable gold or silver deposits. Two decades would pass before Spain would make another serious attempt to settle this territory. In the interim the native population began a transformation due to irreversible processes that the de Soto expedition had set in motion. De Soto's army was merely the vanguard of what would become a European invasion. Thus the great expedition marked both a beginning and an end: the beginning of Spanish involvement in the continental United States and the end of the traditional way of life of its first inhabitants.

References

AGI Archivo General de Indias, Seville
SD Santo Domingo
WLC Woodbury Lowery Collection

Albornoz, Miguel
  1986 *Hernando de Soto: Knight of the Americas.* New York: Franklin Watts.
Bandelier, Fanny, trans.
  1972 *The Narrative of Alvar Núñez Cabeza da Vaca.* Barre, Mass.: The Imprint Society.
Binford, Louis R.
  1972 *An Archaeological Perspective.* New York: Seminar Press.
Boyd, Mark F.
  1949 Diego Peña's Expedition to Apalachee and Apalachicolo in 1716. *Florida Historical Quarterly* 28(1):1–27.
Bryne, Stephen C.
  1986 Apalachee Settlement Patterns. M.A. thesis, Florida State University.
Capilla, Joan Baptista
  1609 Letter to the King, St. Augustine, November 4, 1609. AGI, SD 224, WLC, reel 3 of the copy held by the Strozier Library of Florida State University.
Chaney, Edward E.
  1987 *Report on the 1985 Excavations at the Fountain of Youth Park Site (8SJ31).* Gainesville: Florida State Museum.
Clairborne, J. F. H.
  1880 *Mississippi as a Province, Territory and State.* Vol. 1. Jackson, Miss.
Clayton, Lawrence A., Vernon J. Knight, Jr., and Edward C. Moore, eds.
  1993 *The De Soto Chronicles: The Expedition of Hernando de Soto to North America in 1539–1543.* 2 vols. Tuscaloosa: University of Alabama Press.
Cook, Jeannine, ed.
  1991 *Columbus and the Land of Ayllon: The Exploration and Settlement of the Southeast.* Darien: Carl Vinson Institute of Government, University of Georgia.
Crosby, Alfred W., Jr.
  1986 *Ecological Imperialism: The Biological Expansion of Europe, 900–1900.* New York: Cambridge University Press.

1994 *Germs, Seeds, and Animals: Studies in Ecological History.* Armonk, N.Y.: M. E. Sharpe.

Deagan, Kathleen A.

1981 Downtown Survey: The Discovery of Sixteenth-Century St. Augustine in an Urban Area. *American Antiquity* 46(3):626–34.

1983 *Spanish St. Augustine: The Archaeology of a Colonial Creole Community.* New York: Academic Press.

1987 *Artifacts of the Spanish Colonies of Florida and the Caribbean, 1500–1800.* Vol. 1. Washington: Smithsonian Institution Press.

1988 The Archaeology of the Spanish Contact Period in the Caribbean. *Journal of World Prehistory* 2(2):187–233.

Deagan, Kathleen A., John Bostwick, and Dale Benton

1976 *A Sub-Surface Survey of the St. Augustine City Environs.* Historic St. Augustine Preservation Board.

Defourneaux, Marcelin

1979 *Daily Life in Spain in the Golden Age.* Stanford, Calif.: Stanford University Press.

DePratter, Chester B.

1983 Late Prehistoric and Early Historic Chiefdoms in the Southeastern United States. Ph.D. dissertation, University of Georgia.

Dobyns, Henry F.

1983 *Their Number Become Thinned.* Knoxville: University of Tennessee Press.

Douglas, W.

1873 *Horseshoeing as It Is and as It Should Be.* London: J. Murray.

Duncan, David E.

1995 *Hernando de Soto: A Savage Quest in the Americas.* New York: Crown Publishers, Inc.

Eliot, J. H.

1963 *Imperial Spain, 1469–1716.* Meridian, N.Y.

Eubanks, W., Jr.

1990 Swanton: Four . . . Hudson: Zero, A Response to Hudson, Smith, Anderson, and Chardon. *The Soto States Anthropologist* 90:3–32.

Ewen, Charles R.

1987 From Spaniard to Creole: The Archaeology of Cultural Formation at Puerto Real, Haiti. Ph.D. dissertation, University of Florida.

1990 Soldier of Fortune: Hernando de Soto in the Territory of the Apalachee, 1539–1540. In Thomas 1990, 2:83–92.

1991 *From Spaniard to Creole.* Tuscaloosa: University of Alabama Press.

Ewen, Charles R., Richard Vernon, and Charles B. Poe

1988 *Managing the Archaeological Resources of Leon County.* Historic Tallahassee Preservation Board.

Fernández de Oviedo y Valdés, Gonzalo

1851– *Historia general y natural de Las Indias, islas y tierra-firme del Mar Oce*
1855 *ano.* 4 vols. Madrid: Imprenta de la Real Academia de la Historia.

Ffoulkes, C.

1967 *The Armourer and His Craft: From the XIth to the XVIth Century.* New York: Benjamin Blom.

Foley, V., G. Palmer, and W. Soedel

1985 The Crossbow. *Scientific American* 252(1):104–10.

Fryman, Frank B.

1971 Tallahassee's Prehistoric Political Center. *Archives and History News* 2(3):2–4.

Galloway, Patricia

1995 *Choctaw Genesis 1500–1700.* Lincoln: University of Nebraska Press.

Goggin, John M.

1960 *The Spanish Olive Jar: An Introductory Study.* Yale University Publications in Anthropology 62. New Haven.

1968 *Spanish Majolica in the New World.* Yale University Publications in Anthropology 72. New Haven.

Goodwin, W. B.

1946 *Spanish and English Ruins in Jamaica.* Boston.

Granberry, Julian

1989 *A Grammar and Dictionary of the Timucua Language.* 2d ed. Horseshoe Beach, Fla.: Island Archaeological Museum.

Hamilton, T. E.

1980 *Colonial Frontier Guns.* Chadron, Neb.: The Fur Press.

Hann, John H.

1986 Translation of Governor Rebolledo's 1657 Visitation of Three Florida Provinces and Related Documents. *Florida Archaeology* 2:81–146.

1988 *Apalachee: The Land between the Rivers.* Gainesville: University of Florida Press.

1990 Summary Guide to the Spanish Florida Missions and Visitas with Churches in the Sixteenth and Seventeenth Centuries. *The Americas* 46(4): 417–513.

1992 Heathen Acuera, Murder, and a Potano Cimarrona: The St. Johns River and the Alachua Prairie in the 1670s. *Florida Historical Quarterly* 70:451–74.

1993 The Mayaca and Jororo and Missions to Them. In *The Spanish Missions of La Florida,* ed. Bonnie G. McEwan, 111–40. Gainesville: University Press of Florida.

1996 *Translations of the Accounts of the Panfilo de Narváez Expedition's Experiences in Florida.* Florida Bureau of Archaeological Research, Tallahassee.

Henige, David

1986 The Context, Content, and Credibility of *La Florida del Inca. The Americas* 43:1–24.

Hudson, Charles

1976 *The Southeastern Indians.* Knoxville: University of Tennessee Press.

Hudson, Charles, Chester DePratter, and Marvin T. Smith

    1984 The Hernando de Soto Expedition: From Apalachee to Chiaha. *Southeastern Archaeology* 3(1):65–77.

Irving, T.

    1835 *The Conquest of Florida under Hernando de Soto.* Philadelphia: Carey, Lea, and Irving.

Jesus, Francisco Alonso de

    1630 1630 Memorial of Fray Francisco Alonso de Jesus on Spanish Florida's Missions and Natives. Trans. John H. Hann. *The Americas* 50(1): 85n.105.

Jones, B. Calvin

    1975 Archaeological Resources within the Capitol Center Survey Area. In *Tallahassee Capitol Center Survey,* ed. J. R. Little, 11–18. Miscellaneous Project Report Series no. 30. Tallahassee: Bureau of Historic Sites and Properties, Florida Department of State.

    1982 Southern Cult Manifestations at the Lake Jackson Site, Leon County, Florida: Salvage Archaeology at Mound 3. *Midcontinental Journal of Archaeology* 7:3–44.

    1988 The Dreamer and the de Soto Site. *The Florida Anthropologist* 41(3): 402–4.

Jones, B. Calvin, and Gary N. Shapiro

    1990 Nine Mission Sites in Apalachee. In Thomas 1990, 2:491–509.

Jones, Charles C.

    1880 *De Soto's March through Georgia.* Savannah: Charles C. Jones.

Keith, Donald H.

    1989 Ships of Exploration and Discovery: General Projects. *SHA Newsletter* 22(4):41.

Larsen, Clark S.

    1990 Comments on Report by Storey and Widmer. MS on file, Florida Bureau of Archaeological Research, Tallahassee.

Lister, Florence, and Robert Lister

    1982 *Sixteenth Century Maiolica Pottery in the Valley of Mexico.* Anthropological Papers of the University of Arizona 3. Tuscon.

Lockhart, James

    1972 *The Men of Cajamarca: A Social and Biographical Study of the First Conquerers of Peru.* Austin: University of Texas Press.

Lungwitz, A., and J. W. Adams

    1913 *A Textbook of Horseshoeing for Horseshoers and Veterinarians.* Philadelphia: J. B. Lippincott.

Lussagnet, Suzanne, ed.

    1958 *Les Français en Amérique pendant la deuxième moitié du XVIe siècle. Les Français en Floride.* Paris: Presses Universitaires de France.

Lynch, John

    1984 *Spain under the Hapsburgs.* 2d ed. Vol 1. New York: New York University Press.

Lyon, Eugene
   1979 *Towards a Typology of Spanish Colonial Nails*. Columbia: South Caro-
         lina Institute of Archaeology and Anthropology.
Maples, William R.
   1989 Comments on the report by Storey and Widmer. MS on file, Florida Bu-
         reau of Archaeological Research, Tallahassee.
McAlister, Lyle
   1984 *Spain and Portugal in the New World, 1492–1700*. Minneapolis: Univer-
         sity of Minnesota Press.
McEwan, Bonnie G.
   1983 Spanish Colonial Adaptation on Hispaniola: The Archaeology of Area
         35, Puerto Real, Haiti. M.A. thesis, University of Florida.
   1993 Hispanic Life on the Seventeenth-Century Florida Frontier. In *The Span-
         ish Missions of La Florida*, ed. Bonnie G. McEwan, 295–321. Gaines-
         ville: University Press of Florida.
Méndez de Canzo, Gonzalo
   1601 Letter to the King, St. Augustine, April 24, 1601. AGI, SD 224 (WLC),
         reel 3.
Mendoza, L. C.
   1957 Ceramica de las ruinas de la vega vieja. *Casas Reales* 11:101–13.
Milanich, Jerald T.
   1972 *Excavations at the Richardson Site, Alachua County, Florida: An Early
         17th-Century Potano Indian Village*. Tallahassee: Florida Bureau of His-
         toric Sites and Properties Bulletin 235–61.
   1978 The Western Timucua: Patterns of Acculturation and Change. In *Taca-
         chale: Essays on the Indians of Florida and Southeastern Georgia during
         the Historic Period*, ed. Jerald T. Milanich and Samuel Proctor. Gaines-
         ville: University Presses of Florida.
   1994 *Archaeology of Precolumbian Florida*. Gainesville: University Press of
         Florida.
   1995 *Florida Indians and the Invasion from Europe*. Gainesville: University
         Press of Florida.
Milanich, Jerald T., and Charles Hudson
   1993 *Hernando de Soto and the Indians of Florida*. Gainesville: University
         Press of Florida.
Milanich, Jerald T., and Susan Milbrath, eds.
   1989 *First Encounters: Spanish Explorations in the Caribbean and the United
         States, 1492–1570*. Gainesville: University of Florida Press.
Milburn, W. H.
   1850 *Pioneers, Preachers and People of the Mississippi*. New York: Derby and
         Johnson.
Miller, James J.
   1987 *Acquisition Project Proposal Information—Martin Tract*. Tallahassee:
         Florida Department of Natural Resources, Conservation and Recre-
         ational Lands Program.

Mitchell, Chuck
    1989 *Transcript of Comments.* Florida Archaeological Council, Jacksonville
        Forum.
Mitchem, Jeffrey M.
    1989 Artifacts of Exploration: Archaeological Evidence from Florida. In Mil-
        anich and Milbrath 1989, 99–109.
Morales Patino, Oswaldo, and R. P. d. Acevedo
    1946 El Periódo de transculturación Indo-hispánica. *Revista de arqueología y
        etnología* 1:15–20.
Morison, Samuel E.
    1974 *The European Discovery of America: The Southern Voyages, 1492–1616.*
        New York: Oxford University Press.
Morse, Dan F., and Phyllis Morse
    1983 *Archaeology of the Central Mississippi Valley.* New York: Academic Press.
Nelson, Lee H.
    1968 Nail Chronology as an Aid to Dating Old Buildings. *History News* 19:2,
        reprinted as 24(11). Washington, D.C.: American Association for State
        and Local History Technical Leaflet 48.
Noel Hume, Ivor
    1978 *A Guide to Artifacts of Colonial America.* New York: Alfred A. Knopf.
    1983 *Discoveries in Martin's Hundred.* Williamsburg: The Colonial Williams-
        burg Foundation.
Olds, Dorris L.
    1976 *Texas Legacy from the Gulf.* Miscellaneous Papers 5. Austin: Texas Me-
        morial Museum.
Oré, Luís Gerónimo de
    1936 *The Martyrs of Florida (1513–1616).* Trans. Maynard Geiger. New York:
        Joseph F. Wagner, Inc.
Ortega, Elpidio
    1982 *Arqueología colonial de Santo Domingo.* Serie Científica 4. Santo Do-
        mingo: Fundación Ortega Alvarez, Inc.
Paisley, Clifton
    1989 *The Red Hills of Florida, 1528–1865.* Tuscaloosa: University of Ala-
        bama Press.
Palm, Erwin
    1945 Excavations of La Isabela, White Man's First Town in the Americas. *Acta
        Americana* 3:298–303.
    1952 La Fortaleza de la Concepción de la Vega. *Memoria del V Congreso His-
        tórico Municipal Interamericana* 2:115–18.
Payne, Claudine
    1981 A Preliminary Report of Fort Walton Settlement Patterns in the Tallahas-
        see Red Hills. *Southeastern Archaeological Conference Bulletin* 24:29–
        31.
    1982 Farmsteads and Districts: A Model of Fort Walton Settlement Patterns in

the Tallahassee Hills. Paper presented at the Southeastern Archaeological Conference, Memphis.

Payne-Gallwey, S. R.

1958 *The Crossbow: Medieval and Modern Military and Sporting: Its Construction, History and Management.* New York: Bramwell House.

Peña, Diego

1716 Diario deste viaje de Apalache y de la prov^a de Apalachicolo. AGI, SD 843 (Stetson Collection) (filed under 1717).

Peñaranda, Alonso de

1608 Letter to the King, St. Augustine, January 1608. AGI, SD 224 (WLC), reel 3.

Perete, Frate Francisco, et al.

1676 List of friars, St. Augustine, April 5, 1676. New York Historical Society document. Copy furnished by R. Wayne Childers.

Pickett, A. J.

1896 *History of Alabama, and Incidentally of Georgia and Mississippi, from the Earliest Period.* Sheffield, Ala.: Robert C. Randolph.

Ramenofsky, Anne F.

1987 *Vectors of Death: The Archaeology of European Contact.* Albuquerque: University of New Mexico Press.

Robertson, James Alexander, trans. and ed.

1933 *True Relation of the Hardships Suffered by Governor Fernando de Soto & Certain Portuguese Gentlemen during the Discovery of the Province of Florida. Now Newly Set Forth by a Gentleman of Elvas.* 2 vols. Deland: The Florida State Historical Society.

Rochefort, Charles de

1658 *Histoire naturelle et morale des Isles Antilles del Amérique.* 2d ed. Rotterdam: Chez Arnout Leers.

Rye, W. B., ed.

1851 *The Discovery and Conquest of Terra Florida by Don Fernando de Soto.* London: The Hakluyt Society.

Sale, Kirkpatrick

1990 *The Conquest of Paradise.* New York: Alfred A. Knopf.

Scarry, John F.

1984 Fort Walton Development: Mississippian Chiefdoms in the Lower Southeast. Ph.D. dissertation, Case Western Reserve University.

1985 A Proposed Revision of the Fort Walton Ceramic Typology: A Type-Variety System. *The Florida Anthropologist* 38(3):199–233.

1988 *Stability and Change of the Fort Walton Ceramic Typology: Centralization, Decentralization and Social Reproduction.* Tallahassee: Florida Bureau of Archaeological Research.

1990 The Rise, Transformation, and Fall of the Apalachee. In *Lamar Archaeology,* ed. M. Williams and G. Shapiro, 175–86. Tuscaloosa: University of Alabama Press.

1994a The Late Prehistoric Southeast. In *The Forgotten Centuries*, ed. C. Hudson and C. C. Tesser, 17–35. Athens: University of Georgia Press.

1994b The Apalachee Chiefdom. In *The Forgotten Centuries*, ed. C. Hudson and C. C. Tesser, 156–78. Athens: University of Georgia Press.

Scarry, John F., and Bonnie G. McEwan

1995 Domestic Architecture in Apalachee Province: Apalachee and Spanish Residential Styles in the Late Prehistoric and Early Historic Period Southeast. *American Antiquity* 60(3):482–96.

Shapiro, Gary

1987 *Archaeology at San Luis: Broad Scale Testing*. Florida Archaeology 3. Tallahassee: Florida Bureau of Archaeological Research.

Shelby, Charmion

1993 La Florida by the Inca. History of the Adelantado Hernando de Soto, Governor and Captain General of the Kingdom of La Florida, and of Other Heroic Gentlemen, Spaniards and Indians. Edited by David Bost with footnotes by Vernon J. Knight, Jr. In Clayton, Knight, and Moore 1993.

Shipp, Barnard

1881 *The History of Hernando de Soto and Florida. Or the Record of Events of Fifty-six Years from 1512 to 1568*. Philadelphia: Collins.

Simmons, M., and F. Turley

1980 *Southwestern Colonial Ironwork: The Spanish Blacksmithing Tradition from Texas to California*. Santa Fe: Museum of New Mexico.

Skowronek, Russell K.

1989 A New Europe in the New World: Hierarchy, Continuity and Change in the Spanish Sixteenth-Century Colonization of Hispaniola and Florida. Ph.D. dissertation, Michigan State University.

1991 Return to Peachtree: A Catalogue of Amateur Surface Collections from Cherokee and Clay Counties, N.C. Report submitted to Western Carolina University and the Department of Archives and History for the State of North Carolina, Ann Rogers, P.I.

1995 Reflections on the Quincentennial: Expo '92 and Andalucia in the Construction of the Past. Paper presented at the annual meeting of the Society for Historical Archaeology, Washington.

Smith, Buckingham, ed.

1857 *Colección de varios documentos para la historia de la Florida y tierras adjacentes*. London: Casa Trubner.

1968 *Narratives of De Soto in the Conquest of Florida as Told by a Gentleman of Elvas and in a Relation by Luys Hernández de Biedma*. Gainesville, Fla.: Palmetto Books.

Smith, Hale G.

1951 The Influence of European Cultural Contacts upon the Aboriginal Cultures of North Florida. Ph.D. dissertation, University of Michigan.

Smith, Marion F., and John F. Scarry

1988 Apalachee Settlement Distribution: The View from the Florida Master Site File. *The Florida Anthropologist* 41:351–64.

Smith, Marvin T.

1975 European Materials from the King Site. *Southeastern Archaeological Conference Bulletin* 18: 63–66.

1984 Depopulation and Culture Change in the Early Historic Period Interior Southeast. Ph.D. dissertation, University of Florida.

1987 *Archaeology of Aboriginal Culture Change in the Interior Southeast.* Gainesville: University of Florida Press.

1994 Aboriginal Depopulation in the Postcontact Southeast. In *The Forgotten Centuries,* ed. C. Hudson and C. C. Tesser, 257–75. Athens: University of Georgia Press.

Smith, Marvin T., and M. E. Goode

1982 *Early Sixteenth Century Glass Beads in the Spanish Colonial Trade.* Greenwood, Miss.: Cottonlandia Museum.

Smith, Roger C.

1991 Florida Bureau of Archaeological Research: Pensacola Shipwreck Survey. *SHA Newsletter* 24(2):37.

Smith, Roger C., Donald H. Keith, and Denise C. Lakey

1985 The Highborn Cay Wreck: Further Exploration of a Sixteenth-Century Bahaman Shipwreck. *International Journal of Nautical Archaeology and Underwater Exploration* 14:63–72.

South, Stanley, Russell K. Skowronek, and Richard E. Johnson

1988 *Spanish Artifacts from Santa Elena.* Anthropological Studies 7. Columbia: South Carolina Institute of Archaeology and Anthropology.

Storey, Rebecca, and Randolf J. Widmer

1988 Report on Feature 131 of Site 8LE853. University of Houston.

Swanton, J. R.

1985 *Final Report of the United States De Soto Expedition Commission.* Smithsonian Classics of Anthropology. Washington, D.C.: Smithsonian Institution Press.

Tesar, Louis D.

1980 *The Leon County Bicentennial Survey Report: An Archaeological Survey of Selected Portions of Leon County, Florida.* Miscellaneous Project Report Series 49. Tallahassee: Florida Bureau of Historic Sites and Properties.

Tesar, Louis D., and B. Calvin Jones

1989 In Search of the 1539–40 De Soto Expedition Wintering Site in Apalache. *The Florida Anthropologist* 42:340–60.

Theisen, Gerald, trans.

1972 The Joint Report Recorded by Gonzalo Fernandez de Oviedo y Valdez. In Bandelier 1972.

Thomas, David Hurst, ed.

1990 *Columbian Consequences.* Vol. 2: *Archaeological and Historical Perspectives on the Spanish Borderlands East.* Washington, D.C.: Smithsonian Institution Press.

Thompson, S. M. E.

1986 *Historical and Architectural Survey of the Country Club Estates Neighborhood, Tallahassee, Florida.* Historic Tallahassee Preservation Board.

Valdés, Fernando de

1602 Government Matters. AGI, SD 2533. Stetson Collection (microfilm reel lent by Eugene Lyon) and John Tate Lanning Collection of the Thomas Jefferson Library of the University of Missouri–St. Louis, Collección "Misiones Guale." Trans. John H. Hann. On file at the Florida Bureau of Archaeological Research, Tallahassee.

Varner, John Grier, and Jeannette Johnson Varner, trans. and eds.

1951 *The Florida of the Inca.* University of Texas Press, Austin.

Vega, Garcilaso de

1723 *La Florida del Inca.* En la Oficina Real, y Â Costa de Nicolás Rodrigues Franco, Madrid.

Vicenti, J. A.

1978 *Catalogo general de la moneda Espanola.* Madrid.

Vierra, Bradley J.

1989 *A Sixteenth-Century Campsite in the Tiguex Province.* Laboratory of Anthropology Notes 475. Santa Fe: Museum of New Mexico.

Wilkinson, F.

1970 *Battle Dress: A Gallery of Military Style and Ornament.* Garden City, N.Y.: Doubleday & Company, Inc.

Williams, John L.

1837 *The territory of Florida, or sketches of the topography, civil, and natural history of the country.* New York.

Williams, Jack

1993 Review of *From Spaniard to Creole*, by Charles R. Ewen. *Historical Archaeology* 27(3):118–19.

Willis, Raymond

1984 Empire and Architecture at 16th Century Puerto Real, Hispaniola: An Archaeological Perspective. Ph.D. dissertation, University of Florida.

Worth, John E.

1992 The Timucuan Missions of Spanish Florida and the Rebellion of 1656. Ph.D. dissertation, University of Florida.

Index to Parts I and II

Numbers in italic indicate an illustration.

Index to Part III

Florida Museum of Natural History
The Ripley P. Bullen Series

Jerald T. Milanich, Series Editor

Tacachale: Essays on the Indians of Florida and Southeastern Georgia during the Historic Period, edited by Jerald T. Milanich and Samuel Proctor (1978); first paperback edition, 1994

Aboriginal Subsistence Technology on the Southeastern Coastal Plain during the Late Prehistoric Period, by Lewis H. Larson (1980)

Cemochechobee: Archaeology of a Mississippian Ceremonial Center on the Chattahoochee River, by Frank T. Schnell, Vernon J. Knight, Jr., and Gail S. Schnell (1981)

Fort Center: An Archaeological Site in the Lake Okeechobee Basin, by William H. Sears, with contributions by Elsie O'R. Sears and Karl T. Steinen (1982); first paperback edition, 1994

Perspectives on Gulf Coast Prehistory, edited by Dave D. Davis (1984)

Archaeology of Aboriginal Culture Change in the Interior Southeast: Depopulation during the Early Historic Period, by Marvin T. Smith (1987)

Apalachee: The Land between the Rivers, by John H. Hann (1988)

Key Marco's Buried Treasure: Archaeology and Adventure in the Nineteenth Century, by Marion Spjut Gilliland (1989)

First Encounters: Spanish Explorations in the Caribbean and the United States, 1492–1570, edited by Jerald T. Milanich and Susan Milbrath (1989)

Missions to the Calusa, edited and translated by John H. Hann, with an Introduction by William H. Marquardt (1991)

Excavations on the Franciscan Frontier: Archaeology at the Fig Springs Mission, by Brent Richards Weisman (1992)

The People Who Discovered Columbus: The Prehistory of the Bahamas, by William F. Keegan (1992)

Hernando de Soto and the Indians of Florida, by Jerald T. Milanich and Charles Hudson (1993)

Foraging and Farming in the Eastern Woodlands, edited by C. Margaret Scarry (1993)

Puerto Real: The Archaeology of a Sixteenth-Century Spanish Town in Hispaniola, edited by Kathleen Deagan (1995)

A History of the Timucua Indians and Missions, by John H. Hann (1996)

Archaeology of the Mid-Holocene Southeast, edited by Kenneth E. Sassaman and David G. Anderson (1996)

Bioarchaeology of Native American Adaptation in the Spanish Borderlands, edited by Brenda J. Baker and Lisa Kealhofer (1996)

The Indigenous People of the Caribbean, edited by Samuel M. Wilson (1997)